TERMINATION OF EMPLOYMENT STATUTES

AUSTRALIA
The Law Book Company
Brisbane • Sydney • Melbourne • Perth

CANADA
Carswell
Ottawa • Toronto • Calgary • Montreal • Vancouver

Agents:
Steimatzky's Agency Ltd, Tel Aviv;
N.M. Tripathi (Private) Ltd, Bombay;
Eastern Law House (Private) Ltd, Calcutta;
M.P.P. House, Bangalore;
Universal Book Traders, Delhi;
Aditya Books, Delhi;
MacMillan Shuppan KK, Tokyo;
Pakistan Law House, Karachi, Lahore

TERMINATION
OF
EMPLOYMENT
STATUTES

COMMENTARY BY
ANTHONY KERR

M.A. (Dub.), LL.M. (Lond.)
of King's Inns, Barrister,
Statutory Lecturer in Law,
University College, Dublin

LONDON
SWEET & MAXWELL
1995

Published in 1995 by Sweet and Maxwell Limited of
South Quay Plaza,
183 Marsh Wall, London E14 9FT
Computerset by York House Typographic Ltd, London
Printed in Great Britain by The Bath Press, Bath, Avon

No natural forests were destroyed to make this product, only
farmed timber was used and replanted

**A CIP catalogue record for this book is available from the
British Library**

ISBN 0 421 53080 4

Acknowledgement:
Forms 1, 2 and 3 on pages 207, 208 and 209 are contained
within Statutory Instrument No. 279 of 1994 and are reproduced
with the kind permission of the Controller, Stationery Office,
Dublin and with the consent of the Circuit Court Rules Committee.

The statutory material in this book is reproduced with the kind
permission of the Controller, Stationery Office, Dublin

CONTENTS

FOREWORD

With this publication Tony Kerr has set out to make more accessible that area of Statute Law governing termination of employment. This he has achieved. Everyone involved in the realm of employment rights be they lawyers, employer representatives, trade union officials or otherwise will welcome this worthy addition to Irish legal publishing and will, I know, particularly appreciate the format the author has employed.

The plethora of primary, amending and secondary legislation in this area often makes it difficult to track down specific provisions of Acts which very often interact with one another when an employment relationship is being terminated. This difficulty has in the past led to calls for a Consolidation Act. Mr Kerr's book will greatly ease the problem as the relevant statutes and amendments are now brought together in one volume. As such, it will be a boon to lawyers, academics and industrial relations practitioners and it will allow them to directly access the relevant provisions and case law.

This volume has further benefits. Each of the Acts (Redundancy, Protection of Employment, Minimum Notice, Unfair Dismissal and Employer's Insolvency) are set out in full and are annotated by the Author with helpful commentary and analysis. The reader is given a brief historical résumé on key sections and is guided towards the appropriate case law for further clarification. Despite the vast number of Employment Appeals Tribunal determinations and decisions, Circuit Court, High Court and Supreme Court judgements with which he has had to cope, Mr Kerr has succeeded in providing the practitioner with a comprehensive overview of how the statutory provisions governing termination of employment have been interpreted by the Tribunal and the Courts. He succeeds admirably in elucidating the more important points emerging from this case law analysis.

In addition to the foregoing, there is included in this commendable book all of the Orders and Regulations made pursuant to the statutes in question and, even more helpfully, updated samples of the forms required to initiate claims and appeals under the Acts are provided. The inclusion of the latter will, I have no doubt, make the lot of the employee and employer representatives much easier, especially in cases involving redundancy and insolvency.

vii

Disputes under four of the five legislative enactments covered in this book come before the Employment Appeals Tribunal for adjudication and I anticipate, having regard to the scholarly treatment afforded these legislative provisions by Tony Kerr, that his book will be much in evidence at Tribunal hearings. I wish it and the author every success.

Mary Faherty
Employment Appeals Tribunal
July 31, 1995.

PREFACE

In her concluding remarks to the Seanad following the final debate on the Unfair Dismissals (Amendment) Bill 1993, the then Minister for State at the Department of Enterprise and Employment (Mary O'Rourke T.D.) referred to the "excessive legalism" in the Employment Appeals Tribunal and commented that the increasing role of legal representatives was hindering the Tribunal in providing a fast and inexpensive route for the resolution of disputes (137 *Seanad Debates* Col. 645).

Legal representation in itself is neither objectionable nor undesirable particularly as very important rights are at stake. The Tribunal recently awarded the former head of security at Dunnes Stores £124,800 as compensation for unfair dismissal, a sum more than four times in excess of the current Circuit Court jurisdiction. Such cases are rare however with most awards falling within the current District Court jurisdiction.

The problem of "excessive" or "undue" legalism principally lies in the unnecessary complexity of the legalisation. The increase in the number of statutory provisions has led to calls for the introduction of a consolidating measure. Indeed Senator Dan Neville, the then Fine Gael spokesman on Justice and Law Reform in the Senate, was quoted in the *Irish Times* of December 14, 1993 as saying that the sheer number of labour law provisions had made the area of employer-employee relationships "a minefield". On this ground alone it is not surprising there is increasing resort to legal advice and representation on the part of employers and employees.

It is my modest hope that this book, which contains the up-to-date text of all the legislation concerning termination of employment, will go some way to simplifying things. All amendments, adaptations and repeals are clearly indicated and each section is fully annotated by reference to the available jurisprudence and thoroughly cross-referenced.

Grateful appreciation is due to a large number of individuals for assistance provided and encouragement offered. A considerable debt of gratitude is due to Mary Faherty for her generous foreword and I would specifically like to thank Peter Ward, Declan Madden, Peter Murphy, Kevin Duffy, Dan Sullivan, Liam O'Malley, Bob Clark, Richard Humphreys, Dermot MacCarthy and Geraldine Doyle.

The commentary to the legislation is based on materials and information available to me at June 30, 1995. Although every effort has been made to ensure that the information given in this book is accurate, no legal responsibility, however, is accepted by the author or the publishers for any errors or omissions in that information or otherwise.

This book is dedicated to the memory of Donal Hamilton.

Tony Kerr
Dublin
Bastille Day 1995.

TABLE OF CASES

REDUNDANCY PAYMENTS ACT 1967

(1967 No. 21)

ARRANGEMENT OF SECTIONS

1

An Act to provide for the making by employers of payments to employees in respect of redundancy, to establish a redundancy fund and to require employers and employees to pay contributions towards that fund, to provide for payments to be made out of that fund to employers and employees, to provide financial assistance to certain unemployed persons changing residence, and to provide for other matters (including offences) connected with the matters aforesaid. [*18th December 1967*]

GENERAL NOTE

It has been convincingly demonstrated that the British Redundancy Payments Act 1965, on which this Act is largely based, was "aimed at securing a greater acceptance by employees of the need for more economic, organisational and technological change" (Parker *et al*, *Effects of the Redundancy Payments Act* (1971), p.20). Grunfeld in *The Law of Redundancy* (3rd ed., 1989) writes of the

2

1965 Act's predominant purpose being to mitigate and reduce the resistance of workers to industrial re-organisation and the redeployment of labour. See also Fryer, "The Myths of the Redundancy Payments Act" (1975) 2 I.L.J. 1.

Although the Act provides for a cushion of monetary compensation for the redundant employee, it in no way impinges on the ability of an employer to dismiss for redundancy. The Employment Appeals Tribunal's function is to decide whether there was a redundancy situation; it is not to decide why the redundancy occurred: see *Moon v. Homeworthy Furniture Ltd* [1977] I.C.R. 117. *Quaere* whether the Tribunal is given jurisdiction under the Unfair Dismissals Acts 1977-1993 to decide whether the dismissal was fair: compare *Roche v. Sealink Stena Line Ltd* UD 187/1992 (reported at [1993] E.L.R. 89) and *Boucher v. Irish Productivity Centre* UD 882/1992 (reported at [1994] E.L.R. 205).

An interesting feature of the scheme established by this Act is the spreading of the financial load of redundancy by the subsidisation of redundancy payments through a State fund (the Social Insurance Fund) financed by levies on employers.

The Act, which was described by Kenny J. in *Minister for Labour v. O'Connor*, High Court, March 6, 1973 (reported at (1985) 4 J.I.S.L.L. 72) as being "remarkable for its obscurity", has been amended on a number of occasions, principally in 1971 and 1979.

Citation

See section 1. The collective citation is now the Redundancy Payments Acts 1967-1991.

Commencement

The Act came into operation on January 1, 1968.

Statutory Instruments

Redundancy Payments Act (Appointed Day) Order 1967 (S.I. No. 302 of 1967).
Redundancy (Repayment and Recovery of Payments) Regulations 1968 (S.I. No. 5 of 1968).
Redundancy (Inspection of Records) Regulations 1968 (S.I. No. 12 of 1968).
Redundancy (Redundancy Appeals Tribunal) Regulations 1968 (S.I. No. 24 of 1968).
Redundancy Payments Act (Authorised Officers) Order 1968 (S.I. No. 106 of 1968).
Redundancy (Employment Appeals Tribunal) Regulations 1979 (S.I. No. 114 of 1979).
Redundancy (Inspection of Records) Regulations 1979 (S.I. No. 115 of 1979).
Redundancy (Rebates) Regulations 1990 (S.I. No. 122 of 1990).
Redundancy Certificate Regulations 1991 (S.I. No. 347 of 1991).
Redundancy (Notice of Dismissal) Regulations 1991 (S.I. No. 348 of 1991).
Redundancy Payments (Lump Sum) Regulations 1994 (S.I. No. 64 of 1994).

Parliamentary Debates

228 *Dail Debates* Cols. 1602–1669 (Second Stage)
228 *Dail Debates* Cols. 1937–1994 (Second Stage resumed)

228 *Dail Debates* Cols. 1971–1993 (Second Stage resumed)
230 *Dail Debates* Cols. 1177–1205 (Committee Stage)
230 *Dail Debates* Cols. 1238–1357 (Committee Stage resumed)
230 *Dail Debates* Cols. 1636–1729 (Committee Stage resumed)
230 *Dail Debates* Cols. 1937–1993 (Report and Final Stages)
64 *Seanad Debates* Cols. 24–97 (Second Stage)
64 *Seanad Debates* Cols. 97–298 (Committee and Final Stages)
231 *Dail Debates* Cols. 1755–1762 (Seanad Amendments)

Be it enacted by the Oireachtas as follows:

Short Title

1.—This Act may be cited as the Redundancy Payments Act 1967.

Interpretation

2.—(1) In this Act —

["the Act of 1993" means the Social Welfare (Consolidation) Act 1993];

["adopting parent" means an employee who is an employed adopting mother, an adopting father or sole male adopter within the meaning of the Adoptive Leave Act 1995;]

"business" includes a trade, industry, profession or undertaking, or any activity carried on by a person or body of persons, whether corporate or unincorporate, or by a public or local authority or a Department of State;

"date of dismissal", in relation to an employee, means;

(a) where his contract of employment is terminated by notice given by his employer, the date on which that notice expires,

(b) where his contract of employment is terminated without notice, whether by the employer or by the employee, the date on which the termination takes effect, and

(c) where he is employed under a contract for a fixed term, and that term expires without the contract being renewed, the date on which that term expires,

and cognate phrases shall be construed accordingly;

"employee" means a person who has entered into or works under (or, in the case of a contract which has been terminated, worked under) a contract with an employer, whether the contract is for manual labour, clerical work or otherwise, is express or implied, oral or in writing, and whether it is a

4

contract of service or apprenticeship or otherwise, and "employer" and reference to employment shall be construed accordingly;

"[...]"

"[...]"

"day off" has the meaning assigned to it by section 11(1);

"lump sum" has the meaning assigned to it by section 19;

"the Minister" means the Minister for [Enterprise and Employment];

"prescribed" means prescribed by regulations made by the Minister under this Act;

"rebate" has the meaning assigned to it by section 29;

"redundancy payment" has the meaning assigned to it by section 7;

"short-time" has the meaning assigned to it by section 11(2) [or section 11(3) (as the case may be)];

"sickness" or "illness" includes being incapable of work within the meaning of the Act of [1993];

["the Social Insurance Fund" means the Social Insurance Fund established under section 39 of the Social Welfare Act 1952, and continued in being under section 122 of the Social Welfare (Consolidation) Act 1981 [and further continued in being under section 7 of the Social Welfare (Consolidation) Act 1993];]

"special redundancy scheme" has the meaning assigned to it by section 47;

"the Tribunal" has the meaning assigned to it by section 39(1);

"week", in relation to an employee whose remuneration is calculated weekly by a week ending on a day other than Saturday, means a week ending on that other day and, in relation to any other employee, means a week ending on Saturday, and "weekly" shall be construed accordingly;

"weekly payment" has the meaning assigned to it by section 30.

(2) In this Act a reference to a Part, section or schedule is to a Part or section of, or schedule to, this Act unless it is indicated that reference to some other enactment is intended.

(3) In this act a reference to a subsection, paragraph, subparagraph or other division is to the subsection, paragraph, sub-paragraph or other division of the provision (including a schedule) in which the reference occurs, unless it is indicated that reference to another provision is intended.

(4) For the purposes of the operation of this Act in relation to an employee whose remuneration is payable to him by a person other than his employer, reference in this Act to an employer shall be construed as reference to the person by whom the remuneration is payable.

GENERAL NOTE

The definition of "adopting parent" was inserted by section 27 of the Adoptive Leave Act 1995. The definition of "employer's redundancy contribution" was deleted by section 39(1) of the Social Welfare Act 1991. The definition of "the Employment Service", itself amended by section 19 of the Redundancy Payments Act 1971, was deleted by section 18(4) of the Labour Services Act 1987. The definition of "the Minister" was amended by virtue of the Labour (Transfer of Departmental Administration and Ministerial Functions) Order 1993 (S.I. No. 18 of 1993) and the Industry and Commerce (Alteration of Name of Department and Title of Minister) Order 1993 (S.I. No. 19 of 1993). The words in square brackets were inserted into the definition of "short-time" by section 19 of the 1971 Act. The definition of "the Social Insurance Fund" was inserted by section 26 of the Social Welfare Act 1990, on which see now section 7 of the Social Welfare (Consolidation) Act 1993.

Commencement

3.—This Act shall come into operation on such day as the Minister appoints by order.

GENERAL NOTE

The Redundancy Payments Act (Appointed Day) Order 1967 (S.I. No. 302 of 1967) appointed January 1, 1968 as the day on which the Act came into operation.

Classes of persons to which this Act applies

4.—(1) Subject to this section and to section 47 this Act shall apply to employees employed in employment which is insurable for all benefits under the Social Welfare Acts [...] and to employees who were so employed in such employment in the period of [four] years ending on the date of termination of employment.

(2) This Act shall not apply to a person who is normally expected to work for the same employer for less than [18] hours in a week.

(3)(a) For the purpose of the application of this Act to an employee who is employed in a private household this Act (other than section 20) shall apply as if the household were a business and the maintenance of the household were the carrying on of that business by the employer.

(b) This Act shall not apply to any person in respect of employment where the employer is the father, mother, grandfather, grandmother, stepfather, stepmother, son, daughter, grandson, grand-daughter, stepson, stepdaughter, brother, sister, half-brother or half-sister of the employee, where the employee is a member of the employer's household and the employment is related to a private dwelling house or a farm in or on which both the employer and the employee reside.

[(c) In deducing any relationship for the purposes of paragraph (b) —

(i) a person adopted under the Adoption Acts 1952 [to 1991] shall be considered the legitimate offspring of the adopter or adopters;

(ii) subject to clause (i) of this paragraph, an illegitimate person shall be considered the legitimate offspring of his mother and reputed father;

(iii) a person *in loco parentis* to another shall be considered the parent of that other.]

(4) The Minister may by order declare that this Act shall not apply to a class or classes of persons specified in the order and from the commencement of the order this Act shall not apply to that class or those classes.

(5) Notwithstanding subsection (2), the Minister may by order declare that this Act shall apply to a specified class of worker and from the commencement of the order this Act shall apply to that class.

(6) The Minister may by order amend or revoke an order under this section.

GENERAL NOTE

The word in square brackets in subsection (1) was inserted by section 19 of the Redundancy Payments Act 1971. Insofar as this subsection has the effect of excluding employees from the Act's application by virtue of the Social Welfare (Subsidiary Employments) Regulations 1991 (S.I. No. 73 of 1991), the Social Welfare (Employment of Inconsiderable Extent) (No. 2) Regulations 1991 (S.I. No. 72 of 1991), as amended by S.I. No. 76 of 1994, or any other regulations prescribed by the Minister under section 1(3)(a) of the Worker Protection (Regular Part-time Employees) Act 1991 (the 1991 Act), it must now be read in the light of the provisions of the 1991 Act which apply this Act to employees who have been in the continuous service of their employer for not less than 13 weeks and who are normally expected to work not less than 8 hours a week. Note that section 3 of the Redundancy Payments Act 1971 (as amended and adapted) now provides that, notwithstanding subsection (1), the 1967 Act, with effect from April 6, 1980, shall

7

not apply to a person who on the date of termination of his employment had attained the age which on that date is the pensionable age within the meaning of the Social Welfare (Consolidation) Act 1993.

The word in square brackets in subsection (2) was inserted by section 12 of the Protection of Employees (Employers' Insolvency) Act 1984. By virtue of section 2(3)(b)(i) of the 1991 Act, for the purpose of calculating a period of continuous service, the reference to 18 hours should be read as a reference to 8 hours.

Paragraph (c) of subsection (3) was inserted by section 19 of the Redundancy Payments Act 1971. On the meaning of the expression "in loco parentis" see *Waters v. Cruickshank* [1967] I.R. 378.

Laying of regulations and certain draft orders before Houses of Oireachtas

5.—(1) Whenever an order is proposed to be made under section 4(4), 4(5), 4(6), 19(3), [...], 30(3) or 47 [or section 17 of the Redundancy Payments Act 1971], a draft of the proposed order shall be laid before each House of the Oireachtas and the order shall not be made until a resolution approving of the draft has been passed by each such House.

(2) Every regulation made under this Act shall be laid before each House of the Oireachtas as soon as may be after it is made and, if a resolution annulling the regulation is passed by either such House within the next twenty-one days on which that House has sat after the regulation is laid before it, the regulation shall be annulled accordingly, but without prejudice to the validity of anything previously done thereunder.

GENERAL NOTE

The words in square brackets in subsection (1) were deleted and inserted by section 39(1) of the Social Welfare Act 1991 and section 19 of the Redundancy Payments Act 1971 respectively.

Definitions for Part II

6.—In this Part—

"cease" means cease either temporarily or permanently and from whatever cause;

"lock-out" means the closing of a place of employment, or the suspension of work, or the refusal by an employer to continue to employ any number of persons employed by him in consequence of a dispute, done with a view to compelling those persons, or to aid another employer in compelling persons employed by him, to accept terms or conditions of or affecting employment;

"notice of intention to claim" has the meaning assigned to it by section 12;

"redundancy certificate" has the meaning assigned to it by section 18;

"strike" means the cessation of work by a body of persons employed acting in combination, or a concerted refusal or a refusal under a common understanding of any number of persons employed to continue to work for an employer in consequence of a dispute, done as a means of compelling their employer or any person or body of persons employed, or to aid other employees in compelling their employer or any person or body of persons employed, to accept or not to accept terms or conditions of or affecting employment.

GENERAL NOTE

The definition of "strike" is slightly wider than that contained in the Industrial Relations Act 1990 in that it includes cessations of work done as a means of compelling "any person or body of persons employed" to accept or not to accept terms or conditions of or affecting employment.

General right to redundancy payment

7.—(1) An employee, if he is dismissed by his employer by reason of redundancy or is laid off or kept on short-time for the minimum period, shall, subject to this Act, be entitled to the payment of moneys which shall be known (and are in this Act referred to) as redundancy payment provided—

(a) he has been employed for the requisite period, and

(b) he was an employed contributor in employment which was insurable for all benefits under the Social Welfare Acts [...], immediately before the date of the termination of his employment, or had ceased to be ordinarily employed in employment which was so insurable in the period of [four] years ending on that date.

(2) For the purposes of subsection (1), an employee who is dismissed shall be taken to be dismissed by reason of redundancy if the dismissal is attributable wholly or mainly to—

(a) the fact that his employer has ceased, or intends to cease, to carry on the business for the purposes of which the employee was employed by him, or has ceased or intends to cease, to carry on that business in the place where the employee was so employed, or

[(b) the fact that the requirements of that business for employees to carry out work of a particular kind in the place where he was so employed have ceased or diminished or are expected to cease or diminish, or

(c) the fact that his employer has decided to carry on the business with fewer or no employees, whether by requiring the work for which the employee had been employed (or had been doing before his dismissal) to be done by other employees or otherwise, or

(d) the fact that his employer has decided that the work for which the employee had been employed (or had been doing before his dismissal) should henceforward be done in a different manner for which the employee is not sufficiently qualified or trained, or

(e) the fact that his employer has decided that the work for which the employee had been employed (or had been doing before his dismissal) should henceforward be done by a person who is also capable of doing other work for which the employee is not sufficiently qualified or trained.]

(3) For the purposes of subsection (1), an employee shall be taken as having been laid off or kept on short-time for the minimum period if he has been laid off or kept on short-time for a period of four or more consecutive weeks, or for a period of six or more weeks which are not consecutive but which fall within a period of thirteen consecutive weeks.

(4) Notwithstanding any other provision of this Act, where an employee who has been serving a period of apprenticeship training

10

with an employer under an apprenticeship agreement is dismissed within one month after the end of that period, that employee shall not, by reason of that dismissal, be entitled to redundancy payment.

[(4A) In ascertaining, for the purposes of subsection (2)(c), whether an employer has decided to carry on a business with fewer or no employees, account shall not be taken of the following members of the employer's family—

> father, mother, stepfather, stepmother, son, daughter, adopted child, grandson, granddaughter, stepson, stepdaughter, brother, sister, half-brother, half-sister.]

(5) In this section "requisite period" means a period of [104] weeks' continuous employment (within the meaning of Schedule 3) of the employee by the employer who dismissed him, laid him off or kept him on short-time, but excluding any period of employment with that employer before the employee had attained the age of 16 years.

GENERAL NOTE

The word in square brackets in paragraph (b) of subsection (1) was substituted by virtue of section 19 of the Redundancy Payments Act 1971. Paragraphs (b)–(e) of subsection (2) were inserted by virtue of section 4 of the 1971 Act. Paragraph (4A) was inserted by virtue of section 4 of the 1971 Act. The figure in square brackets in subsection (5) was substituted by virtue of section 19 of the 1971 Act. Section 40(2) of the Maternity Protection Act 1994 provides that an employee, who is entitled to return to work following absence on "protective leave" but is not permitted to do so, shall be deemed to have been dismissed by reason of redundancy, the date of dismissal being deemed to be the expected date of return. See also section 29 of the Adoptive Leave Act 1995 which provides in similar terms for an "adopting parent".

The definition, as amended in 1971, is wider than what is commonly regarded as constituting redundancy. It goes beyond an excess of manpower resulting from mechanisation, rationalisation, or from a decrease in business activity and requiring a permanent reduction in the number of persons employed. It is significantly different to the definition in the equivalent British and Northern Irish legislation, particularly in not requiring that workers adapt themselves to new methods and techniques (see *Limerick Health Authority v. Ryan* [1969] I.R. 194 which would now be decided differently in this jurisdiction). The focus is not just on the kind of work but also on the type of employee. Consequently the Employment Appeals Tribunal has held that night work is different to day work and that temporary work is different to full time work: see *Dinworth v. Southern Health Board* 284/1977 and *Kelleher v. St. James's Hospital* 64/1977.

According to the Tribunal (Chairman: Dermot MacCarthy S.C.) in *St Ledger v. Frontline Distributors Ireland Ltd* UD56/1994, the statutory definition of "redundancy" has two important characteristics, namely "impersonality" and "change".

11

"Impersonality runs throughout the five definitions in the Act. Redundancy impacts on the job and only as a consequence of the redundancy does the person involved lose his job. It is worthy of note that the E.C. Directive on Collective Redundancies uses a shorter and simpler definition: "one or more reasons not related to the individual workers concerned".

Change also runs through all five definitions. This means change in the workplace. The most dramatic change of all is a complete close down. Change may also mean a reduction in needs for employees, or a reduction in number. Definition (d) and (e) involve change in the way the work is done or some other form of change in the nature of the job. Under these two definitions change in the job must mean qualitative change. Definition (e) must involve, partly at least, work of a different kind, and that is the only meaning we can put on the words "other work". More work or less work of the same kind does not mean "other work" and is only quantitative change."

In this case the claimant was a warehouse supervisor who was dismissed and replaced by a person who was better able to handle the increased volume of work. The Tribunal did not accept that this was a redundancy. In the first place, the quantitative change was in the wrong direction. A *downward* change in the volume of work might imply redundancy under definition (b) but an *upward* change did not. Secondly the Tribunal emphasised that training was not the same as ability. It was irrelevant the claimant's replacement was better able to do the work previously done by the claimant. "To hold otherwise", the Tribunal concluded, "would be to deny the essential impersonality of redundancy".

The meaning of the words "attributable wholly or mainly to" in the equivalent British legislation was considered in *Hindle v. Percival Boats Ltd* [1969] 1 W.L.R. 174 where the Court of Appeal divided 2–1 as to whether the Tribunal should have been concerned with the cause of the dismissal or with the employer's motive. Sachs L.J. (with whom Widgery L.J. concurred in the result) took the view that the onus of proving that dismissal was not attributable to redundancy was discharged if the employer satisfied the Tribunal that the reason he gave was genuine and was the main reason for the dismissal even although that reason was based on a mistaken view of the facts. Lord Denning M.R., however, was firmly of the view that the Tribunal should not have concerned itself with the employer's motives or beliefs but with the cause of the dismissal.

If an employer is overstaffed and for that reason dismisses some employees, is that a dismissal by reason of redundancy? This question was answered affirmatively by Lord Denning in *Hindle* and by the Northern Ireland Court of Appeal in *McCrea v. Cullen & Dawson Ltd* [1988] I.R.L.R. 30. The late Gibson L.J., with whom Lord Lowry C.J. (as he then was) and O'Donnell L.J. agreed, said that what the Northern Ireland equivalent of paragraph (b) was directed to was not a diminution in the work but a diminution in the requirement for employees to do that work. Even if the diminution was foreseen at the time of engagement, there can still be a redundancy: *Lee v. Nottinghamshire County Council* [1980] I.C.R. 635.

In paragraphs (a) and (b) of subsection (2) the phrases "where the employee was so employed" and "where he was so employed" are used. The meaning of such phrases in the equivalent British legislation was considered in *Sutcliffe v. Hawker Siddely Ltd* [1973] I.C.R. 560 where it was held that they meant "where under his contract of employment he could be required to work". In the more recent decision in *Bass Leisure Ltd v. Thomas* [1994] I.R.L.R. 104, the English E.A.T. has ruled, however, that the place where an employee was employed for redundancy payment purposes does not extend to any place where he or she could be contractually required to work. The place of employment was to be established "by a factual inquiry, taking into account the employee's fixed or changing place or places of work and any contractual terms which go to evidence or define the place of employment and its extent, but not those (if any) which make provision for the employee to be transferred to another." In this case the fact that the contract provided that the company reserved the right to transfer any employee to a suitable alternative place of work did not result in the claimant losing her right to a redundancy payment when she resigned after being relocated to a depot some 20 miles away.

In *Keenan v. Gresham Hotel Co. Ltd* UD478/1988, the Tribunal (chaired by the late David Butler S.C.) emphasised that redundancy can only arise in the situations defined in subsection (2) as amended. In the instant case, the employer submitted that its requirements for employees to carry out work which the claimant was required to do had diminished or were expected to diminish. The Tribunal held, however, that such diminution

> must be expected to occur at or within a very short time after the time of the alleged redundancy, as otherwise an employer who merely expects that his requirements for employees to do work of a particular kind may diminish at some distant time in the future could greatly reduce the redundancy entitlements of such employees by serving R.P.1 forms on them prematurely.

The meaning of the words "continuous employment" in subsection (5) was considered by Murphy J. in *Irish Shipping Ltd v. Adams* High Court, January 30, 1987 (reported at (1987) 6 J.I.S.L.L. 186). Here the claimants were all seamen who served on the appellant's ships in the years prior to December 1984 when the appellant company was ordered to be wound up. An examination of the certificates of discharge of each claimant showed varying periods of engagement in respect of different ships and also varying periods elapsing between engagements. What was the relationship between the seamen and the shipping company in the period between engagements? The Tribunal took the view that the periods were merely lay-offs and did not affect continuity. Schedule 3 provides *inter alia* where an employee's period of service is interrupted by a period of not more than 26 consecutive weeks by reason of holidays, lay-offs or any cause (other than the voluntary leaving of his employment by the employee) authorised by the employer continuity of employment shall not be broken. On appeal to the High Court, Murphy J. held that, on the basis of the evidence, the Tribunal was entitled as a matter of law to conclude that, in the circumstances of this case, the periods spent ashore by the claimants constituted for the first part holidays and, to the extent that the employee was not re-engaged when he sought to resume his service, lay-off and that the balance of the period was another similar cause authorised by the employer. Accordingly Murphy J. concluded that, on the basis of the evidence accepted, the Tribunal was entitled as a matter of law to come to the decision it did and he dismissed the appeal.

Qualification of general right under section 7

8.—(1) Notwithstanding anything in section 7, where an employee who has been dismissed by reason of redundancy or laid off has, during the period of the four years immediately preceding

13

the date of dismissal or the lay-off, been laid off for an average annual period of more than twelve weeks, the following provisions shall have effect:

(a) that employee shall not become entitled to redundancy payment by reason of dismissal or lay-off until a period equal to the average annual period of lay-off over the said four-year period in relation to that employee has elapsed after the date of dismissal or lay-off;

(b) if, before the termination of the period required to elapse under paragraph (1), that employee resumes work with the same employer, that employee shall not be entitled to redundancy payment in relation to that dismissal or lay-off;

(c) if, before the termination of the period required to elapse under paragraph (a), the employer offers to re-employ that employee and that employee unreasonably refuses the offer, he shall not be entitled to redundancy payment in relation to that dismissal or lay-off.

(2) In a case where this section applies, the period of four weeks first referred to in section 12 or the period of thirteen weeks referred to in that section shall not commence until the expiration of the period (referred to in subsection (1)(a)) equal to the appropriate average annual period of lay-off.

Dismissal by employer

9.—(1) For the purposes of this Part an employee shall, subject to this Part, be taken to be dismissed by his employer if but only if—

(a) the contract under which he is employed by the employer is terminated by the employer, whether by or without notice, or

(b) where under the contract under which he is employed by the employer he is employed for a fixed term, that term expires without being renewed under the same or a similar contract, or

(c) the employee terminates the contract under which he is employed by the employer [...] in circumstances (not falling within subsection (5)) such that he is entitled so to terminate it by reason of the employer's conduct.

(2) An employee shall not be taken for the purposes of this Part to be dismissed by his employer if his contract of employment is renewed, or he is re-engaged by the same employer under a new contract of employment, and—

    (a) in a case where the provisions of the contract as renewed or of the new contract as to the capacity and place in which he is employed, and as to the other terms and conditions of his employment, do not differ from the corresponding provisions of the previous contract, the renewal or re-engagement takes effect immediately on the ending of his employment under the previous contract, or

    (b) in any other case, the renewal or re-engagement is in pursuance of an offer in writing made by his employer before the ending of his employment under the previous contract, and takes effect either immediately on the ending of that employment or after an interval of not more than four weeks thereafter.

(3)(a) An employee shall not be taken for the purposes of this Part as having been dismissed by his employer if—

    (i) he is re-engaged by another employer (hereinafter referred to as the new employer) immediately on the termination of his previous employment,

    (ii) the re-engagement takes place with the agreement of the employee, the previous employer and the new employer,

    (iii) before the commencement of the period of employment with the new employer the employee receives a statement in writing on behalf of the previous employer and the new employer which—

        (A) sets out the terms and conditions of the employee's contract of employment with the new employer,

        (B) specifies that the employee's period of service with the previous employer will, for the purposes of this Act, be regarded by the new employer as service with the new employer,

        (C) contains particulars of the services mentioned in clause (B), and

        (D) the employee notifies in writing the new employer that the employee accepts the statement required by this sub-paragraph.

(b) Where in accordance with this subsection an employee is re-engaged by the new employer, the service of that employee [with the previous employer] shall for the purposes of this Act be deemed to be service with the new employer.

(4) For the purposes of the application of subsection (2) to a contract under which the employment ends on a Friday, Saturday or Sunday—

(a) the renewal or re-engagement shall be treated as taking effect immediately on the ending of the employment under the previous contract if it takes effect on or before the next Monday after that Friday, Saturday or Sunday, and

(b) the interval of four weeks mentioned in subsection (2)(b) shall be calculated as if the employment has ended on that Monday.

(5) When an employee terminates his contract of employment without notice, being entitled to do so by reason of a lock-out by his employer, subsection (1)(c) shall not apply to that termination.

(6) Where by virtue of subsection (2) an employee is treated as not having been dismissed by reason of a renewal or re-engagement taking effect after an interval, then, in determining for the purposes of section 7(1) whether he has been continuously employed for the requisite period, the period of that interval shall count as a period of employment.

(7) In determining for the purposes of this Act whether at a particular time before the commencement of this Act an employee was dismissed by his employer, the appropriate provisions of this section shall apply as if the matter to be decided occurred after such commencement.

GENERAL NOTE

The words in square brackets in paragraph (c) of subsection (2) were deleted by virtue of section 19 of the Redundancy Payments Act 1971. The words in square brackets in paragraph (b) of subsection (3) were substituted by virtue of section 19 of the 1971 Act. It should be noted that the definition of "dismissal" in subsection (1)(c) is not as extensive as the equivalent definition in the Unfair Dismissals Act 1977, on which see *infra*, p.157, in that it only applies where the employee is "entitled" to terminate the contact: see *Western Excavating ECC Ltd v. Sharp* [1978] I.C.R. 221.

Employee anticipating expiry of employer's notice

10.—(1) This section shall have effect where—

(a) an employer gives notice to an employee to terminate his contract of employment, and

(b) at a time within the obligatory period of that notice, the employee gives notice in writing to the employer to terminate the contract of employment on a date earlier than the date on which the employer's notice is due to expire.

(2) Subject to subsection (3), in the circumstances specified in subsection (1) the employee shall, for the purposes of this Part, be taken to be dismissed by his employer and the date of dismissal in relation to that dismissal shall be the date on which the employee's notice expires.

(3) If, before the employee's notice is due to expire, the employer gives him notice in writing—

(a) requiring him to withdraw his notice terminating the contract of employment as mentioned in subsection (1)(b) and to continue in the employment until the date on which the employer's notice expires, and

(b) stating that, unless he does so, the employer will contest any liability to pay to him a redundancy payment in respect of the termination of his contract of employment,

but the employee unreasonably refuses to comply with the requirements of that notice, the employee shall not be entitled to a redundancy payment by virtue of subsection (2).

[(3A) Where an employer agrees in writing with an employee to alter the date of dismissal mentioned in a notice under subsection (1)(a) given by him to that employee so as to ensure that the employee's notice under subsection (1)(b) will be within the obligatory period in relation to the notice under subsection (1)(a), the employee's entitlement to redundancy payment shall be unaffected and the employee shall, for the purposes of this Part, be taken to be dismissed by his employer, the date of dismissal in relation to that dismissal being the date on which the employee's notice expires.]

(4) In this section—

(a) if the actual period of the employer's notice (that is to say, the period beginning at the time when the notice is given

17

and ending at the time when it expires) is equal to the minimum period which (whether by virtue of any enactment or otherwise) is required to be given by the employer to terminate the contract of employment, "the obligatory period", in relation to that notice, means the actual period of the notice;

(b) in any other case, "the obligatory period", in relation to an employer's notice, means that period which, being equal to the minimum period referred to in paragraph (a), expires at the time when the employer's notice expires.

GENERAL NOTE

Subsection (3A) was inserted by virtue of section 9 of the Redundancy Payments Act 1979. The Department have issued Form RP6 (reproduced *infra* at p.107) for the purposes of this section.

Lay-off and short time

11.—(1) Where [...] an employee's employment ceases by reason of his employer's being unable to provide the work for which the employee was employed to do, and—

(a) it is reasonable in the circumstances for that employer to believe that the cessation of employment will not be permanent, and

(b) the employer gives notice to that effect to the employee prior to the cessation,

that cessation of employment shall be regarded for the purposes of this Act as lay-off.

[(2) Where—

(a) for any week an employee's remuneration is less than one-half of his normal weekly remuneration or his hours of work are reduced to less than one-half of his normal weekly hours,

(b) the reduction in remuneration or hours of work is caused by a diminution either in the work provided for the employee by his employer or in other work of a kind which under his contract the employee is employed to do,

(c) it is reasonable in the circumstances for the employer to believe that the diminution in work will not be permanent and he gives notice to that effect to the employee prior to the reduction in remuneration or hours of work,

18

the employee shall, for the purposes of this Part, be taken to be kept on short-time for that week.]

[(3) Where by reason of a diminution in the work provided for an employee by his employer (being work of a kind which under his contract the employee is employed to do) the employee's reduced hours of work for any week are less than one-half of his normal weekly hours, he shall for the purposes of this Part be taken to be kept on short-time for that week].

GENERAL NOTE

The words in square brackets in subsection (1) were deleted by virtue of section 19 of the Redundancy Payments Act 1971. Subsection (2) was substituted by virtue of section 10 of the Redundancy Payments Act 1979. Subsection (3) was added by virtue of section 19 of the 1971 Act.

In *Industrial Yarns Ltd v. Greene* [1984] I.L.R.M. 15, Costello J. thought it important to stress that the operation of subsection (1) did not involve a termination of the contract of employment. The employment ceases but the contract of employment continues until the section 12 procedure has been utilised. If it can be shown, as in *Industrial Yarns*, that the statutory condition for the initiation of the lay-off procedure—a reasonable belief that the cessation of employment would not be permanent—is not fulfilled then, it seemed to Costello J., that the employee is entitled to treat the repudiation of the contract (ceasing to employ the employee and refusing to pay him wages) as terminating the contract and to base his claim for a redundancy payment on that fact.

Part A of Form RP9 (reproduced *infra* at p.110) may be used to notify an employee of temporary lay-off/short-time.

Right to redundancy payment by reason of lay-off or short-time

[**12.**—(1) An employee shall not be entitled to redundancy payment by reason of having been laid off or kept on short-time unless—

(a) he has been laid off or kept on short-time for four or more consecutive weeks or, within a period of thirteen weeks, for a series of six or more weeks of which not more than three were consecutive, and

(b) after the expiry of the relevant period of lay-off or short-time mentioned in paragraph (a) and not later than four weeks after the cessation of the lay-off or short-time, he gives to his employer notice (in this Part referred to as a notice of intention to claim) in writing of his intention to claim redundancy payment in respect of lay-off or short-time.

(2) Where, after the expiry of the relevant period of lay-off or short-time mentioned in subsection (1)(a) and not later than four

19

weeks after the cessation of the lay-off or short-time, an employee to whom that subsection applies, in lieu of giving to his employer a notice of intention to claim, terminates his contract of employment either by giving him the notice thereby required or, if none is so required, by giving him not less than one week's notice in writing of intention to terminate the contract, the notice so given shall, for the purposes of this Part and of Schedule 2, be deemed to be a notice of intention to claim given in writing to the employer by the employee on the date on which the notice is actually given.]

GENERAL NOTE

Section 12 was substituted by virtue of section 11 of the Redundancy Payments Act 1971. Part B of Form RP9 (reproduced *infra* at p.112) may be used to notify the employer of an intention to claim a redundancy lump sum in a lay off or short time situation.

Right of employer to give counter-notice

13.—(1) Subject to subsection (2), an employee shall not be entitled to a redundancy payment in pursuance of a notice of intention to claim if, on the date of service of that notice, it was reasonably to be expected that the employee (if he continued to be employed by the same employer) would, not later than four weeks after that date, enter upon a period of employment of not less than thirteen weeks during which he would not be laid off or kept on short-time for any week.

(2) Subsection (1) shall not apply unless, within seven days after the service of the notice of intention to claim, the employer gives to the employee notice (in this Part referred to as a counter-notice) in writing that he will contest any liability to pay to him a redundancy payment in pursuance of the notice of intention to claim.

(3) If, in a case where an employee gives notice of intention to claim and the employer gives a counter-notice, the employee continues or has continued, during the next four weeks after the date of service of the notice of intention to claim, to be employed by the same employer, and he is or has been laid off or kept on short-time for each of those weeks, it shall be conclusively presumed that the condition specified in subsection (1) was not fulfilled.

(4) Fur the purposes of section 12 and for the purposes of subsection (3)—

    (a) it is immaterial whether a series of weeks (whether it is four weeks, or four or more weeks, or six or more weeks) consists wholly of weeks for which the employee is laid off or

20

wholly of weeks for which his is kept on short-time or partly of the one and partly of the other;

(b) no account shall be taken of any week for which an employee is laid off or kept on short-time where the lay-off or short-time is wholly or mainly attributable to a strike or a lock-out, whether the strike or lock-out is in the trade or industry in which the employee is employed or not and whether it is in the State or elsewhere.

GENERAL NOTE

An employer may use Part C of Form RP9 (reproduced *infra* at p.112) to give the requisite counter notice.

Disentitlement to redundancy payment because of dismissal for misconduct

14.—(1) Subject to subsection (2), an employee who has been dismissed shall not be entitled to redundancy payment if his employer, being entitled to terminate that employee's contract of employment without notice by reason of the employee's conduct, terminates the contract because of the employee's conduct—

(a) without notice,

(b) by giving shorter notice than that which, in the absence of such conduct, the employer would be required to give to terminate the contract, or

(c) by giving notice (other than such notice as is mentioned in sub-paragraph (b)) which includes, or is accompanied by, a statement in writing that the employer would, by reason of such conduct, be entitled to terminate the contract without notice.

(2) When an employee who has received the notice required by section 17 takes part, before the date of dismissal, in a strike and his employer by reason of such participation, terminates the contract of employment with the employee in a manner mentioned in subsection (1), that subsection shall not apply to such termination.

(3) Where an employee who has given notice to terminate his contract of employment by reason of lay-off or short-time takes part, before the expiry of the notice, in a strike and, by reason of such participation, is dismissed, subsection (1) shall not apply.

21

GENERAL NOTE

As to when an employer is entitled to terminate a contract of employment without notice, see General Note to section 8 of the Minimum Notice and Terms of Employment Act 1973 (*infra* at p.141).

Disentitlement to redundancy payment for refusal to accept alternative employment

15.—(1) An employee [. . .] shall not be entitled to a redundancy payment if [. . .]

(a) his employer has offered to renew that employee's contract of employment or to re-engage him under a new contract of employment,

(b) the provisions of the contract as renewed, or of the new contract, as to the capacity and place in which he would be employed and as to the other terms and conditions of his employment would not differ from the corresponding provisions of the contract in force immediately before [the termination of his contract],

(c) the renewal or re-engagement would take effect on or before the date of [the termination of his contract], and

(d) he has unreasonably refused the offer.

(2) An employee [. . .] shall not be entitled to a redundancy payment if [. . .]

(a) his employer has made to him in writing an offer to renew the employee's contract of employment or to re-engage him under a new contract of employment,

(b) the provisions of the contract as renewed, or of the new contract, as to the capacity and place in which he would be employed and as to the other terms and conditions of his employment would differ wholly or in part from the corresponding provisions of his contract in force immediately before [the termination of his contract].

(c) the offer constitutes an offer of suitable employment in relation to the employee,

(d) the renewal or re-engagement would take effect not later than four weeks after the date of [the termination of his contract], and

(e) he has unreasonably refused the offer.

22

[(2A) Where an employee who has been offered suitable employment and has carried out, for a period of not more than four weeks, the duties of that employment, refuses the offer, the temporary acceptance of that employment shall not solely constitute an unreasonable refusal for the purposes of this section.]

[(2B) Where—

(a) an employee's remuneration is reduced substantially but not to less than one-half of his normal weekly remuneration, or his hours of work are reduced substantially but not to less than one-half of his normal weekly hours, and

(b) the employee temporarily accepts the reduction in remuneration or hours of work and indicates his acceptance to his employer,

such a temporary acceptance for a period not exceeding 52 weeks shall not be taken to be an acceptance by the employee of an offer of suitable employment in relation to him.]

[(3) Where a person who is entitled to a weekly payment has unreasonably refused suitable employment offered or approved by [An Foras Aiseanna Saothair], that person shall be disqualified from receiving any further payments.]

GENERAL NOTE

The words in square brackets in subsections (1) and (2) were deleted or substituted, as the case may be, by virtue of section 19 of the Redundancy Payments Act 1971. Subsection (2A) was inserted by virtue of section 19 of the 1971 Act. In *O'Connor v. Ormond Printing Co. Ltd.* 629/1988, the Tribunal observed that, although the new subsection mentioned a period of four weeks, it was not a "necessary corollary" that a trial period longer than four weeks "would necessarily disentitle an employee under the Acts". Subsection (2B) was inserted by virtue of section 11 of the Redundancy Payments Act 1979. Subsection (3) was substituted by virtue of section 19 of the 1971 Act with the words in square brackets therein being substituted by virtue of section 18(4) of the Labour Services Act 1987.

The question of whether the "new" contract involves working in the same place has been considered many times by the Tribunal. So in *Broderick v. Dorothea Fashions Ltd* 11/1978 the Tribunal held that East Arran St. was not the same place as Churchtown.

As to whether there has been an unreasonable refusal of an offer of suitable alternative employment, see *McCann v. St Laurence's Hospital* UD348/1988. In *Cambridge & District Co-operative Society Ltd v. Ruse* [1993] I.R.L.R. 156 the English E.A.T., when considering the similarly worded provisions of the British legislation, said, at 158, that the question of "the suitability of the employment is an objective matter, whereas the reasonableness of the employee's refusal depends on factors personal to him and is a subjective matter to be considered from the employee's point of view".

Associated companies

16.—(1) Where the employer is a company, any reference in this Part to re-engagement by the employer shall be construed as a reference to re-engagement by that company or by an associated company, and any reference in this Part to an offer made by the employer shall be construed as including a reference to an offer made by an associated company.

(2) Subsection (1) shall not affect the operation of section 20 in a case where the previous owner and new owner (as defined by that section) are associated companies; and where that section applies, subsection (1) shall not apply.

(3) Where an employee is dismissed by his employer, and the employer is a company (in this subsection referred to as the employing company) which has one or more associated companies, then if—

(a) [none of the conditions specified in sections 7(2) is fulfilled, but]

(b) one or other of these conditions would be fulfilled if the business of the employing company and the business of the associated company (or, if more than one, each of the associated companies) were treated as together constituting one business, that condition shall for the purposes of this Part be taken to be fulfilled in relation to the dismissal of the employee.

(4) For the purposes of this section two companies shall be taken to be associated companies if one is a subsidiary of the other, or both are subsidiaries of a third company, and "associated company" shall be construed accordingly.

(5) In this section—

"company" includes any body corporate;

"subsidiary" has the same meaning as, by virtue of section 155 of the Companies Act 1963, it has for the purposes of that Act.

GENERAL NOTE

The words in square brackets in subsection (2)(a) were substituted by virtue of section 19 of the Redundancy Payments Act 1971.

Section 155(1) of the Companies Act 1963 provides that a company shall be deemed to be a subsidiary of another company if that other is a member of it and controls the composition of its board of directors, or if that other holds more than half in nominal value of its equity share capital, or if that other holds more than half in nominal value of its shares carrying voting rights.

24

Notice of proposed dismissal for redundancy

17.—(1) An employer who proposes to dismiss by reason of redundancy an employee who has not less than [104 weeks] service with that employer shall, not later than two weeks before the date of dismissal, give to the employee notice in writing of the proposed dismissal and send to the Minister a copy of that notice.

(2) The Minister may make regulations for giving effect to this section and, without prejudice to the generality of the foregoing, regulations under this section may relate to all or any of the following matters—

  (a) the particulars to be stated in the notice,
  (b) the method of service of the notice,
  (c) the furnishing to the Minister of a copy of the notice and the time for furnishing such a copy.

(3) An employer who fails to comply with this section or who furnishes false information in a notice under this section shall be guilty of an offence and shall be liable on summary conviction to a fine not exceeding [£300]

GENERAL NOTE

The words in square brackets in subsections (1) and (3) were substituted respectively by virtue of section 10 of the Redundancy Payments Act 1971 and section 17 of the Redundancy Payments Act 1979.

In exercise of the powers conferred upon him by this section the Minister has made the Redundancy (Notice of Dismissal) Regulations 1991 (S.I. No. 348 of 1991), reproduced *infra* at p.104.

Redundancy certificate

18.—[(1) When an employer dismisses by reason of redundancy an employee who has not less than 104 weeks' continuous employment, he shall give to the employee not later than the date of the dismissal a certificate (in this Part referred to as a redundancy certificate).

(2) Whenever an employee who has not less than 104 weeks' continuous employment gives notice of intention to claim in accordance with section 12, his employer shall, subject to section 13, give him, not later than seven days after the service of the notice of intention to claim, a redundancy certificate.]

(3) The Minister may make regulations for giving effect to this section and, without prejudice to the generality of the foregoing,

may prescribe the particulars to be stated on a redundancy certificate.

(4) An employer who fails to comply with this section or who furnishes false information in a redundancy certificate shall be guilty of an offence shall be liable on summary conviction to a fine not exceeding [£300].

GENERAL NOTE

Subsections (1) and (2) were substituted by virtue of section 19 of the Redundancy Payments Act 1971. The figure in square brackets in subsection (4) was substituted by virtue of section 17 of the Redundancy Payments Act 1979.

In exercise of the power conferred upon him by this section the Minister has made the Redundancy Certificate Regulations 1991 (S.I. No. 347 of 1991), reproduced *infra* at p.100.

This section was considered by Kenny J. in *Minister for Labour v. O'Connor* High Court March 6, 1973 (reported at (1985) 4 J.I.S.L.L. 72) who said that the calculation of the statutory lump sum was "an involved, difficult process" and that one of the purposes of the certificate was "to enable the employee to see how it has been calculated". It also has the purpose that it establishes that the lump sum has been paid so that the employer can claim a payment of the rebate from the Social Insurance Fund (on which see section 29 *infra* at p.34). In this case the employee was dismissed for reasons of redundancy and his statutory entitlement was £132. The employee was paid £500 by way of compensation and a dispute arose as to whether this included his statutory lump sum. The employee had not been given the prescribed certificate. Kenny J. said that, if an employer agrees to pay a larger sum to which the employee is statutorily entitled but does not get the certificate signed by the employee, the employee's right to payment of the lump sum is not lost unless the employer establishes that:

i) the employee knew the amount of the statutory lump sum before or at the time of dismissal, and

ii) the employee agreed to accept the sum offered in discharge of the employer's statutory liability to pay the lump sum and of the claim which the employee believed he had against the employer for compensation for dismissal.

See also the Tribunal's determination in *Ward v. MCM Builders Ltd* 40/1990.

Payment of lump sum by employer

19.—(1) Upon the dismissal by reason of redundancy of an employee who is entitled under this Part to redundancy payment, [or where by virtue of section 12 an employee becomes entitled to redundancy payment,] his employer shall pay to him an amount which is referred to in this Act as the lump sum.

(2) Schedule 3 shall apply in relation to the lump sum.

(3) The Minister may by order amend Schedule 3.

GENERAL NOTE

The words in square brackets in subsection (1) were inserted by virtue of section 19 of the Redundancy Payments Act 1971. Section 4(2) of the Redundancy Payments Act 1979 provides that the Minister may, by regulations made with the consent of the Minister for Finance, both vary the amount referred to in paragraph 2 of Schedule 3, and alter the method of calculation of a lump sum under this Act. By virtue of the Redundancy Payments (Lump Sum) Regulations 1994 (S.I. No. 64 of 1994) the ceiling on annual reckonable earnings to be taken into account in the calculation of the lump sum is now £15,600.

Change of ownership of business

20.—(1) This section shall have effect where—

(a) a change occurs (whether by virtue of a sale or other disposition or by operation of law) in the ownership of a business for the purposes of which a person is employed, or of a part of such a business, and

(b) in connection with that change the person by whom the employee is employed immediately before the change occurs (in this section referred to as the previous owner) terminates the employee's contract of employment, whether by or without notice.

(2) If, by agreement with the employee, the person (in this section referred to as the new owner) who immediately after the change occurs is the owner of the business or of the part of the business in question as the case may be renews the employee's contract of employment (with the substitution of the new owner for the previous owner) or re-engages him under a new contract of employment, section 9(2) shall have effect as if the renewal or re-engagement had been a renewal or re-engagement by the previous owner (without any substitution of the new owner for the previous owner).

(3) If the new owner offers to renew the employee's contract of employment (with the substitution of the new owner for the previous owner) or to re-engage him under a new contract of employment, but the employee refuses the offer, section 15(1) or section 15(2) (as may be appropriate) shall have effect, subject to subsection (4) of this section, in relation to that offer and refusal as it would have had effect in relation to the like offer made by the previous owner and a refusal of that offer by the employee.

27

(4) For the purpose of the operation, in accordance with subsection (3) of this section, of section 15(1) or 15(2) in relation to an offer made by the new owner,—

(a) the offer shall not be treated as one whereby the provisions of the contract as renewed, or of the new contract, as the case may be, would differ from the corresponding provisions of the contract as in force immediately before the dismissal by reason only that the new owner would be substituted for the previous owner as the employer, and

(b) no account shall be taken of that substitution in determining whether the refusal of the offer was unreasonable.

(5) Subsections (1) to (4) shall have effect (subject to the necessary modifications) in relation to a case where—

(a) the person by whom a business, or part of a business, is owned immediately before a change is one of the persons by whom (whether as partners, trustees or otherwise) it is owned immediately after the change, or

(b) the persons by whom a business, or part of a business, is owned immediately before a change (whether as partners, trustees or otherwise) include the person by whom, or include one or more of the persons by who, it is owned immediately after the change,

as those provisions have effect where the previous owner and the new owner are wholly different persons.

[(5A) In a case mentioned in subsection (1)(a), the new owner shall be estopped from denying that an employee was in continuous employment (within the meaning of Schedule 3) unless, within 26 weeks of the change of ownership, he notifies the employee of his intention so to deny.]

(6) Nothing in this section shall be construed as requiring any variation of a contract of employment by agreement between the parties to be treated as constituting a termination of the contract.

GENERAL NOTE

Subsection (5A) was inserted by virtue of section 5 of the Redundancy Payments Act 1971. Section 6 of the 1971 Act extends the application of this section to cases where there is a change relating to the control or management of a business but a change in the ownership of the business does not occur. Note that paragraph 2 of Schedule 2 provides that this section shall not apply to any change whereby the ownership of the business passes to a deceased employer's personal representative.

In *Minister for Labour v. Devoy* High Court, March 6, 1973 (reported at (1985) 4 J.I.S.L.L. 76) Kenny J. said that section 20 related to changes in the ownership of a business which occurred after the Act came into operation on January 1, 1968.

Implied or constructive termination of contract

21.—(1) Where, in accordance with any enactment or rule of law, any act on the part of an employer or any event affecting an employer (including, in the case of an individual, his death) operates so as to terminate a contract under which an employee is employed by him, that act or event shall for the purposes of this Act be treated as a termination of the contract by the employer, if apart from this subsection, it would not constitute a termination of the contract by him.

(2) Where—

(a) subsection (1) applies,
(b) the employee's contract of employment is not renewed, and
(c) he is not re-engaged under a new contract, as provided by section 9(2),

he shall for the purposes of this Act be taken to be dismissed by reason of redundancy if the circumstances in which the contract is not renewed and he is not re-engaged (as provided by the said section 9(2)) are wholly or mainly attributable to a fact specified in section [7(2)].

(3) For the purposes of subsection (2), section 7(2)(a), in so far as it relates to the employer ceasing or intending to cease to carry on the business, shall be construed as if the reference to the employer included a reference to any person to whom, in consequence or the act or event in question, power to dispose of the business has passed.

(4) In this section reference to section 9(2) includes reference to that section as applied by section 20(2).

GENERAL NOTE

Subsection (2) was amended by virtue of section 19 of the Redundancy Payments Act 1971. Paragraph 6 of Schedule 2 (*see infra* p.56) provides that, where by virtue of section 21 the death of the employer is to be treated as a termination by him of the contract of employment, any reference in subsection (2) to section 9(2) shall be construed as including a reference to paragraph 3 of Schedule 2.

Application of this Part upon employer's or employee's death

22.—(1) Part 1 of Schedule 2 shall have effect in relation to the death of an employer.

(2) Part 2 of Schedule 2 shall have effect in relation to the death of an employee.

Modification of right to redundancy payment where previous redundancy payment has been paid

23.—(1) This section shall apply where—

(a) a lump sum is paid to an employee under section 19, whether in respect of dismissal, lay-off or short-time,

(b) the contract of employment under which he was employed (in this section referred to as the previous contract) is renewed, whether by the same or another employer, or he is re-engaged under a new contract of employment, whether by the same or another employer, and

(c) the circumstances of the renewal or re-engagement are such that, in determining for the purposes of section 7(1) or Schedule 3 whether at any subsequent time he has been continuously employed for the requisite period, or for what period he has been continuously employed, the continuity of his period of employment would, apart from this section, be treated as not having been broken by the termination of his previous contract and the renewal or re-engagement.

(2) In determining for the purposes of section 7(1) or section 19 in a case to which this section applies whether at any subsequent time an employee has been continuously employed for the requisite period, or for what period he has been continuously employed, the continuity of the period of employment shall be treated as having been broken at the date which was the date of dismissal in relation to the lump sum mentioned in subsection (1)(a), and any time before that date shall be disregarded.

(3) For the purposes of this section a lump sum shall be treated as having been paid if the whole of the payment has been paid to the employee by the employer or if the Minister has paid a sum, to the employee in respect of the redundancy payment under section 32.

[(4) This section shall not apply in any case to which section 19 of the Unfair Dismissals Act 1977 applies.]

GENERAL NOTE

Subsection (4) was inserted by virtue of section 17 of the Redundancy Payments Act 1979. Section 19 of the Unfair Dismissals Act 1977 provides that, where an employee is reinstated or re-engaged in pursuance of a determination or order under the 1977 Act (as amended), any payments made under the Redundancy Payments Acts shall be repaid.

Time-limit on claims for redundancy payment

24.—(1) Notwithstanding any other provision of this Act, an employee shall not be entitled to a lump sum unless before the end of the period of [52] weeks beginning on the date of dismissal or the date of termination of employment—

(a) the payment has been agreed and paid, or
(b) the employee has made a claim for the payment by notice in writing given to the employer, or
(c) a question as to the right of the employee to the payment, or as to the amount of the payment, has been referred to the Tribunal under section 39.

[(2) Notwithstanding any provision of this Act, an employee shall not be entitled to a weekly payment unless he has become entitled to a lump sum.]

[(2A) Where an employee who fails to make a claim for a lump sum within the period of 52 weeks mentioned in subsection (1) (as amended) makes such a claim before the end of the period of 104 weeks beginning on the date of dismissal or the date of termination of employment, the Tribunal, if it is satisfied that the employee would have been entitled to the lump sum and that the failure was due to a reasonable cause, may declare the employee to be entitled to the lump sum and the employee shall thereupon become so entitled.]

[(3) Notwithstanding subsection (2A), where an employee establishes to the satisfaction of the Tribunal—

(a) that failure to make a claim for a lump sum before the end of the period of 104 weeks mentioned in that subsection was caused by his ignorance of the identity of his employer or employers or by his ignorance of a change of employer involving his dismissal and engagement under a contract with another employer, and

31

(b) that such ignorance arose out of or was contributed to by a breach of a statutory duty to give the employee either notice of his proposed dismissal or a redundancy certificate,

the period of 104 weeks shall commence from such date as the Tribunal at its discretion considers reasonable having regard to all the circumstances.]

GENERAL NOTE

The time limit in subsection (1) was originally 30 weeks but was increased to 52 by section 12(2) of the Redundancy Payments Act 1971. Section 12(1) of the 1971 Act amended section 24 by inserting subsection (2). Section 12(2) of the 1971 Act also amended section 24 by inserting subsection (2A). Subsection (3) was inserted by virtue of section 13 of the Redundancy Payments Act 1979.

On whether the failure to lodge a claim in time was due to a "reasonable cause" see *Clancy v. Beau Monde Ltd* 945/1977; *Comiskey v. Beau Monde Ltd* 99/1978; *Weldon v. Beau Monde Ltd* 236/1978; *Kelly v. Kenna* 20/1982; *Finucane v. Pat Dowling (Electrical Contractors) Ltd* 111/1982 and *Doherty v. John Grant and Co. Ltd* 51/1983.

Employment wholly or partly abroad

25.—(1) An employee shall not be entitled to redundancy payment if on the date of dismissal he is outside the State, unless under his contract of employment he ordinarily worked in the State.

(2) [Notwithstanding subsection (1), an employee] who under his contract of employment ordinarily works outside the State shall not be entitled to redundancy payment unless, immediately before he commenced to work outside the State, he was domiciled in the State and was in the employment of the employer concerned and unless—

(a) he was in the State in accordance with the instructions of his employer on the date of dismissal, or
(b) he had not been afforded a reasonable opportunity by his employer of being in the State on that date.

(3) In computing, for the purposes of this Act, for what period of service a person was in continuous employment, any period of service in the employment of the employer concerned while the employee was outside the State shall be deemed to have been service in the employment of that employer within the State.

(4) Where an employee who has worked for his employer outside the State becomes entitled to redundancy payment under this Act, the employer in making any lump sum payment due to the

employee under section 19 shall be entitled to deduct from that payment any redundancy payment to which that employee may have been entitled under a statutory scheme relating to redundancy in the State which he was working.

GENERAL NOTE

Subsection (2) was amended by virtue of section 19 of the Redundancy Payments Act 1971. As to whether a person is domiciled in the State see Binchy, *Irish Conflict of Laws* (1988), pp. 45–96.

PART III

[SOCIAL INSURANCE] FUND

Establishment of the Redundancy Fund

26. [*Repealed by section 29 of the Social Welfare Act 1990*]

[Social Insurance Fund]

[**27.** All moneys received by the Minister under this Act shall be paid into the Social Insurance Fund and all payments made pursuant to this Act shall be made out of that Fund.]

GENERAL NOTE

This section was inserted by virtue of section 39 of the Social Welfare Act 1991.

Amount of contribution

28. [*Repealed by section 39(1) of the Social Welfare Act 1991*]

Rebates to employers

[**29.**—(1) Subject to this Part, the Minister shall make from the [Social Insurance] Fund a payment to an employer of such sum (in this Part referred to as a rebate) as is equivalent in amount to 60 per cent of each lump sum paid by that employer under section 19.

(2) Notwithstanding subsection (1), whenever an employer fails to comply with any provision of section 17, the Minister may at his discretion reduce the amount of the rebate payable in respect of the lump sum paid under section 19 to that employer, but the amount of rebate when so reduced shall not be less than 40 per cent of the lump sum.

(3) The Minister may by regulation, made with the consent of the Minister for Finance, vary a rate of rebate specified in this section.]

GENERAL NOTE

This section (as amended by section 26 of the Social Welfare Act 1990) was inserted by virtue of section 13 of the Redundancy Payments Act 1971. An employer who makes an error in the calculation of the redundancy lump sum leaves itself open to having an application for a rebate refused: see *Secretary of State for Employment v. Cheltenham Computer Bureau Ltd* [1985] I.R.L.R. 333 where Waite J. said that the Secretary of State was not obliged to pay a rebate if the redundancy lump sum was not calculated in accordance with the precise formula even where the parties had agreed this sum and had it endorsed by an industrial tribunal. It should also be noted that a rebate is only repayable in respect of the statutory payment.

Weekly payments to employees from [Social Insurance] Fund

30.—(1) Upon his dismissal by reason of redundancy [or where by virtue of section 12 he becomes entitled to redundancy payment], an employee who is entitled to redundancy payment shall be entitled, subject to this Act, to a weekly payment (in this Act referred to as a weekly payment) from the [Social Insurance] Fund.

(2) The provisions of Schedule 1 shall apply to a weekly payment.

(3) The Minister may by order amend Schedule 1.

GENERAL NOTE

The words in square brackets in subsection (1) were inserted by virtue of section 19 of the Redundancy Payments Act 1971.

Schedule 1 was amended by the Redundancy Payments (Weekly Payments and Lump Sum) Order 1974 (S.I. No. 82 of 1974) and the Redundancy Payments (Weekly Payments) Order 1976 (S.I. No. 126 of 1976). Note that section 4(4) of the Redundancy Payments Act 1979 provides that these two orders shall cease to have effect from April 6, 1979 and section 8 of that Act further provides that this section shall similarly cease to have effect from the same date save for those persons who were in receipt of weekly payments at that time.

Regulations as to entitlement to weekly payment and to allowance under Industrial Training Act 1967

31.—(1) The Minister may by regulations provide, in relation to cases where a person is entitled to an allowance under section 9(1)(g) of the Industrial Training Act 1967, and to a weekly payment, for adjusting the amount of such allowance or the amount of such weekly payment.

(2) Notwithstanding any other provision of this Act, regulations under this section may provide that a person to whom the regulations apply shall not be entitled to a weekly payment either at all or for a specified period.

GENERAL NOTE

Section 8 of the Redundancy Payments Act 1979 provides that this section shall cease to have effect from April 6, 1979, save for those persons who were in receipt of weekly payments at that time.

Other payments to employees from [Social Insurance] Fund

[**32.**—(1) When an employee claims that an employer is liable to pay to him a lump sum under section 19 and that—

(a) the employee has taken all reasonable steps (other than legal proceedings) to obtain the payment of the lump sum from the employer and the employer has refused or failed to pay it or has paid part of it and has refused or failed to pay the balance, [or]

(b) the employer is insolvent and the whole or part of the lump sum remains unpaid, or

(c) the employer has died and neither probate of his will has, nor letters of administration in respect of his estate have, been granted, and the whole or part of the lump sum remains unpaid,

the employee may apply to the Minister for a payment under this section.

(2) If on an application under this section the Minister is satisfied that an employee is entitled to a lump sum under section 19 which remains unpaid either in whole or in part, the Minister shall pay to the employee out of the [Social Insurance] Fund so much of the lump sum as remains unpaid.

(3) Upon the payment by the Minister of a payment under this section all rights and remedies of the employee with respect to the lump sum concerned or, if the Minister has paid part of it, with respect to that part, shall thereupon stand transferred to and become vested in the Minister and any moneys recovered by the Minister by virtue of this subsection shall be paid into the [Social Insurance] Fund.

(4) Where, in a case falling within subsection (1)(a), the Minister makes a payment to an employee under subsection (2), the Minister shall claim from the employer a sum equal to the amount of the payment made by the Minister under subsection (2) less the amount of the rebate that would have been payable to the employer from the [Social Insurance] Fund under section 29 if the employer had paid the lump sum to the employee, save that, where it appears to the Minister that the refusal or failure of the employer was without reasonable excuse, the Minister may either withhold any rebate to which the employer would otherwise have been entitled to reduce the amount of that rebate to such extent as the Minister thinks appropriate, and in either such case the amount of

the Minister's claim against the employer under this subsection may be increased accordingly.

(5) Where, in a case falling within subsection (1)(b), the Minister makes a payment to an employee under subsection (2), the Minister shall be entitled to claim in the bankruptcy, arrangement, administration of the insolvent estate or winding up (as the case may be) in respect of, and only in respect of, a sum equal to the amount of the payment made by the Minister under subsection (2) less the amount of the rebate that would have been payable to the employer from the [Social Insurance] Fund under section 29 if the employer had paid the lump sum to the employee.

(6) Where, in a case falling within subsection (1)(c), the Minister makes a payment to an employee under subsection (2), the Minister shall be entitled to claim from the deceased employer's estate in respect of, and only in respect of, a sum equal to the amount of the payment made by the Minister under subsection (2) less the amount of the rebate that would have been payable to the deceased employer's estate from the [Social Insurance] Fund under section 29 if the employee had been paid the lump sum from the estate of the deceased employer.

(7) For the purpose of this section an employer shall be deemed to be insolvent if—

(a) the employer has been adjudicated bankrupt, has filed a petition for arrangement or has executed a deed of arrangement (within the meaning of section 4 of the Deeds of Arrangement Act 1887).

(b) the employer has died and his estate, being insolvent, is being administered in accordance with the rules set out in Part I of the First Schedule to the Succession Act 1965, or

(c) the employer is a company, and the company is insolvent and being wound up.]

GENERAL NOTE

This section was inserted by virtue of section 17 of the Redundancy Payments Act 1979. Form RP14 (reproduced *infra* at p.113) may be used when applying to the Minister for payment of a redundancy lump sum from the Social Insurance Fund. Form RP77 (reproduced *infra* at p.115) may be used to apply to the employer for payment.

Regulations as to payment of contributions

33. [*Repealed by section 39(1) of the Social Welfare Act 1991*]

Preparation and issue of redundancy stamps, etc.

34. [*Repealed by section 18 of the Redundancy Payments Act 1979*]

Persons employed by more than one employer, etc.

35.—(1) In relation to persons who—

(a) are employed by more than one employer in any week, or

(b) work under the general control or management of some person other than their immediate employer,

and in relation to any other cases for which it appears to the Minister that special provision is needed, regulations may provide that for the purposes of this Act the prescribed person shall be treated as their employer.

(2) Regulations made relating to persons mentioned in subsection (1)(b) may provide for adjusting the rights between themselves of the person prescribed as the employer, the immediate employer and the persons employed.

GENERAL NOTE

The following Regulations have been made under this section all of which provide that, for the purpose of calculating redundancy payments entitlements of workers disemployed under schemes of decasualisation and rationalisation for the Ports of Dublin, Dundalk, Galway, Limerick and Waterford, their periods of service with various firms can be aggregated.

Redundancy Payments (Dublin Port Dockers) Regulations 1971 (S.I. No. 301 of 1971)

Redundancy Payments (Dublin Port Dockers) Regulations 1973 (S.I. No. 42 of 1973)

Redundancy Payments (Dundalk Port Dockers) Regulations 1973 (S.I. No. 95 of 1973)

Redundancy Payments (Galway Port Dockers) Regulations 1973 (S.I. No. 26 of 1973)

Redundancy Payments (Limerick Port Dockers) Regulations 1974 (S.I. No. 59 of 1974)

Redundancy Payments (Waterford Port Dockers) Regulations 1975 (S.I. No. 73 of 1975)

Regulations for Part III

36.—(1) The Minister may make regulations for giving effect to this Part.

(2) Without prejudice to the generality of subsection (1), regulations under this section may make provision in relation to all or any of the following matters:

- (a) requiring an employer entitled to a rebate to make a claim therefor and prescribing the time within which such a claim is to be made;
- (b) requiring an employer who has made a claim for a rebate to produce such evidence and other information as may be prescribed and to produce for examination on behalf of the Minister such documents as may be prescribed and are in that employer's custody or under his control;
- (c) requiring, in connection with an application made to the Minister under section 32, the employer concerned to produce for examination on behalf of the Minister such documents as may be prescribed and are in the employer's custody or under his control;
- (d) [. . .]
- (e) prescribing the method, time and place for the making of weekly payments.

(3) A person who fails to comply with a regulation under subsection (2)(b) or (2)(c) or who, in relation to a regulation requiring information, furnishes false information shall be guilty of an offence and shall be liable on summary conviction to a fine not exceeding [£300].

GENERAL NOTE

The words in square brackets in paragraph (d) of subsection (2) were deleted by virtue of section 18 of the Redundancy Payments Act 1979. The figure in square brackets in subsection (3) was inserted by virtue of section 17 of the Redundancy Payments Act 1979.

The Redundancy (Rebates) Regulations 1990 (S.I. No. 122 of 1990)—reproduced *infra* at p.96—provide that a claim for a rebate should be made in the prescribed form before the expiration of six months from the date on which the employer made the relevant lump sum payment.

PART IV

MISCELLANEOUS PROVISIONS

Deciding officers

37. The Minister may appoint [...] such and so many persons as he thinks proper to be deciding officers for the purposes of this Act, and every person so appointed shall hold office as a deciding officer during the pleasure of the Minister.

GENERAL NOTE

The words in square brackets were deleted by virtue of section 19 of the Redundancy Payments Act 1979.

Decisions by deciding officers

38.—(1) Subject to this Act and in accordance with any relevant regulations, every question arising—

(a) in relation to a claim for a weekly payment,
(b) as to whether a person is disqualified for a weekly payment,
(c) as to the period of any disqualification for a weekly payment,
(d) [...]
(e) as to who is the employer of an employee, or
(f) on any such other matter relating to this Act as may be prescribed,

shall be decided by a deciding officer.

(2) A reference in this section to a question arising in relation to a claim for a weekly payment includes a reference to a question whether a weekly payment is or is not payable.

GENERAL NOTE

The words in square brackets in paragraph (d) of subsection (1) were deleted by virtue of section 39(1) of the Social Welfare Act 1991.

[Employment] Appeals Tribunal and appeals and references thereto

39.—(1) There shall be a Tribunal (which shall be known as the [Employment] Appeals Tribunal and is in this section hereinafter referred to as the Tribunal) to determine the appeals provided for in this section.

(2) The Tribunal shall consist of the following members—

[(a) a chairman who before his appointment shall have had not less than 7 years' experience as a practising barrister or practising solicitor.]

[(b) not more than 5 vice-chairman, and

(c) not less than 12 and not more than 30 ordinary members.]

(3) The members of the Tribunal shall be appointed by the Minister and shall be eligible for re-appointment.

[(3A) Notwithstanding subsection (2), whenever the Minister is of the opinion that for the speedy despatch of the business of the Tribunal it is expedient that there should be added further vice-chairmen or further ordinary members (or both further vice-chairmen and further ordinary members), he may make such additional appointments, and the reference in subsection (4) shall include a reference to this subsection.]

(4) The appointments pursuant to subsection (3) of the ordinary members of the Tribunal shall be made—

(a) as to one-half of those members, being persons nominated for that purpose by an organisation representative of trade unions of workers, and

(b) as to the other half of those members, from among persons nominated for that purpose by a body or bodies representative of employers.

(5) The term of office of a member of the Tribunal shall be such period as is specified by the Minister when appointing such member.

(6)(a) A member of the Tribunal may, by letter addressed to the Minister, resign his membership.

(b) A member of the Tribunal may be removed from office by the Minister.

(7)(a) Whenever a vacancy occurs in the membership of the Tribunal and is caused by the resignation, removal from office or death of an ordinary member mentioned in subsection (4)(a), the vacancy shall be filled by the Minister by appointment in the manner specified in that subsection.

(b) Whenever a vacancy occurs in the membership of the Tribunal and is caused by the resignation, removal from office or death of an ordinary member mentioned in subsection (4)(b), the vacancy shall be filled by the Minister by appointment in the manner specified in that subsection.

(8) In the case of a member of the Tribunal filling a vacancy caused by the resignation, removal from office or death of a member before the completion of the term of office of the last-mentioned member, the member filling that vacancy shall hold office for the remainder of the term of office of the period who so resigned, died or was so removed from office.

(9) A vice-chairman of the Tribunal shall act as chairman thereof when so required by the chairman or the Minister and when so acting shall have all the powers of the chairman.

(10) A member of the Tribunal shall be paid such remuneration (if any) and allowances as may be determined by the Minister with the consent of the Minister for Finance.

(11) Whenever the chairman of the Tribunal is of the opinion that, for the speedy dispatch of the business of the Tribunal, it is expedient that the Tribunal should act by divisions, he may direct accordingly and, until he revokes his direction, the Tribunal shall be grouped as so directed.

(12) Each division of the Tribunal shall consist of either the chairman or a vice-chairman of the Tribunal, an ordinary member of the Tribunal mentioned in subsection (4)(a) and an ordinary member of the Tribunal mentioned in subsection (4)(b).

(13) The Minister may, with the consent of the Minister for Finance, appoint such officers and servants of the Tribunal as he considers necessary to assist the Tribunal in the performance of its functions, and such officers and servants shall hold office on such terms and receive such remuneration as the Minister for Finance determines.

(14) The decision of the Tribunal on any question referred to it under this section shall be final and conclusive, save that any person dissatisfied with the decision may appeal therefrom to the High Court on a question of law.

(15) Any employer who is dissatisfied with a decision given by the Minister in relation to a rebate or with any decision given by a deciding officer in relation to any question specified in section [. . .] 38(1)(e) or 38(1)(f), or any employee who is dissatisfied with a decision given by a deciding officer under section 38 or with any decision of an employer under this Act [may appeal to the Tribunal against the decision]; provided however, that the Tribunal shall not

be competent to decide whether or not an employee is or was at the material times in employment which is or was insurable for all benefits under the Social Welfare Acts [. . .].

(16) A deciding officer may if he so thinks proper, instead of deciding it himself, refer in the prescribed manner to the Tribunal for a decision thereon any question which falls to be decided by him under section 38.

(17) (a) The Tribunal shall, on the hearing of any matter referred to it under this section, have power to take evidence on oath and for that purpose may cause to be administered oaths to persons attending as witnesses at such hearing.

(b) Any person who, upon examination on oath authorised under this subsection, wilfully and corruptly gives false evidence or wilfully and corruptly swears anything which is false, being convicted thereof, shall be liable to the penalties for wilful and corrupt perjury.

(c) The Tribunal may, by giving notice in that behalf in writing any person, require such person to attend at such time and place as is specified in the notice to give evidence in relation to any matter referred to the Tribunal under this section or to produce any documents in his possession, custody or control which relate to any such matter.

(d) A notice under paragraph (c) may be given either by delivering it to the person to whom it relates or by sending it by post in a prepaid registered letter addressed to such person at the address at which he ordinarily resides.

(e) A person to whom a notice under paragraph (c) has been given and who refuses or wilfully neglects to attend in accordance with the notice or who, having so attended, refuses to give evidence or refuses or wilfully fails to produce any document to which the notice relates shall be guilty of an offence and shall be liable on summary conviction thereof to a fine not exceeding [£150].

(18) The Tribunal shall submit an annual report to the Minister which shall be published.

(19) The Minister may make regulations giving effect to this section and such regulations may, in particular but without prejudice to the generality of the foregoing, provide for all or any of the following matters—

(a) the procedure to be followed regarding the submission of appeals to the Tribunal,

(b) the times and places of hearings by the Tribunal,

(c) the representation of parties attending hearings by the Tribunal,

(d) procedure regarding the hearing of appeals by the Tribunal,

(e) publication and notification of decisions of the Tribunal,

(f) notices relating to appeals or hearings by the Tribunal,

(g) the award by the Tribunal of costs and expenses and the payment of such awards,

(h) an official seal of the Tribunal,

(i) for treating the Minister as a party to any proceedings before the Tribunal where he would not otherwise be a party to them and entitling him to appear and be heard accordingly.

GENERAL NOTE

By virtue of section 18 of the Unfair Dismissals Act 1977, the Tribunal established by this section (the Redundancy Appeals Tribunal) shall be known as the Employment Appeals Tribunal. Subsection (2) was amended as to paragraph (a) by section 7 of the Redundancy Payments Act 1971 and as to paragraphs (b) and (c) by section 17 of the Redundancy Payments Act 1979.

The Tribunal presently consists of the Chairman and thirteen Vice-Chairmen (all with legal qualifications) and a panel of forty other members. Subsection (15) was amended by virtue of section 17 of the Redundancy Payments Act 1979. The figure in square brackets in paragraph (e) of subsection (17) was inserted by virtue of section 17 of the Redundancy Payments Act 1979 although it should be noted that section 8(9) of the Unfair Dismissals Act 1977, as amended by section 7(c) of the Unfair Dismissals (Amendment) Act 1993, provides that this subsection shall apply in relation to proceedings before the Tribunal under the Unfair Dismissals Acts as they apply to matters referred to it under this section with the substitution in paragraph (e) of subsection (17) of "a fine not exceeding £1,000" for the fine herein specified (see also to similar effect section 8(5) of the Terms of Employment (Information) Act 1994). The relevant regulations under subsection (19) are the Redundancy (Redundancy Appeals Tribunal) Regulations 1968 (S.I. No. 24 of 1968)—reproduced *infra* at p.000—as amended by the Redundancy (Employment Appeals Tribunal) Regulations 1979 (S.I. No. 114 of 1979). Note also that section 12 of the Unfair Dismissals (Amendment) Act 1993 provides that a document signed by the Chairman or a Vice-Chairman of the Tribunal, stating details of the alleged offence, shall be admitted as evidence of the matters so stated without further proof.

Section 15(1) of the Redundancy Payments Act 1971 provides that any dispute arising under a special redundancy scheme may be referred by a party to the scheme to the Tribunal and shall be deemed to be a question referred under section 39 to the Tribunal for a decision on the question. Section 7(5) of the Redundancy Payments Act 1979 provides that any dispute arising under that section shall be deemed to be a decision referred to in subsection (15). The Tribunal also has jurisdiction under the Minimum Notice and Terms of Employment Act 1973, the Unfair Dismissals Act 1977, the Protection of Employees (Employers' Insolvency) Act 1984, the Payment of Wages Act 1991, the Worker Protection (Regular Part-Time Employees) Act 1991, the Terms of Employment (Information) Act 1994, the Maternity Protection Act 1994 and the Adoptive Leave Act 1995.

According to the *Twenty Sixth Annual Report* (1993) of the Tribunal it is "an independent body bound to act judicially" which "endeavours to provide a relatively quick and inexpensive method for individuals to seek remedies for alleged infringements of their statutory rights". During that year a total of 967 claims under the Redundancy Payments Acts were referred to the Tribunal, the majority of which were appeals by employees for redundancy payments on the grounds that they were dismissed by reason of redundancy. Other areas of dispute related to questions of whether alternative employment offered was suitable, lay-off and short-time, change of ownership of trade or business, continuity of employment and calculation of lump sums and normal weekly remuneration.

Reference and appeal to the High Court

[40.—(1) Where any question, other than a question specified in section 38(1)(a), 38((1)(b) or 38(1)(c), is referred to the Tribunal, the Minister may, on the request of the Tribunal, refer the question for the decision of the High Court.

(2) Where the Minister refers a question for the decision of the High Court under this section, or where a person appeals to the High Court under section 39(14), the court may, at its discretion, order the payment by the Minister from the [Social Insurance] Fund of the costs (in whole or in part as so ordered) when taxed of a party involved.

(3) Where the Minister refers a question for the decision of the High Court under this section, he may be represented as a party in that court at the hearing of the question.]

GENERAL NOTE

This section was substituted by virtue of section 9 of the Redundancy Payments Act 1971.

Revision of decisions

41.—(1) A deciding officer may, at any time and from time to time, revise any decision of a deciding officer, it appears to him that the decision was erroneous in the light of new evidence or of new facts which have been brought to his notice since the date on which it was given or by reason of some mistake having been made with respect to the law or the facts, or if it appears to him in a case where a weekly payment has been payable that there has been any relevant change of circumstances since the decision was given, and the provisions of this Act as to appeals shall apply to such revised decision in the manner as they apply to an original decision.

(2) Subsection (1) shall not apply to a decision relating to a matter which is on appeal or reference under section 39 unless the revised decision would be in favour of a claimant for a weekly payment.

(3) A revised decision given by a deciding officer shall take effect as follows—

    (a) where redundancy payment will, by virtue of the revised decision, be disallowed or reduced and the revised decision is given owing to the original decision is given owing to the original decision having been given, or having continued in effect, by reason of any statement or representation (whether written or oral) which was to the knowledge of the person making it false or misleading in a material respect or by reason of the wilful concealment of any material fact, it shall take effect as from the date on which the original decision took effect, but, in a case in which the redundancy payment is by way of periodical payment, the original decision may, in the discretion of the deciding officer continue to apply to any period covered by such original decision to which such false or misleading statement or representation or such wilful concealment of any material fact does not relate;

    (b) in any other case, it shall take effect as from the date considered appropriate by the deciding officer, but any payment already made at the date of the revision shall not be affected.

(4) Regulations may provide for the treating of any redundancy payment paid to an employee under a decision of a deciding officer, which it is subsequently decided officer, which it is subsequently decided was not payable, as paid on account of any other redundancy payment which it is decided was payable to that employee or for the repayment of any such payment and the recovery thereof by deduction or otherwise.

(5) Reference in this section to revision includes reference to revision consisting of a reversal.

GENERAL NOTE

In exercise of the powers conferred upon him by this section, the Minister has made the Redundancy (Repayment and Recovery of Payments) Regulations 1968 (S.I. No. 5 of 1968) reproduced *infra* at p.84.

Provisions relating to winding up and bankruptcy

42.—[(1) There shall be included among the debts which, under section 285 of the Companies Act 1963, are, in the distribution of the assets of a company being wound up, to be paid in priority to all other debts, all contributions [. . .] payable by the company under this Act during the twelve months before the commencement of the winding up or the winding-up order and any lump sum (or portion of a lump sum) payable under this Act by such a company, and the said section 285 shall have effect accordingly, and formal proof of the debts to which priority is given under this subsection shall not be required except in cases where it may otherwise be provided by rules made under the Companies Act 1963].

(2) Subsection (1) shall not apply where a company is wound up voluntarily merely for the purposes of reconstruction or of amalgamation with another company.

[(3) There shall be included among the debts which, under [section 81 of the Bankruptcy Act 1988] are, in the distribution of the property of a bankrupt or arranging debtor, to be paid in priority to all other debts, all contributions [. . .] payable under this Act by the bankrupt or arranging debtor during the twelve months before the date of the order of adjudication in the case of a bankrupt or the filing of the petition for arrangement in the case of an arranging debtor and any lump sum (or portion of a lump sum) payable under this Act by a bankrupt or arranging debtor, and the said [section 81] shall have effect accordingly, and formal proof of the debts to which priority is given under this subsection shall not be required except in cases where it may otherwise be provided by general orders made under the [Bankruptcy Act 1988].]

(4) Every assignment of or charge on, and every agreement to assign or charge, a weekly payment shall be void and on the bankruptcy of any person entitled to a weekly payment the weekly payment shall not pass to the official assignee in bankruptcy or any trustee or other person acting on account of the creditors.

(5) Nothing in [section 57 of the Bankruptcy Act 1988], or in section 286 of the Companies Act 1963, shall apply to any redundancy payments made by an employer.

GENERAL NOTE

Subsections (1) and (3) were inserted by virtue of section 14 of the Redundancy Payments Act 1971 and subsequently amended, by the deletion of the words in square brackets, by section 39(1) of the Social Welfare Act 1991. Both subsections

(3) and (5) have also been amended to take account of the repeal of the Bankruptcy Ireland Amendment Act 1872 and the Preferential Payments in Bankruptcy (Ireland) Act 1889.

Recovery of sums due to [Social Insurance] Fund

[43. All moneys due to the [Social Insurance] Fund under this Act shall be recoverable as debts due to the State and, without prejudice to any other remedy, may be recovered by the Minister as a debt under statute in any court of competent jurisdiction.]

GENERAL NOTE

This section was substituted by virtue of section 26 of the Social Welfare Act 1990.

Application of [section 213 of the Act of 1993]

[44. [Section 213] of the Social Welfare (Consolidation) Act [1993] shall apply in relation to benefits under this Act as it applies to benefits and other payments under the Social Welfare (Consolidation) Act [1993].]

GENERAL NOTE

This section, which was inserted by virtue of section 39(1) of the Social Welfare Act 1991, referred originally to section 115 of the Social Welfare (Consolidation) Act 1981. Section 115 was repealed by the Social Welfare Act 1993 and its provisions were replaced by section 27 of that Act. The provisions of section 27, in turn, are now to be found in section 213 of the Social Welfare (Consolidation) Act 1993, the marginal note to which is "False statements and offences, including offences relating to bodies corporate".

Application of [section 224 of the Act of 1993]

45. [Section 224 of the Act of 1993] shall apply in relation to offences under this Act or under regulations thereunder as it applies to offences under the Act of [1993] or to offences under regulations thereunder, save that in the said application reference in the said [section 224] to the Minister for Social Welfare shall be construed as reference to the Minister.

GENERAL NOTE

This section originally referred to section 53 of the Social Welfare Act 1952, which became section 116 of the Social Welfare (Consolidation) Act 1981 and is now section 224 of the Social Welfare (Consolidation) Act 1993.

Aid to unemployed persons changing residence

46.—[(1) The Minister may, for the purpose of promoting national economic policy, make with the consent of the Minister for Finance regulations providing for financial assistance out of moneys provided by the Oireachtas—

(a) to persons who are obliged to change their normal place of residence in order to take up employment offered or approved by [Foras Aiseanna Saothair], or

(b) to enable persons to travel for selection for training at approved training centres or to undertake course of training at such centres.]

(2) Without prejudice to the generality of subsection (1), regulations under this section—

(a) may provide for the payment or recoupment, in whole or in part, of the costs of transport (including the transport of household effects) arising out of a change of residence and for allowances in respect of lodgings, and

(b) may impose conditions, time limits and financial limits in respect of any moneys payable under the regulations.

(3) Notwithstanding anything contained in section 4, regulations under this section may apply to workers belonging to a class excluded from this Act by the said section 4.

GENERAL NOTE

A number of resettlement assistance regulations were made between 1968 and 1982 but the relevant regulations were all revoked by the Redundancy (Resettlement Assistance((Revocation) Regulations 1982 (S.I. No. 251 of 1982).

Special redundancy schemes for employees excluded from Act

47.—(1) The Minister may, in respect of a class of employee excluded from this Act by section 4 or by an order made thereunder, and after consultation with representatives of employers interested in the form of work normally carried on by employees of that class and with representatives of employees so interested, prepare and cause to be carried out a scheme (in this Act referred to

49

as a special redundancy scheme) providing in accordance with the terms of the special redundancy scheme for redundancy payment to employees of that class.

(2) Whenever the Minister has prepared a special redundancy scheme he shall, as soon as he thinks fit after such preparation, make an order providing for the carrying into effect on a specified date of that special redundancy scheme, and from that date that scheme shall be so carried into effect.

Provision for officers and servants of Coras Iompair Eireann and Ostlanna Iompair Eireann Teoranta

48.—(1) Section 9 of the Transport Act 1964 shall not apply to a person who, after the commencement of this Act, becomes an officer or servant or the Board unless such person was, or but for a casual interruption of his employment, would have been, an officer or servant of the Board at such commencement and continues to be an officer or servant of the Board except for casual interruptions of employment.

(2) Where, before the commencement of this Act, a person is in receipt of compensation under section 9 of the Transport Act 1964 subsection (1) shall not operate to diminish his right to such compensation.

(3) Where a person, on or after the commencement of this Act, becomes entitled to compensation under section 9(4) of the Transport Act 1964, in consequence of the termination of his employment with the Board or with the Company, he shall, notwithstanding any other provision of this Act, stand disqualified, as on and from the date of such entitlement, for redundancy payment in respect of such employment and all contributions under this Act paid in respect of that person as an employee of the Board or of the company shall be refunded to the person who paid such contributions.

(4) In this section—

"the Board" means Coras Iompair Eireann;
"the Company" means Ostlanna Iompair Eireann Teoranta.

GENERAL NOTE

Section 9 of the Transport Act 1964 provides for the payment of compensation for employees of the Board or the Company in cases of dismissal and transfer.

Power to modify or wind-up existing schemes and arrangements for the provision of superannuation and redundancy payments

49. Any scheme or arrangement for the provision of pensions, compensation for redundancy or other benefits (including any scheme or arrangement established or provided by or under, or having statutory force by virtue of, any enactment and any scheme evidenced only by one or more policies of insurance) may be modified, or wound up, in connection with the establishment under this Act of a scheme for the provision of redundancy payments by agreement between the parties concerned in the scheme or arrangement.

Application of Probation of Offenders Act 1907

50. [*Repealed by section 39(1) of the Social Welfare Act 1991*]

GENERAL NOTE

See now section 217 of the Social Welfare (Consolidation) Act 1993.

Voidance of purported exclusion of provisions of this Act

51. Any provision in an agreement (whether a contract of employment or not) shall be void in so far as it purports to exclude or limit the operation of any provision of this Act.

GENERAL NOTE

The scope of this section was considered by McWilliam J. in *Minister for Labour v. Clarke*, High Court, February 11, 1977 (reported (1985) 4 J.I.S.L.L. 79) who said that the section did not confine its scope to reductions in or avoidance of redundancy payments. It applied to the operation of any provision of the Act. Consequently the inclusion of a condition in a contract between a company and an employee which purported to exclude the operation of section 9(2) of the Act, as applied by section 20, was void.

Offences by bodies corporate

52. Where an offence under this Act committed by a body corporate is proved to have been committed with the consent or connivance of, or to be attributable to any neglect on the part of, any director, manager, secretary or other officer of the body corporate or any person who was purporting to act in any such capacity, he as well as the body corporate shall be guilty of that offence and shall be liable to be proceeded against and punished accordingly.

Provisions regarding notices

53.—(1) Any notice which under this Act is required or authorised to be given by an employer to an employee may be given by being delivered to the employee, or left for him at his usual or last-known place of residence, or sent by post addressed to him at that place.

(2) Any notice which under this Act is required or authorised to be given by an employee to an employer may be given either by the employee himself or by a person authorised by him to act on his behalf, and, whether given by or on behalf of the employee,—

(a) may be given by being delivered to the employer, or sent by post addressed to him at the place where the employee is or was employed by him, or

(b) if arrangements in that behalf have been made by the employer, may be given by being delivered to a person designated by the employer in pursuance of the arrangements, or left for such a person at a place so designated, or sent by post to such a person at an address so designated.

(3) In this section reference to the delivery of a notice shall, in relation to a notice not required by this Act to be in writing, be construed as including a reference to the oral communication of the notice.

(4) Any notice which, in accordance with this section, is left for a person at a place referred to in this section shall, unless the contrary is proved, be presumed to have been received by him on the day on which it was left there.

(5) Nothing in subsection (1) or (2) shall be construed as affecting the capacity of an employer to act by a servant or agent for the purposes of any provision (including either of those subsections) of this Act.

Certificate of decision by deciding officer

54. A document purporting to be a certificate of a decision made pursuant to this Act or regulations by a deciding officer and to be signed by him shall be prima facie evidence of the making of the said decision, and of the terms thereof, without proof of the signature of such officer or of his official capacity.

Power to remove difficulties

55.—(1) If in any respect any difficulty arises in bringing into operation this Act or any amendment or repeal effected by this Act, the Minister may by order do anything which appears to be necessary or expedient for bringing this Act into operation, and any such order may modify a provision of this Act so far as may appear necessary or expedient for carrying the order into effect.

(2) Every order made by the Minister under this section shall be laid before each House of the Oireachtas as soon as may be after it is made, and if a resolution is passed by either House of the Oireachtas within the next twenty-one days on which that House has sat after the order is laid before it annulling such order, the order shall be annulled accordingly, but without prejudice to the validity of anything previously done under the order.

(3) No order maybe made under this section after the expiration of one year after the commencement of this Act.

GENERAL NOTE

In exercise of the powers conferred upon him by this section, the Minister made the Redundancy Payments Act (Authorised Officers) Order 1968 (S.I. No. 106 of 1968)—reproduced *infra* at p.95.

Expenses of Minister

56.—(1) Any expenses incurred by the Minister or any other Minister in carrying this Act into effect shall, to such extent as may be sanctioned by the Minister for finance, be paid out of moneys provided by the Oireachtas.

(2) There shall be paid to the Minister for Finance out of the [Social Insurance] Fund, at such times and in such manner as the Minister for Finance may direct, such sums as the Minister may estimate, on such basis as may be agreed upon between him and the Minister for Finance, to be the part of the said expenses of the Minister or any other Minister in carrying into effect section 39 [and section 40], and any sums so paid shall be appropriated in aid of moneys provided by the Oireachtas for carrying this Act into effect.

(3) In estimating expenses for the purposes of subsection (2), there shall be included such amount as, in the opinion of the Minister for Finance, represents the amount of the accruing liability in respect of any superannuation or other retiring allowances, lump

sums or gratuities accruing in respect of the employment of any officer or other person for the purposes of this Act.

GENERAL NOTE

The insertion of the words "and section 40" in subsection (2) was required by virtue of section 19 of the Redundancy Payments Act 1971.

Regulations regarding keeping of records, furnishing of information and inspection of records

57. For the purpose of ensuring the effective operation of this Act the Minister may make regulations providing for the keeping of records and the furnishing of information by employers and for the inspection by authorised officers of the Minister of records or other documents in the custody or under the control of employers.

GENERAL NOTE

In exercise of the powers conferred upon him by this section, the Minister has made the Redundancy (Inspection of Records) Regulations 1968 (S.I. No. 12 of 1968) reproduced *infra* at p.85.

Regulations providing for offences

58. The Minister may by regulations provide for offences consisting of contraventions of or failure to comply with a provision of this Act or of contraventions of or failure to comply with regulations under this Act and for the recovery on summary conviction of such offences of fines not exceeding specified amounts not exceeding [£50], together with, in the case of continuing offences, further such fines in respect of each of the days on which the offences are continued.

GENERAL NOTE

The figure in square brackets was inserted by virtue of section 17 of the Redundancy Payments Act 1979. In exercise of the powers conferred upon him by this section, the Minister has made the Redundancy (Inspection of Records) Regulations 1968 (S.I. No. 12 of 1968), the Redundancy (Inspection of Records) Regulations 1979 (S.I. No. 115 of 1979), the Redundancy Certificate Regulations 1991 (S.I. No. 347 of 1991) and the Redundancy (Notice of Dismissal) Regulations 1991 (S.I. No. 348 of 1991).

SCHEDULE 1

WEEKLY PAYMENTS FROM THE [SOCIAL INSURANCE] FUND

[omitted]

SCHEDULE 2

DEATH OF EMPLOYER OR EMPLOYEE

Part 1

1. This Part shall have effect in relation to an employee where his employer (in this Part referred to as the deceased employer) dies.

2. Section 20 shall not apply to any change whereby the ownership of the business, for the purposes of which the employee was employed by the deceased employer, passes to a personal representative of the deceased employer.

3. Where, by virtue of section 21, the death of the deceased employer is to be treated for the purposes of this Act as a termination by him of the contract of employment, the employee shall nevertheless not be treated for those purposes as having been dismissed by the deceased employer if—

    (a) his contract of employment is renewed by a personal representative of the deceased employer, or he is re-engaged under a new contract of employment by such a personal representative, and

    (b) the renewal or re-engagement takes effect not later than eight weeks after the death of the deceased employer.

4. Where, by reason of the death of the deceased employer, the employee is treated for the purposes of this Act as having been dismissed by him, he shall not be entitled to a redundancy payment in respect of that dismissal if—

    (a) a personal representative of the deceased employer has made to him an offer in writing to renew his contract of employment or to re-engage him under a new contract,

    (b) in accordance with the particulars specified in that offer the renewal or re-engagement would take effect not later than eight weeks after the death of the deceased employer,

(c) either—

    (i) the provisions of the contract as renewed, or of the new contract, as to the capacity and place in which he would be employed and as to the other terms and conditions of his employment would not differ from the corresponding provisions of the contract in force immediately before the death, or

    (ii) if, notwithstanding that in accordance with the particulars specified in that offer the provisions mentioned in subparagraph (i) would differ (wholly or in part) from the corresponding provisions of the contract in force immediately before the death, the offer constitutes an offer of suitable employment in relation to the employee,

and

(d) the employee has unreasonably refused that offer.

5. For the purposes of paragraph 4—

(a) an offer shall not be treated as one whereby the provisions of the contract as renewed, or of the new contract, would differ from the corresponding provisions of the contract in force immediately before the death of the deceased employer by reason only that the personal representative would be substituted as the employer for the deceased employer, and

(b) account shall not be taken of that substitution in determining whether the refusal of the offer was unreasonable.

6. Where by virtue of section 21 of the death of the deceased employer is to be treated as a termination by him of the contract of employment, any reference in section 21(2) to section 9(2) shall be construed as including a reference to paragraph 3 of this Schedule.

7. Where the employee has before the death of the deceased employer been laid off or kept on short-time for one or more than one week, but has not given to the deceased employer notice of intention to claim, then if after the death of the deceased employer—

(a) his contract of employment is renewed, or he is re-engaged under a new contract, as mentioned in paragraph 3(a) or 3(b) of this Schedule, and

(b) after the renewal or re-engagement, he is laid off or kept on short-time for one or more weeks by the personal representative of the deceased employer,

sections 12 and 13 shall apply as if the week in which the deceased employer died and the first week of the employee's employment by the personal representative were consecutive weeks, and any reference in those sections to four weeks or thirteen weeks shall be construed accordingly.

8. Paragraph 9 or (as the case may be) paragraph 10 shall have effect where the employee has given to the deceased employer notice of intention to claim, and—

(a) the deceased employer has died before the end of the next four weeks after the service of that notice, and

(b) the employee has not terminated the contract of employment by notice expiring before the death of the deceased employer.

9. If in the circumstances specified in paragraph 8 the employee's contract of employment is not renewed by a personal representative of the deceased employer before the end of the next four weeks after the service of the notice of intention to claim, and his is not re-engaged under a new contract by such a personal representative before the end of those four weeks, sections 12(1) and 12(2) and section 13(4) shall apply as if—

(a) the deceased employer had not died, and

(b) the employee had terminated the contract of employment by a week's notice (or, if under the contract he is required to give more than a week's notice to terminate the contract, he had terminated it by the minimum notice which he is so required to give) expiring at the end of those four weeks,

but sections 12(1) to 13(3) shall not apply.

10. (1) This paragraph shall have effect where, in the circumstances specified in paragraph 8, the employee's contract of employment is renewed by a personal representative of the deceased employer before the end of the next four weeks after the service of the notice of intention to claim, or he is re-engaged under a new contract by such a personal representative before the end of those four weeks, and—

(a) he was laid off or kept on short-time by the deceased employer for one or more of those weeks, and

(b) he is laid off or kept on short-time by the personal representative for the week, or for the next two or more weeks, following the renewal or re-engagement.

(2) Where the conditions specified in subparagraph (1) are fulfilled, sections 12 and 13 shall apply as if all the weeks for which the employee was laid off or kept on short-time as mentioned in the said subparagraph (1) were consecutive weeks during which he was employed (but laid off or kept on short-time) by the same employer.

11. In paragraphs 7 to 10 "week" and "notice of intention to claim" have the meanings respectively assigned to them by sections 2 and 12.

12. Where by virtue of paragraph 3 the employee is treated as not having been dismissed by reason of a renewal or re-engagement taking effect after the death of the deceased employer, then, in determining, for the purposes of section 7, whether he has been continuously employed for the requisite period, the interval between the death and the date on which the renewal or re-engagement takes effect shall count as a period of employment with the personal representative of the deceased employer, if, apart from this paragraph, it would not count for that purpose as such a period of employment.

13. For the purposes of the application, in accordance with section 4(3), of any provisions of this Act to an employee who was employed in a private household, any reference to a personal representative in this Part shall be construed as including a reference to any person to whom, otherwise than in pursuance of a sale or other disposition for valuable consideration, the management of the household has passed in consequence of the death of the deceased employer.

14. Subject to the preceding provisions of this Part, in relation to an employer who has died—

(a) any reference in this Act to the doing of anything by, or in relation to, an employer shall be construed as including a reference to the doing of that thing by, or in relation to, any personal representative of the deceased employer, and

(b) any reference in this Act to a thing required or authorised to be done by, or in relation to, an employer shall be construed as including a reference to anything which, in accordance with any provision of this Act as modified by this Part (including sub-paragraph (a)), is required or authorised to be done by, or in relation to, any personal representative of his.

15. Where by virtue of any provision of this Act, as modified by this Part, a personal representative of the deceased employer is liable to pay a redundancy payment, or part of a redundancy payment, and that liability had not accrued before the death of the deceased employer, it shall be treated for all purposes as if it were a liability of the deceased employer which had accrued immediately before his death.

Part II

16. Where an employer has given notice to an employee to terminate his contract of employment and before that notice expires the employee dies, Part II of this Act shall apply as if the contract had been duly terminated by the employer by notice expiring on the date of the employee's death.

17. Where an employer [before the termination of an employee's contract of employment] has offered to renew his contract of employment, or to re-engage him under a new contract, then if—

(a) the employee dies without having either accepted or refused the offer, and
(b) the offer has not been withdrawn before his death,

section 15(1) or 15(2) (as the case may be) shall apply as if for "the employee has unreasonable refused" there were substituted "it would have been unreasonable on the part of the employee to refuse".

18. (1) Where, in the circumstances specified in sections 10(1)(a) and 10(1)(b), the employee dies before the notice given by him under section 10(1)(b) is due to expire and before the employer has given him notice under section 10(3), section 10(3) and section 10(4) shall apply as if the employer had given him such notice and he had complied with it.

(2) Where, in the circumstances specified in sections 10(1)(a) and 10(1)(b), the employee dies before his notice given under section 10(1)(b) is due to expire but after the employer has given him notice under section 10(3), sections 10(3) and 10(4) shall apply as if the circumstances were that the employee had not died and had complied with the last-mentioned notice.

19. (1) [...]

(2) Where an employee, who has given notice of intention to claim, dies within seven days after the service of that notice, and before the employer has given a counter-notice, the provisions of sections 12 and 13 shall apply as if the employer had given a counter-notice, the provisions of sections 12 and 13 shall apply as if the employer had given a counter-notice within those seven days.

(3) In this paragraph "notice of intention to claim" and "counter-notice" have the meanings respectively assigned to them by sections 12 and 13.

20. [. . .]

21. Subject to the preceding provisions of this Part, in relation to an employee who has died—

    (a) any reference in this Act to the doing of anything by, or in relation to, an employee shall be construed as including a reference to the doing of that thing by, or in relation to, any personal representative of the deceased employee, and

    (b) any reference in this Act to a thing required or authorised to be done by, or in relation to, an employee shall be construed as including a reference to anything which, in accordance with any provision of this Act as modified by this Part (including sub-paragraph (a)), is required or authorised to be done by, or in relation to, any personal representative of his.

22. Any right to a redundancy payment which had not accrued before the employee's death shall devolve on his personal representative.

23. In relation to any case where, under any provision contained in Part II of this Act, as modified by the preceding provisions of this Part, the Tribunal has power to determine that an employer shall be liable to pay to a personal representative of a deceased employee either—

    (a) The whole of a redundancy payment to which he would have been entitled apart from another provision therein mentioned, or]

    (b) such part of such a redundancy payment as the Tribunal thinks fit,

any reference in paragraph 22 to a right to a redundancy payment shall be construed as including a reference to any right to receive the whole or part of a redundancy payment if the Tribunal determines that the employer shall be liable to pay it.

GENERAL NOTE

The words in square brackets in paragraph 17 were inserted by section 19 of the Redundancy Payments Act 1971. The words in square brackets in paragraphs 19(1) and 20 were also deleted by virtue of section 19 of the 1971 Act.

SCHEDULE 3

AMOUNT OF LUMP SUM

1. The amount of the lump sum shall be equivalent to the aggregate of the following—

(a) the product of one-half of the employee's normal weekly remuneration and the number of years of continuous employment, with the employer in whose employment he was on the date of dismissal [or by whom he was employed when he gave notice of intention to claim under section 12], between the date on which the employee attained the age of sixteen years and the date on which he attained the age of forty-one years, and

(b) the product of the employee's normal weekly remuneration [...] and the number of years of continuous employment, with the employer in whose employment he was on the date of dismissal [or by whom he was employed when he gave notice of intention to claim under section 12], after the employee had attained the age of forty-one years, [and

(c) a sum equivalent to the employee's normal weekly remuneration.]

[2. In calculating the amount of the lump sum any part of an employee's earnings per annum in excess of [£15,600] shall be disregarded.]

3. (a) For the purpose of ascertaining, for the purposes of paragraph 1, the number of years of continuous employment, the number of weeks in the period of continuous employment shall be ascertained in accordance with this Schedule and the result shall be divided by 52.

(b) In ascertaining the number of weeks in the period of continuous employment, a week which under this Schedule is not allowable as reckonable service shall be disregarded.

(c) When the division required under subparagraph (a) produces a remainder of 26 or more weeks, this remaining period of 26 (or more) weeks shall be counted as a year of continuous employment but if that division produces a remainder of less than 26 weeks that period shall be disregarded.

(d) When the total number of years of continuous employment as ascertained in accordance with sub-paragraphs (a) to (c) falls to be divided for the purposes of paragraphs 1(a) and 1(b), any remaining parts of a year in those divisions shall be aggregated and the number of full years represented by this aggregation (when calculated in accordance with sub-paragraphs (a) to (c)) shall be added to the period of employment mentioned in paragraph 1(a).

CONTINUOUS EMPLOYMENT

4. For the purposes of this Schedule employment shall be taken to be continuous unless terminated by dismissal or by the employee's voluntarily leaving the employment [, but for the purposes of this paragraph "dismissal" does not include a dismissal within the meaning of the Unfair Dismissals Act 1977 and in respect of which redress has been awarded under section 7(1)(a) or 7(1)(b) of that Act].

[4A. Notwithstanding anything in paragraph 4 (and anything in clause (b) of the definition "date of dismissal" in section 2), the period of notice due to an employee under section 4(2)(a) of the Minimum Notice and Terms of Employment Act 1973, but not given by the employer, shall, where the Tribunal so orders, be allowed as continuous service for redundancy purposes where, but for the failure of the employer to comply with the provisions of that Act, the employee would have qualified for redundancy payment.]

5. (1) Where an employee's period of [employment is or was] interrupted by any one of the following—

(a) a period of not more than 78 consecutive weeks by reason of sickness [(including an injury)],

[(ai) any period by reason of service by the employee in the Reserve Defence Force,]

(b) a period of not more than 26 consecutive weeks by reason of—

(i) lay-off,

(ii) holidays,

(iii) [. . .]

(iv) any cause (other than the voluntary leaving of his employment by the employee) not mentioned in clauses (i) to (iii) but authorised by the employer,

(c) any period during which an employee was absent from work because of a lock-out by his employer or because the employee was participating in a strike, whether such absence occurred before or after the commencement of this Act,

[(d) a period during which an employee was absent from her work while on protective leave or natal care absence within the meaning of Part IV of the Maternity Protection Act 1994,]

[(e) a period during which an adopting parent was absent from her work while on adoptive leave or additional adoptive leave under the Adoptive Leave Act 1995,]

continuity of employment shall not be broken by such interruption whether or not notice of termination of the contract of employment has [or had] been given.

(2) During the year 1968 subparagraph (1)(b) shall have effect as if "52 consecutive weeks" were substituted for "26 consecutive weeks".

[(5A) If an employee is dismissed by reason of redundancy before attaining the period of 104 weeks referred to in section 7(5) (as amended) of the Principal Act and resumes employment with the same employer within 26 weeks, his employment shall be taken to be continuous.]

[6. Where a trade or business or an undertaking (whether or not it be an undertaking established by or under an Act of the Oireachtas), or part of a trade or business or of such an undertaking, was or is transferred from one person to another, the period of employment of an employee in the trade, business or undertaking (or in the part of the trade, business or undertaking) at the time of the transfer shall count as a period of employment with the transferee, and the transfer shall not break the continuity of the period of employment.]

RECKONABLE SERVICE

7. For the purposes of this Schedule, a week falling within a period of continuous employment and during which (or during any

part of which) the employee concerned either was actually at work, or as absent therefrom by reason of sickness, [a dismissal within the meaning of the Unfair Dismissals Act 1977, and in respect of which redress has been awarded under section 7(1)(a) or 7(1)(b) of that Act,] holidays or any other arrangement with his employer shall, subject to paragraph 8, be allowable as reckonable service.

8. None of the following absences from work shall be allowable as reckonable service—

> (a) absence in excess of 52 consecutive weeks by reason of an occupational accident or disease within the meaning of the Social Welfare [(Consolidation) Act 1993],
> (b) absence in excess of 26 consecutive weeks by reason of any illness not referred to in subparagraph (a),
> (c) absence in excess of 13 weeks in a period of 52 weeks and caused by any reason not referred in subparagraph (a) or (b) but being an absence authorised by the employer,
> (d) absence by reason of lay-off by the employer.

9. Absence from work by reason of a strike in the business or industry in which the employee concerned is employed and which occurred before the commencement of this Act shall be allowable as reckonable service.

10. Absence from work by reason of a strike in the business or industry in which the employee concerned is employed and which occurred after the commencement of this Act shall not be allowable as reckonable service.

11. Absence from work by reason of a lock-out shall be allowable as reckonable service.

12. Absence from work by reason of a strike or lock-out in a business or industry other than that in which the employee concerned is employed shall be allowable as reckonable service if it occurred before the commencement of this Act.

Normal Weekly Remuneration

13. For the purposes of this Schedule, in the case of an employee who is paid wholly by an hourly time rate or by a fixed wage or salary, and in the case of any other employee whose remuneration does not vary in relation to the amount of work done by him, his normal weekly remuneration shall be taken to be his earnings (including any regular bonus or allowance which does not vary in relation to the amount of work done [and any payment in kind]) for his normal weekly working hours as at the date on which he was declared redundant, together with, in the case of [an employee

who is normally expected to work overtime], his average weekly overtime earnings as determined in accordance with paragraph 14.

14. For the purpose of paragraph 13 the average weekly overtime earnings shall be determined by ascertaining the total amount of overtime earnings of the employee concerned in the period of 26 weeks which ended 13 weeks before the date on which the employee was declared redundant and dividing that amount by 26.

15. For the purpose of paragraph 14 any week during which the employee concerned did not work shall be disregarded and the most recent week before the 26-week period mentioned in paragraph 14 shall be taken into account instead of the week during which the employee did not work.

16. (i) In the case of an employee who is paid wholly or partly by piece rates, bonuses or commissions (being piece rates, bonuses or commissions related directly to his output) and in the case of any other employee whose remuneration varies in relation t the amount of work done by him, his normal weekly remuneration shall be taken to be the amount as calculated in accordance with subparagraph (ii).

(ii) For the purposes of subparagraph (i) normal weekly remuneration shall be calculated by dividing the remuneration to be taken into account in accordance with subparagraph (iii) by the number of hours ascertained in accordance with subparagraph (vi) and multiplying the resulting hourly rate by the normal weekly working hours of the employee concerned at the date on which he was declared redundant.

(iii) The remuneration to be taken into account for the purposes of subparagraph (ii) shall be the total remuneration paid to the employee concerned for all the hours worked in the period of 26 weeks which ended 13 weeks before the date on which the employee was declared redundant, adjusted in respect of any variations in the rates of pay which became operative during the period of 13 weeks ending on the date on which the employee was declared redundant.

(iv) For the purposes of subparagraph (iii), weeks worked with different employers may be taken into account if the change of employer did not affect the employee's continuous employment as provided by paragraphs 4 to 6.

(v) For the purposes of subparagraph (iii), any week during which the employee did not work shall be disregarded and the most recent week before the 26-week period mentioned in subparagraph (iii) shall be taken into account instead of the week during which the employee did not work.

(vi) The number of hours to be taken into account for the purposes of subparagraph (ii) shall be the total number of hours worked in the period of 26 weeks mentioned in subparagraph (iii).

17. Where an employee receives additional remuneration for working more than a fixed number of hours, that fixed number of hours shall, for the purposes of paragraphs 13 and 16(ii), be taken to be his normal weekly working hours, unless by his contract of employment he is required to work for more than that fixed number of hours, and in the last mentioned case the higher number of hours required by the contract shall be taken to be his normal weekly working hours.

18. Where in a particular week an employee qualifies for a payment of a bonus, pay allowance or commission which relates to more than the work done in that week, the appropriate portion of the payment may be taken into account under paragraphs 13 and 16(iii).

19. An employee who is normally employed on a shift cycle and whose remuneration varies in relation to the particular shift he works, and an employee whose remuneration for his normal number of working hours varies in relation to the day of the week or the times of the day or night over which those hours are spread, shall be taken to be each an employee who is paid wholly or partly by piece-rates.

20. For the purposes of this Schedule, in the case of an employee who has no normal working hours, his normal weekly remuneration shall be taken to be the average weekly remuneration, including any bonus, pay allowance or commission, received by the employee concerned over the period of 52 weeks during which he was actually working immediately prior to the date on which he was declared redundant.

21. The date on which an employee is declared redundant shall for the purposes of this Schedule be taken to be the date on which a notice of proposed dismissal was given to the employee in accordance with section 17 or, where a redundancy payment is claimed in accordance with section 12, the first day of the series of weeks of lay-off or short-time referred to in section 7(3).

22. Where under this Schedule account is to be taken of remuneration or other payments for a period which does not coincide with the periods for which the remuneration or other payments are calculated, part of the remuneration or other payments shall be duly apportioned in such manner as may be just.

23. For the purposes of paragraphs 13 and 16, account shall not be taken of any sums paid to an employee by way of recoupment of expenses necessarily incurred by him in the proper discharge of the duties of his employment.

MISCELLANEOUS

24. In this Schedule—

[. . .]

"strike" and "lock-out" have the meanings respectively assigned to them by section 6.

GENERAL NOTE

The words in square brackets in paragraphs 1(a) and (b) were inserted and deleted by virtue of section 19 of the Redundancy Payments Act 1971. Paragraph 2 was inserted by virtue of section 4 of the Redundancy Payments Act 1979 and the figure in square brackets therein was substituted by virtue of the Redundancy Payments (Lump Sum) Regulations 1994 (S.I. No. 64 of 1994), which Regulations came into effect on May 1, 1994. The words in square brackets in paragraph 4 were inserted by virtue of section 17 of the Redundancy Payments Act 1979, as was paragraph 4A. The words in square brackets in paragraph 5(a) were inserted by virtue of section 19 of the Redundancy Payments Act 1971, as was paragraph 5(ai). The words in square brackets in paragraph 5(b) were deleted by virtue of section 19 of the Redundancy Payments Act 1971 and paragraph 5(d) (inserted by the Maternity Protection of Employees Act 1981) was substituted by virtue of section 39 of the Maternity Protection Act 1994. Paragraph 5(e) was inserted by virtue of section 28 of the Adoptive Leave Act 1995. Paragraph 5A was inserted by virtue of section 19 of the Redundancy Payments Act 1971. Paragraph 6 was substituted by virtue of section 19 of the Redundancy Payments Act 1971. The words in square brackets in paragraph 7 were inserted by virtue of section 17 of the Redundancy Payments Act 1979. The words in square brackets in paragraph 13 were inserted by virtue of section 19 of the Redundancy Payments Act 1971. The words in square brackets in paragraph 24 were deleted by virtue of section 19 of the Redundancy Payments Act 1971.

Paragraphs 4 and 5 were considered by McWilliam J. in *Harte v. Telecord Holdings Co. Ltd* (High Court, May 18, 1979, reported at (1985) 4 J.I.S.L.L. 84) where it was argued unsuccessfully that the continuity of the claimant's employment was broken by her absence from July 1961 to August 1962. McWilliam J. thought it clear that the cause of the interruption in the claimant's employment was sickness and the fact that she went to America to recover from it and, while there, took up another employment, did not appear to him to be relevant "unless there is some circumstance from which it should be inferred that she intended to leave the employment permanently."

Paragraph 6 must be read in conjunction with the European Communities (Safeguarding of Employees' Rights on Transfer of Undertakings) Regulations 1980 (S.I. No. 306 of 1980) which ensure that, in any transfer of a business or undertaking or part thereof, the employment of the existing workers is preserved or, if their employment terminates by reason of the transfer, that their rights arising out of that termination are effectively safeguarded.

Paragraphs 13 and 21 were considered in *Nokia Ltd v. Minister for Labour* 435/1983 in which an important point as to the computation of redundancy pay arose. The company had appealed the Minister's decision to refuse it a redundancy rebate on the ground that the employees in question had not been paid their full statutory entitlements. Seventeen employees had been dismissed at a time when the statutory ceiling for the purpose of calculating redundancy pay was £96.15. On June 1, 1981 the ceiling was raised to £163.45. The Minister contended that the wage to be taken into account when calculating redundancy pay was the wage at the date of the expiry of the statutory notice period under the Minimum Notice and Terms of Employment Act 1973. In the case of each of the seventeen employees this would have been after June 1. Their redundancy lumpsums had been calculated using the old, not the increased ceiling. The company argued successfully, however, that under paragraph 13 of Schedule 3 the wage to be taken into account was the wage applying "as at the date on which he was declared redundant". Furthermore paragraph 21 defines the date an employee is declared redundant as to the date on which the notice of a proposed dismissal was given to the employee. The Employment Appeals Tribunal ruled that, as the employees had been declared redundant prior to June 1, the company was correct in calculating the lump sums using the old ceiling. The Minister appealed this decision to the High Court but Costello J., in an *ex tempore* judgment delivered March 30, 1983 (1983 No. 455 Sp), dismissed the appeal.

REDUNDANCY PAYMENTS ACT 1971

(1971 No. 20)

An Act to amend and extend the Redundancy Payments Act 1967 and to provide for other matters connected with the matter aforesaid. [*27th July 1971*]

GENERAL NOTE

The main purpose of this Act was to provide for a new definition of redundancy to counter the decision of the High Court in *Limerick Health Authority v. Ryan* [1969] I.R. 194 which gave what was perceived as being a restricted interpretation to the word "redundancy" and to provide for the compensation of workers adversely affected by that decision. The Act also provided for improvements in the rates of redundancy payments and made a number of other technical amendments.

Citation

See section 20.

Commencement

This Act came into operation on September 1, 1971, although section 19(2) provides that that section should be deemed to have come into operation on January 22, 1971.

Statutory Instruments

Redundancy Payments Act 1971 Commencement Order 1971 (S.I. No. 230 of 1971).

Parliamentary Debates

251 *Dail Debates* Cols. 941–986 (Second Stage)
253 *Dail Debates* Cols. 81–109 (Committee Stage)
253 *Dail Debates* Cols. 236–273 (Committee Stage resumed)
253 *Dail Debates* Cols. 533–558 (Committee Stage resumed)
253 *Dail Debates* Cols. 580–638 (Committee Stage resumed)
253 *Dail Debates* Cols. 786–793 (Committee Stage resumed)
254 *Dail Debates* Cols. 776–824 (Report and Final Stages)
70 *Seanad Debates* Cols. 393–408 (Second Stage)
70 *Seanad Debates* Cols. 434–470 (Second Stage resumed)
70 *Seanad Debates* Cols. 623–690 (Committee Stage)
70 *Seanad Debates* Cols. 1196–1211 (Report and Final Stages)

Be it enacted by the Oireachtas as follows:

Definition

1. In this Act, "the Principal Act" means the Redundancy Payments Act 1967.

Extension of application of certain provisions of Acts

2. In relation to an employee whose employment is terminated by reason of redundancy on or after the commencement of this Act, any provision or the Principal Act or this Act which affects or relates to the preservation of continuity of the employee's employment shall apply to periods of employment before the 1st day of January, 1968, as they apply to such periods after that date.

Provisions relating to persons [reaching qualifying age for old age pension]

[**3.** Notwithstanding section 4(1) of the Principal Act, that Act shall, with effect from the 6th day of April, 1980, not apply to a person who on the date of termination of his employment had attained the age which on that date is the pensionable age within the meaning of the [Social Welfare (Consolidation) Act 1993].]

GENERAL NOTE

This section was substituted by virtue of section 5 of the Redundancy Payments Act 1979.

Amendment of section 7 of Principal Act

4. [. . .]

Amendment of section 20 of Principal Act

5. [. . .]

Application of section 20 of Principal Act

6.—(1) Where—

(i) a change relating to the control or management of a business (or part thereof) for the purposes of which a person is employed occurs, but a change in the ownership of the business (or part thereof) does not occur,

(ii) section 20 of the Principal Act would have applied to that change if it were a change in the ownership of that business (or part thereof), and

(iii) an employee of the previous owner accepts, before, on or within four weeks of the termination of his contract of employment with the previous owner, an offer by the new owner of employment in the same place of employment and on terms which are either the same as, or not materially less advantageous to the employee than, his existing terms of employment,

the said section 20 shall apply to that change as if a change of ownership of that business (or part thereof) had occurred.

(2) In this section "previous owner" and "new owner" mean, respectively, the persons who would have been the previous owner and the new owner within the meaning of the said section 20 if a

71

change of ownership of a business (or part thereof) had occurred.

Amendment of section 39 of Principal Act

7. [...]

Redundancy payment to certain employees dismissed before commencement of Act

8.—(1) Where an employee who was dismissed before the commencement of this Act was not entitled to redundancy payment under the Principal Act in respect of the dismissal solely because the requirements of the business carried on by his employer for employees to carry out work of a particular kind, or to carry out such work in the place where the employee had been so employed, had not ceased or diminished or were not expected to cease or diminish, the Minister may, at his discretion and notwithstanding the Principal Act, pay to that employee out of the [Social Insurance] Fund a sum equal in amount to the sum to which he would have been entitled under the Principal Act if the said requirements had ceased or diminished or were expected to cease or diminish.

(2) In relation to the amendments of the Principal Act referred to in section 19(2), the Minister may, in respect of a dismissal or a termination of employment in the period beginning on the 22nd day of January 1971 and ending on the commencement of this section and notwithstanding the Principal Act, pay to an employee out of the [Social Insurance] Fund any moneys to which the employee may become entitled by virtue of the said section 19(2).

Reference and appeal to the High Court

9. [*Amending section 40 of the Redundancy Payments Act 1967*]

Presumptions by Tribunal

10.—For the purposes of a reference to the Tribunal—

    (a) a person's employment during any period shall, unless the contrary is proved, be presumed to have been continuous;

    (b) an employee who has been dismissed by his employer shall, unless the contrary is proved, be presumed to have been so dismissed by reason of redundancy;

(c) the Tribunal shall, after consultation with any person or body charged by statute with the fixing or determination or minimum wages or rates of pay, or the registration or employment agreements under the Industrial Relations [Acts 1946-1990], have regard to any such minimum as is appropriate or relevant.

GENERAL NOTE

The British Redundancy Payments Act 1965 created a presumption that an employee who has been dismissed shall, unless the contrary be proved, be presumed to have been so dismissed by reason of redundancy. This was not in the 1967 Act and Kenny J. in *Limerick Health Authority v. Ryan* [1969] I.R. 194, 201 was of the view that such a presumption could not be implied. Paragraph (b) rectifies this situation.

Right to redundancy payment by reason of lay-off or short-time

11. [*Amending section 12 of the Redundancy Payments Act 1967*]

Time-limit on claims for redundancy payment

12. [*Amending section 24 of the Redundancy Payments Act 1967*]

Rebates to employers from [Social Insurance] Fund

13. [*Amending section 29 of the Redundancy Payments Act 1967*]

Other payments to employees from [Social Insurance] Fund

14. [*Amending section 32 of the Redundancy Payments Act 1967*]

Provisions relating to special redundancy schemes.

15.—(1) Any dispute arising under a special redundancy scheme may be referred by a party to the scheme to the Tribunal and shall be deemed to be a question referred under section 39 of the Principal Act to the Tribunal for a decision on the question.

[(2) For the purpose of providing moneys for making payments which under this Act are to be made out of a fund established under a special redundancy scheme, there shall be paid into that fund—

(a) as may be provided in that scheme, contributions by employers, and

(b) advances as provided for in subsections (3) and (4).]

(3) The Minister for Finance may from time to time, on the recommendation of the Minister, advance to any fund established under a special redundancy scheme moneys to enable payments required under the scheme to be made out of the fund, and any advance under this subsection shall be made out of the Central Fund or the growing produce thereof and shall be on such terms as to interest and repayment as the Minister for Finance may determine.

[(4) The Minister may, with the consent of the Minister for Finance, from time to time authorise the transfer of moneys from the [Social Insurance] Fund to any fund established under a special redundancy scheme, and any moneys transferred under this subsection shall be repayable to the [Social Insurance] Fund on such terms (including terms as to interest) as the Minister for Finance may determine.]

(5)(a) A fund established under a special redundancy scheme shall comprise a current account, to be managed and controlled by the Minister, and an investment account, to be managed and controlled by the Minister for Finance.

(b) Save where otherwise specifically provided, sums payable into a fund established under a special redundancy scheme shall be paid into the current account of that fund and sums payable out of that fund shall be paid out of that account.

(c) Moneys standing to the credit of the current account of a fund established under a special redundancy scheme and not required to meet current expenditure shall be transferred to the investment account of that fund.

(d) Whenever the moneys in the current account of a fund established under a special redundancy scheme are insufficient to meet the liabilities of that account there shall be transferred to that account from the investment account of that fund such sums as may be necessary for the purpose of discharging those liabilities.

(e) Subject to paragraph (d), moneys standing to the credit of the investment account of a fund established under a special redundancy scheme shall be invested by the Minister for Finance, and income arising from any such investment shall be paid into that account.

(f) An investment pursuant to paragraph (e) may be in any securities in which trustees are for the time being by law empowered to invest trust funds or in any of the stocks, funds and securities as are for the time being authorised by law as investments for the Post Office Savings Bank funds.

(g) The accounts of a fund established under a special redundancy scheme shall be prepared in such form, in such matter and at such times as the Minister for Finance may direct and the Comptroller and Auditor General shall examine and certify every such account and a copy thereof, together with the report thereon of the Comptroller and Auditor General, shall be laid before each House of the Oireachtas.

Offences relating to payments under Principal Act

16.—(1) A person who fraudulently claims a weekly payment, fraudulently applies to the Minister for a payment under section 32 of the Principal Act or fraudulently makes a claim for a rebate, shall be guilty of an offence and shall be liable on summary conviction to a fine not exceeding [£300].

(2) A person who aids, abets, counsels or procures another person to commit an offence under subsection (1) of this section shall be guilty of an offence and shall be liable on summary conviction to a fine not exceeding [£300].

(3) Notwithstanding any provision in any Act specifying the period within which summary proceedings may be commenced, proceedings in respect of an offence under this section may be commenced at any time within the period of three months from the date on which evidence, sufficient in the opinion of the Minister to satisfy a prosecution for the offence, comes to his knowledge, or within the period of twelve months after the commission of the offence, whichever period last expires.

GENERAL NOTE

The figures in square brackets were substituted by virtue of section 18 of the Redundancy Payments Act 1979.

Reciprocal arrangements

17.—(1) The Minister may make such orders as may be necessary to carry out any reciprocal or other arrangements, made with the proper authority under any other Government, in respect of matters relating to redundancy payments, and may be any such order make such adaptations of an modifications in the Principal Act as he considers necessary.

(2) The Minister may by order amend or revoke an order under this section.

Aid to persons changing residence or undergoing certain training

18. [*Amending section 46 of the Redundancy Payments Act 1967*]

Miscellaneous amendments of Principal Act

19.—(1) Each provision of the Principal Act mentioned in column (1) of the Schedule to this Act is hereby amended in the manner stated in column (2) of that Schedule opposite the mention of that provision in column (1).

(2) Notwithstanding section 20(3), this section, in so far as it relates to the first amendment of section 7 of that Act, the fifth amendment of Schedule 1 of that Act and the fourth amendment of Schedule 3 of that Act, shall be deemed to have come into operation on the 22nd day of January 1971.

Short title, construction, collective citation and commencement

20.—(1) This Act may be cited as the Redundancy Payments Act 1971.

(2) The Principal Act and this Act shall be construed as one Act and may be cited together as the Redundancy Payments Act 1967 and 1971.

(3) This Act shall come into operation on such day as the Minister appoints by order.

GENERAL NOTE

By virtue of S.I. No. 230 of 1971, the Act came into operation on September 1, 1971.

[*Schedule omitted*]

REDUNDANCY PAYMENTS ACT 1979

(1979 No. 7)

An Act to amend and extend the Redundancy Payments Acts 1967 to 1973 and to provide for other connected matters. [*20th March 1979*].

GENERAL NOTE

This Act makes various changes to the 1967 and 1971 Acts, principal amongst them being the discontinuance of weekly payments, the simplification of the rebate system, the abolition of workers' contributions and the provision of time-off to look for new employment.

Citation

See section 21.

Commencement

This Act came into operation on April 6, 1979.

Statutory Instruments

Redundancy Payments Act 1979 Commencement Order 1979 (S.I. No. 195 of 1979).
Redundancy Payments (Lump Sum) Regulations 1994 (S.I. No. 64 of 1994).

Parliamentary Debates

311 *Dail Debates* Cols. 1016–1052 (Second Stage)
311 *Dail Debates* Cols. 1623–1660 (Committee Stage)
311 *Dail Debates* Cols. 1705–1708 (Committee Stage resumed)
312 *Dail Debates* Cols. 442–445 (Report and Final Stages)
91 *Seanad Debates* Cols. 474–512 (Second Stage)
91 *Seanad Debates* Cols. 629–668 (Committee and Final Stages)

Be it enacted by the Oireachtas as follows:

Definitions

1.—In this Act—

"the Act of 1971" means the Redundancy Payments Act 1971;

"the Minister" means the Minister for [Enterprise and Employment];

"the Principal Act" means the Redundancy Payments Act 1967.

Financing of [Social Insurance] Fund

2. [*Amending section 27 of the Redundancy Payments Act 1967*]

Contributions to [Social Insurance] Fund

3. [*Amending section 28 of the Redundancy Payments Act 1967 (as amended by the Redundancy Payments Act 1973)*]

Provisions relating to lump sum under Principal Act and consequential provisions

4.—(1) [Amending Schedule 3 of the Redundancy Payments Act 1967 (as amended by the Redundancy Payments Act 1971).]

(2) The Minister may by regulations made with the consent of the Minister for Finance—

(a) vary the amount of [£15,600] referred to in paragraph 2 of Schedule 3 of the Principal Act (inserted by this section), and

(b) alter the method of calculation of a lump sum under the Principal Act.

(3) When making regulations under subsection (2) of this section, the Minister shall take into account any changes in the average earning of workers in the transportable good industries as recorded by the Central Statistics Office since the date by reference to which the sum specified in subsection (1) of this section was last determined.

(4)(a) Subject to paragraph (b) of this subsection, the Redundancy Payments (Weekly Payments and Lump Sum) Order 1974 (S.I. No. 82 of 1974), and the Redundancy Payments (Weekly Payments) Order 1976 (S.I. No. 126 of 1976), shall cease to have effect from the commencement of this section.

(b) Notwithstanding paragraph (a) of this subsection but subject to section 8 of this Act, an employee who at the commencement of this section is in receipt of weekly payments shall continue to receive such payments as if that paragraph were not enacted.

GENERAL NOTE

Subsection (2), as originally enacted, specified an amount of £5,000 as being the maximum lump sum payable. This figure has been increased from time to time and now stands at £15,600 which figure was inserted into Schedule 3 of the 1967 Act by virtue of the Redundancy Payments (Lump Sum) Regulations 1994 (S.I. No. 64 of 1994).

The discontinuance of weekly payments commenced on April 6, 1979 by virtue of the Redundancy Payments Act 1979 (Commencement) Order 1979 (S.I. No. 195 of 1979).

Provisions relating to persons reaching qualifying age for old age pension

5. [*Amending section 3 of the Redundancy Payments Act 1971*]

Rebates to employers from [Social Insurance] Fund

6. [*Amending section 29 of the Redundancy Payments Act 1967 (inserted by the Redundancy Payments Act 1971)*]

Employee's right to time off for certain purposes while under notice of dismissal for redundancy

7.—(1) This section applies to an employee who has not less than 104 weeks' service with an employer and has been given notice of proposed dismissal by reason of redundancy.

(2) An employee to whom this section applies shall be entitled during the two weeks ending on the expiration of his notice of dismissal to be allowed by his employer reasonable time off during the employee's working hours in order to look for new employment or make arrangements for training for future employment.

(3) An employee who is allowed time off under this section shall be entitled to be paid remuneration by his employer for the period of absence at the appropriate hourly rate obtaining on the date of his notice of dismissal and to remuneration equal to this amount in a case where the employer unreasonably refuses time off under this section.

(4) The employer of an employee to whom this section applies may require the employee to furnish him with such evidence as he requests of arrangements made by the employee relating to effort to obtain new employment or training for future employment, and the employee shall furnish any evidence so requested if it is no prejudicial to the employee's interest.

(5) Any dispute arising under this section shall be deemed to be a decision referred to in section 39(15) of the Principal Act, and any amount ordered by the Employment Appeals Tribunal to be paid by an employer to an employee shall be recoverable as a simple contract debt in a court of competent jurisdiction.

Termination of entitlement to weekly payments

8.—(1) Subject to subsection (2) of this section, sections 30 and 31 of the Principal Act shall cease to have effect from the commencement of this section.

(2) Notwithstanding subsection (1) of this section, an employee who at the commencements of this section is in receipt of weekly

payments shall continue to receive such payments as if that subsection were not enacted, but (notwithstanding any other provision of the Redundancy Payments Acts 1967 to 1979) if before the exhaustion of such payments payment of them ceases for any reason the employee shall not subsequently be or become entitled to any weekly payment.

(3) For the purposes of subsection (2) of this section, in the case of any employee whose employment is terminated by reason of redundancy in the period of two weeks ending at the commencement of this section, that employee shall be deemed to be in receipt of weekly payments if his claim for such payments is made not later than two weeks after such commencement and is duly decided under the Principal Act to be payable.

(4) An employee whose employment terminates by reason of redundancy before the commencement of this section and who has claimed weekly payments before such commencement, but whose claim for such payments is not before such commencement decided on, shall for the purposes of subsection (2) of this section be deemed to be in receipt of weekly payment if his claim is upheld.

Amendment of section 10 of Principal Act

9. [. . .]

Amendment of section 11 of Principal Act

10. [. . .]

Amendment of section 15 of Principal Act

11. [. . .]

Application to certain cases of sections 10 and 11.

12.—Where—

- (a) a dismissal (or termination of employment) occurred before the commencement of this section,
- (b) the employee concerned would have been entitled to redundancy payment if section 10 or 11 of this Act had been in operation on the date of dismissal or termination of employment, and

(c) the employee concerned had appealed to the Tribunal before the 1st day of January, 1979, but a decision relating to that appeal had not been made before the commencement of this section,

the Tribunal shall, as soon as practicable after the commencement of this section, make a decision relating to that appeal as if section 10 and 11 of this Act had been in operation on the date of dismissal or termination of employment.

Amendment of section 24 of Principal Act

13. [...]

Amendment of section 42 of Principal Act

14. [...]

Amendment of section 15 of Act of 1971

15. [...]

Power to remove difficulties

16.—(1) If in any respect any difficulty arises in bringing into operation this Act or any amendment or repeal effect by this Act, the Minister may by order do anything which appears to be necessary or expedient for bringing this Act into operation, and any such order may modify a provision of this Act so far as may appear necessary or expedient for carrying the order into effect.

(2) Every order made by the Minister under this section shall be laid before each House of the Oireachtas as soon as may be after it is made, and if a resolution is passed by either House of the Oireachtas within the next 21 days on which that House has sat after the order is laid before it annulling such order, the order shall be annulled accordingly but without prejudice to the validity of anything previously done under the order.

(3) No order may be made under this section after the expiration of one year after the commencement of this section.

Miscellaneous amendments of Principal Act

17. Each provision of the Principal Act mentioned in column (1) of the Schedule to this Act is amended in the manner stated in column (2) of that Schedule, opposite the mention of the provision in column (1).

Amendment of section 16 of Act of 1971

18. Section 16 of the Act of 1971, which relates to fraudulent claims to payments under the Principal Act, is amended by the substitution of "£300" for "fifty pounds" in subsections (1) and (2).

Repeals

19. Sections 34 and 36(2)(d) of the Principal Act are repealed.

Expenses

20. Any expenses incurred by the Minister or any other Minister of the Government in carrying this Act into effect shall, to such extent as may be sanctioned by the Minister for Finance, be paid out of monies provided by the Oireachtas.

Short title, construction, collective citation and commencement

21.—(1) This Act may be cited as the Redundancy Payments Act 1979.

(2) The Redundancy Payments Act 1967 to 1973, and this Act shall be construed together as one Act and may be cited together as the Redundancy Payments Acts 1967 to 1979.

(3) This Act shall come into operation on such day or days as may be fixed by order or orders of the Minister, and different days may be so fixed for different provisions of this Act.

GENERAL NOTE

By virtue of S.I. No. 195 of 1979, the Act came into operation on April 6, 1979.

[Schedule omitted]

REDUNDANCY (REPAYMENT AND RECOVERY OF PAYMENTS) REGULATIONS 1968

S.I. No. 5 of 1968

1. These Regulations may be cited as the Redundancy (Repayment and Recovery of Payments) Regulations 1968.

2. Where under section 41 of the Redundancy Payments Act 1967,

> (a) a decision of a deciding officer is revised so as to disallow or reduce redundancy payment paid or payable to a person, and
> (b) the revised decision is given because the original decision had been given, or had continued in effect, by reason of any statement or representation (whether written or oral) which was to the knowledge of the person making it false or misleading in a material respect or by reason of the wilful concealment of any material fact,

any redundancy payment paid in pursuance of the original decision shall be repayable to the [Social Insurance] Fund to the extent to which it would not have been payable if the revised decision had been given in the first instance and such person (and either any other person to whom the benefit was paid on behalf of such person or the personal representative of such person) shall be liable to pay to the Fund on demand by the Minister the sum so repayable.

3. Any benefit repayable in accordance with paragraph 2 may be recovered by deduction from any redundancy payment to which the person concerned (or any other person on the death of such person) then is or becomes entitled.

GENERAL NOTE

The purpose of these Regulations is to provide for the recovery to the Social Insurance Fund of payments, or overpayments, where a deciding officer's decision is revised because the original decision was based on information which was, to the knowledge of the person giving it, false or misleading.

REDUNDANCY (INSPECTION OF RECORDS) REGULATIONS 1968

S.I. No. 12 of 1968

1. These Regulations may be cited as the Redundancy (Inspection of Records) Regulations 1968.

2. In this Act—

"the Act" means the Redundancy Payments Act 1967 (No. 21 of 1967);

"eligible", in relation to an employee, means an employee to whom, by virtue of section 4 of the Act or an order thereunder, the Act applies;

"the Minister" means the Minister for [Enterprise and Employment];

"officer" means an authorised officer of the Minister.

3. An officer may—

    (a) enter any premises or place for the purpose of inspecting any documents or records liable to inspection under these Regulations,

    (b) make such inspection of such documents or records as may be necessary for the purpose of ascertaining whether the Act (or any order thereunder) is being or has been complied with by the employer concerned,

    (c) examine, either alone or in the presence of another person as the officer thinks fit, any person whom he finds in any premises or place entered by the officer under these Regulations with respect to any matter relating to the Act on which the officer may reasonably require information for the purpose of ensuring that the Act (or any order thereunder) is being effectively operated,

    (d) require any person examined under subparagraph (c) to sign a declaration of the truth of any matter in respect of which that person has been so examined.

4. The occupier of any premises or place in which documents or records liable to inspection under these Regulations are deposited,

and any person who is or has been employing a person who is or was an eligible employee, and the servants and agents of any such occupier or other person, and any such eligible employee, shall furnish to an officer all such information and shall produce to an officer for inspection all such registers, cards, wages sheets, records of wages and other documents as the officer may reasonably require for the purpose of ascertaining whether the Act (or any order thereunder) is being or has been complied with.

5. Any person who—

    (a) wilfully delays or obstructs an officer in the exercise of any power under these Regulations,

    (b) refuses or neglects to answer any question or to furnish any information or to produce any document when required so to do under these Regulations, or

    (c) conceals or prevents or attempts to conceal or prevent any other person from appearing before or being examined by an officer,

shall be guilty of an offence and shall be liable on summary conviction thereof to a fine not exceeding [£50].

6. An officer shall, while exercising powers under these Regulations, have in his possession a certificate of his appointment as such officer, and shall, on applying for admission to any premises or place under these Regulations, if so required, produce the certificate.

7.—(1) An employer shall, on receipt by him from an officer of a notice in writing addressed to the employer at the address at which he resides or carries on business and incorporating or having annexed to it a form of declaration, furnish on the said form of declaration such information as is demanded in the notice in respect of any eligible employee who is or has been in his employment and shall sign and duly complete the declaration and deliver the same by hand or by registered post to the officer, within the time specified by the officer, not being less than six days from the date of the notice.

(2) Where a notice under subparagraph (1) is sent by post it shall be deemed to have been received by the person to whom it is addressed on the date on which it would be received in the ordinary course of post, unless the contrary is proved.

GENERAL NOTE

The purpose of these Regulations is to specify the powers of authorised officers in regard to the entry of premises, inspection of records and procurement of information for the purpose of ensuring the effective operation of the legislation.

The figure in Regulation 5 was substituted by virtue of the Redundancy (Inspection of Records) Regulations 1979 (S.I. No. 115 of 1979).

REDUNDANCY (REDUNDANCY APPEALS TRIBUNAL) REGULATIONS 1968

S.I. No. 24 of 1968

GENERAL

1. These Regulations may be cited as the Redundancy (Redundancy Appeals Tribunal) Regulations 1968.
2. In these Regulations—

"the Act" means the Redundancy Payments Act 1967 (No. 21 of 1967);

"the Minister" means the Minister for [Enterprise and Employment];

"notice of appeal" means the notice of appeal required by paragraph 3;

"the Tribunal" means the [Employment] Appeals Tribunal.

ORIGINATING APPLICATION

[3. Where a person (in these Regulations referred to as the appellant) desires to appeal under section 39(15) of the Act to the Tribunal he shall give written notice of appeal to the Secretary of the Tribunal.]

4. The notice of appeal shall be given on the form provided by the Minister for the purpose and shall be accompanied by a statement of the facts and contentions on which the appellant intends to rely.

TIME LIMIT FOR AND WITHDRAWAL OF APPEALS

[5. No appeal shall be entertained by the Tribunal unless the appropriate notice of appeal has been submitted to the Tribunal within 21 days after the receipt by the appellant of the decision which constitutes the subject of the appeal; provided that notice of appeal given after that period may, with the consent of the Tribunal, be accepted.

6. An appellant may withdraw an appeal to the Tribunal by sending notice of withdrawal to the Tribunal.]

FORWARDING OF APPEALS

7.[(1) In the case of an appeal against a decision of a deciding officer and in the case of an employer who is appealing against a decision given by the Minister in relation to a rebate, the Secretary of the Tribunal shall forward to the Minister the notice of appeal together with a copy of the statement by the appellant required under paragraph 4, and the Minister shall, as soon as he may be after receipt by him of such copy appeal and statement, cause to be furnished to the Secretary of the Tribunal a counter-statement given by or on behalf of the deciding officer or the Minister (as the case may be) showing to what extent the facts and contentions advanced by the appellant are admitted or disputed.]

(2) On receipt of the notice of appeal and the counter-statement, the Secretary of the Tribunal shall forward a copy of the counter-statement to the appellant.

[8. In the case of an employee who is appealing against a decision given by an employer under the Redundancy Payments Acts 1967 to [1991], the Secretary of the Tribunal shall on receipt of the notice of appeal forward to the employer concerned (in these Regulations referred to as "the respondent") a copy of the notice of appeal and of the statement by the appellant required under paragraph 4.]

APPEARANCE BY RESPONDENT

9. (1) A respondent shall within 14 days of receiving a copy of the appropriate notice of appeal enter an appearance to the proceedings by sending to the Secretary of the Tribunal a statement (on the form provided by the Minister for the purpose) indicating whether he intends to contest the appeal and, if so, to what extent the facts and contentions advanced by the appellant are admitted or disputed.

(2) Subject to subparagraph (3), a respondent who has not submitted a notice of appearance as required by subparagraph (1) shall not be entitled to take any part in the appeal proceedings or to be represented thereat.

(3) A respondent may apply within the 14-day-period mentioned in subparagraph (1) for an extension of the time in which to enter an appearance.

(4) When the Secretary of the Tribunal receives a notice of appearance from the respondent, he shall forthwith send a copy thereof to the appellant.

HEARINGS BY THE TRIBUNAL

10. The chairman of the Tribunal shall from time to time fix dates, times and places for the hearing of appeals by the Tribunal and notice thereof shall be given by the Secretary to the Tribunal to all persons appearing to the chairman to be concerned.

11. The hearing of an appeal by the Tribunal shall take place in public unless the Tribunal decides at the request of either party to the appeal to hear the appeal in private.

12. Parties summoned to attend a hearing of the Tribunal may appear and be heard in person or may be represented by counsel or solicitor or by a representative of a trade union or of an employers' association or, with the leave of the Tribunal, by any other person.

PROCEDURE AT HEARINGS

13. A party to an appeal heard by the Tribunal may—

    (a) make an opening statement,
    (b) call witnesses,
    (c) cross-examine any witnesses called by any other party,
    (d) give evidence on his own behalf, and
    (e) address the Tribunal at the close of the evidence.

14. The Tribunal may postpone or adjourn the hearing of an appeal from time to time.

15. The Tribunal may admit any duly authenticated written statement as prima facie evidence of any fact whenever it thinks it just and proper so to do.

16. If, after notice of a hearing has been duly given, any of the parties fails to appear at the hearing, the Tribunal may determine the question under appeal or may adjourn the hearing to a later date: provided that before determining the question under appeal the Tribunal shall consider all the evidence before it at the time of the hearing.

17.(1) A decision of the Tribunal may be taken by a majority of the members thereof.

(2) A decision of the Tribunal shall be recorded in a document signed by the chairman and sealed with the seal of the Tribunal.

(3) A decision of the Tribunal shall be entered in a Register of Appeals and a copy of the decision shall be sent to the appellant and to any other person concerned.

(4) The Register of Appeal shall be open to inspection by any person without charge during normal business hours.

(5) The chairman of the Tribunal may by certificate under his hand correct any clerical mistake, error or omission in a decision of the Tribunal, and the correction shall be duly entered in the Register of Appeals and a copy of the corrected decision shall be sent to the appellant and to any other person concerned.

NOTICES

18. (1) Any notice required by these Regulations shall be in writing, and all notices and documents required or authorised by these Regulations to be sent or given to any person may be deemed to be duly sent if sent by registered post and directed—

(i)   in the case of the Minister, to the head office of the Department of [Enterprise and Employment],
(ii) in the case of the Secretary of the Appeals Tribunal, to the office of the Secretary,
(iii) in the case of an appellant, to the address given by him in the notice of appeal,
(iv) in the case of any other person, to his usual or last-known address or his place of business,
(v)   in the case of a body corporate, to its registered office.

(2) A notice or document if sent or given to the authorised representative of a person shall be deemed to have been sent or given to that person.

(3) A party to an appeal may at any time by notice to the Tribunal and to any other party or parties concerned in the appeal change his address for service under these Regulations.

COSTS AND EXPENSES

19. (1) Subject to paragraph (2), the Tribunal shall not award costs against any party to an appeal.

(2) Where in the opinion of the Tribunal a party to the proceedings (and, if he is a respondent, whether or not he has entered an appearance) has acted frivolously or vexatiously, the Tribunal may make an order that that party shall pay to another party a specified amount in respect of travelling expenses and any other costs or

expenses reasonably incurred by that other party in connection with the hearing.

(3) Notwithstanding subparagraph (2), costs shall not be awarded in respect of the costs or expenses in respect of the attendance of counsel, solicitors, officials of a trade union or of any employers' association appearing before the Tribunal in a representative capacity.

(4) Where the Tribunal has made an order under subparagraph (2), the amount referred to in the order shall be recoverable as a simple contract debt.

20. (1) The Tribunal may award to a person appearing before it a sum in respect of travelling expenses and subsistence allowance in accordance with such scale as the Minister, with the consent of the Minister for Finance, may from time to time determine.

(2) A sum awarded under subparagraph (1) shall be paid out of the [Social Insurance] Fund.

[20A.(1) Subject to subparagraph (2), the Tribunal may, at its discretion, award to a person appearing before it and whose attendance is deemed essential by the Tribunal such sum in respect of expenses for loss of remunerative time as it considers reasonable.

(2) The Tribunal shall not make an award under subparagraph (1) in respect of the attendance before the Tribunal of—

(a) appellants or respondents,
(b) any of the following persons appearing in a representative capacity—counsel, solicitors, officials or a trade union, officials of an employer's association.

(3) A sum awarded under subparagraph (1) shall be paid out of the [Social Insurance] Fund.]

Miscellaneous

21. (1) The Tribunal shall have an official seal which shall be judicially noticed.

(2) When affixed to any document the official seal of the Tribunal shall be authenticated by the signature of the chairman or vice-chairman of the Tribunal or by the secretary or such officer of the Tribunal as is authorised for that purpose by the chairman.

(3) Every document issued by the Tribunal and sealed with the official seal of the Tribunal shall be received in evidence without further proof.

22. (1) Where the Minister would not otherwise be a party to any proceedings before the Tribunal, he may request the Tribunal to treat him as a party to the proceedings and, where the Minister makes such a request, he shall be treated as such a party and be entitled to appear and be heard accordingly.

(2) Where under subparagraph (1) the Minister is treated as a party to proceedings, he may for the purposes of appearing or being heard before the Tribunal be represented by a person appointed by him.

23. The Tribunal may consider and decide any question duly referred to it for consideration and determination, notwithstanding the failure or neglect of any person to comply with an requirement of these Regulations.

[23A. The Tribunal may consider and decide any appeal duly made to it notwithstanding the failure or neglect of any person to comply with any requirement of these Regulations.]

24. The Tribunal may require any party to an appeal to furnish in writing further particulars with regard to the facts and contentions contained in either the notice of appeal or the notice of appearance and when the required particulars have been received by the Secretary of the Tribunal he shall furnish the other party to the appeal with a copy of the particulars provided.

25. A reference by a deciding officer to the Tribunal under section 39(16) of the Act shall be made on the form provided by the Minister for that purpose.

GENERAL NOTE

These Regulations, as amended, prescribe the procedure to be followed in relation to the submission and hearing of appeals against decisions given under the Redundancy Payments Acts 1967 to 1991. They also provide for matters incidental to the hearing of appeals, including notifications of decisions, the keeping of a Register of Appeals, the use of an official seal and the awarding of costs and expenses.

Regulations 3, 5, 6, 7(1), 8, 20A and 23A were substituted or inserted, as the case may be, by virtue of the Redundancy (Employment Appeals Tribunal) Regulations 1979 (S.I. No. 114 of 1979).

The form referred to in Regulation 4 is Form RP51A which is reproduced *infra* at p.275.

The Tribunal's powers under Regulation 14 were considered in *Concannon v. Geraghty* UD1148/1992 (reported at [1994] E.L.R. 229). The case, which had been part heard and then settled, came before a division of the Tribunal for mention on September 29, 1994. The claimant applied to have the case adjourned to a date after August 31, 1995 and the respondent applied to have the case struck out. The Tribunal (Chairman: Iarfhlaith O'Neill S.C.) were of the opinion that it had no jurisdiction to strike out a claim or appeal on the application of the respondent. The only way in which a claim or appeal could be removed from the jurisdiction of the Tribunal was either by way of a withdrawal pursuant to

Regulation 4 of the Unfair Dismissals (Claims and Appeals) Regulations 1977 (*see infra* at p.197) or by way of a determination of the Tribunal. Because the claimant was unwilling to withdraw his application prior to the end of August 1995 it "necessarily" followed that his case could not be struck out or extinguished by the Tribunal within that time. Accordingly the Tribunal exercised its jurisdiction to adjourn, as provided for in Regulation 14, but added that it did not have jurisdiction to "adjourn generally". It could only adjourn from "time to time", which was construed as meaning "to adjourn to a definite time in the future".

As to whether a claimant had acted "frivolously or vexatiously" within the meaning of Regulation 19(2) *see Sherry v. Panther Security Ltd* UD 465/1990 (reported at [1991] E.L.R. 239) and *Sheehan v. M & M Keating & Sons Ltd* UD 534/1991 (reported at [1993] E.L.R. 12).

REDUNDANCY PAYMENTS ACT (AUTHORISED OFFICERS) ORDER 1968

S.I. No. 106 of 1968

1. This Order may be cited as the Redundancy Payments Act (Authorised Officers) Order 1968.

2. The Minister for [Enterprise and Employment] may, with the consent of another Minister, designate an officer of that other Minister to be a duly authorised officer of the Minister for (Enterprise and Employment) for the purposes of the Redundancy Payments Act 1967 (No. 21 of 1967).

GENERAL NOTE

This Order empowers the Minister to designate officers of other Ministers to be duly authorised officers of the Minister for the purposes of the legislation.

REDUNDANCY (REBATES) REGULATIONS 1990

S.I. No. 122 of 1990

1. These Regulations may be cited as the Redundancy (Rebates) Regulations 1990, and shall come into operation on the 23rd day of May, 1990.

2. In these Regulations—

"the Acts" means the Redundancy Payments Acts 1967 to [1991];

"the Minister" means the Minister for [Enterprise and Employment];

"rebate" has the meaning assigned to it by section 29 of the Redundancy Payments Act 1967 (No. 21 of 1967).

3. A claim for a rebate shall be made—

(a) by the employee in the form set out in the Schedule to these Regulations (or a form substantially to the like effect) and shall contain the appropriate particulars referred to in that form,

(b) to the Minister for [Enterprise and Employment] addressed to his office, in Dublin,

(c) before the expiration of six months from the date on which the employer made the relevant lump sum payment or, where a claimant proves that there was good cause for his failure to make the claim before the expiration of that period, within such further period as the Minister may in any particular case or class of cases allow, and

(d) in writing and accompanied by the copy of the redundancy certificate on which the employee concerned has signed a receipt for the lump sum payment, except that where in a particular case a claimant proves to the satisfaction of the Minister that that copy cannot be produced the Minister may, at his discretion, accept in lieu of the certificate such other evidence as he thinks fit of the payment of the lump sum.

4. An employer who has made a claim for a rebate shall, if required to do so by the Minister, produce evidence of the following matters—

    (a) the period of continuous employment of the employee concerned, with the employer,

    (b) the normal weekly remuneration of the employee concerned,

    (c) the numbers of employees employed on material dates by the employer, and

    (d) the receipt by the employee concerned of the lump sum in respect of which the rebate is claimed.

5. An employer who has made a claim for a rebate shall, if required to do so by the Minister, produce for examination on behalf of the Minister any or all such registers, cards, wages sheets, other records of wages and records of employment which may contain particulars of the employment of the employee or employees concerned with the employer and which are in the custody of the employer or under his control.

6. The Redundancy (Rebates) Regulations 1984 (S.I. No. 222 of 1984) are hereby revoked.

SCHEDULE

FORM RP3

AN ROINN FIONTAR **AGUS FOSTAIOCHTA**	**DEPARTMENT OF ENTERPRISE** **AND EMPLOYMENT**

EMPLOYER'S CLAIM FOR REBATE FROM THE SOCIAL INSURANCE FUND
REDUNDANCY PAYMENTS ACTS 1967 TO 1991

Notes: Before completing this form please refer to explanatory booklet. A claim for rebate must be sent to the Minister for [Enterprise and Employment] addressed to his office in Dublin within six months of the date of payment of the redundancy lump sum.

PLEASE COMPLETE THIS FORM IN BLOCK CAPITALS

EMPLOYER'S PAYE REGISTERED NUMBER _____

BUSINESS NAME OF EMPLOYER _____
_____

BUSINESS ADDRESS _____
_____
_____

To the Minister for [Enterprise and Employment]:—

I certify that the employees whose names are listed overleaf (and on continuation sheets numbered   to   )—

   (i) ceased employment on the dates on the attached Redundancy Certificates,

  (ii) in accordance with the terms of the Redundancy Payments Acts 1967 to 1991, were paid lump sums for which they have signed receipts on the attached copies of redundancy certificates and that these redundancy certificates are true copies of the certificates given to the employees concerned.

I understand that in order to establish my right to any rebate it may be necessary for you to refer to information given by me to the Revenue Commissioners and other Government Departments, and I hereby give my consent to the disclosure of such information for this purpose only. I also certify that none of the redundancy payments to which this claim refers is awaiting the decision of an Appeals Tribunal.

I claim rebate amounting to £ and declare that no other claim for rebate has been made in respect of the service of these employees between the dates of commencement and termination on the attached redundancy certificates.

SIGNATURE OF EMPLOYER _____

POSITION HELD IN COMPANY _____

DATE _____

R P 3

CLAIM FOR REBATE FROM THE SOCIAL INSURANCE FUND

Employee's Revenue and Social Insurance (RSI) Number	Employees		Amount of Rebate claimed
	Surname	First Name	

GENERAL NOTE

The purpose of these Regulations is to set out the procedures which must be followed by employers when claiming rebates on lump-sum payments consequent on the amalgamation of the Redundancy and Employers' Insolvency Fund with the Social Insurance Fund. The place at which the claims must be made, the procedures and the time limit for the making of the claims are also prescribed. The Regulations also provide that claimants for rebates must, if required to do so by the Minister, produce evidence in support of the claims.

REDUNDANCY CERTIFICATE REGULATIONS 1991

S.I. No. 347 of 1991

1. These Regulations may be cited as the Redundancy Certificate Regulations 1991, and shall come into operation on the 30th day of December, 1991.

2. A redundancy certificate shall be in the form set out in the Schedule to these Regulations, or in a form substantially to like effect, and shall contain—

    (a) the appropriate particulars referred to in that form,

    (b) a declaration or declarations (as appropriate) by the employer concerned in the terms set out in that form, and

    (c) a receipt, if appropriate, in the terms set out in that form, by the employee concerned for the lump sum payment referred to in that form.

3. An employer who fails to comply with these Regulations shall be guilty of an offence and shall be liable on summary conviction to a fine not exceeding £50.

4. The Redundancy Certificate Regulations 1984 (S.I. No. 221 of 1984) are hereby revoked.

SCHEDULE

FORM RP2

REDUNDANCY CERTIFICATE
REDUNDANCY PAYMENTS ACTS 1967 to 1991

AN ROINN FIONTAR AGUS FOSTAIOCHTA	**DEPARTMENT OF ENTERPRISE AND EMPLOYMENT**

Note: Before completing this form please refer to explanatory booklet.

PLEASE COMPLETE THIS FORM IN BLOCK CAPITALS

EMPLOYER'S PAYE REGISTERED NUMBER   Figures   Letter

BUSINESS NAME OF EMPLOYER _____

BUSINESS ADDRESS _____

EMPLOYER'S REVENUE AND SOCIAL INSURANCE NUMBER   Figures   Letter

To: **SURNAME** _____ FIRST NAME _____

SOCIAL WELFARE INSURANCE NUMBER

SEX

Male	
Female	

Tick
Appropriate
Box

DATE OF BIRTH   **OCCUPATION**

For Official Use

MANCO

101

DATE OF COMMENCEMENT **DATE OF TERMINATION** **NUMBER OF HOURS NORMALLY EXPECTED TO WORK PER WEEK**

Day Month Year   Day Month Year

PERIODS OF NON RECKONABLE SERVICE

Day Month Year   Day Month Year   Reason

From   To

Day Month Year   Day Month Year   Reason

From   To

Day Month Year   Day Month Year   Reason

From   To

1. CALCULATION OF STATUTORY LUMP SUM PAYMENT

Note: Regard should be had to ceiling on normal weekly remuneration.

Years

(i)   Total Reckonable Service _____

(Exclude service before age of 16 and other non-reckonable service)

weeks

(ii) Number of weeks pay due _____

(iii) Amount of Normal Week's Pay:

Gross weekly wage £   Average regular overtime £   Benefits in kind £

Total £

(iv) State ceiling on earnings applied for purposes of calculation if the statutory ceiling is lower than normal week's pay _____ £

(v)   Amount of statutory lump sum payment to which employee is entitled _____ £

102

2. EMPLOYEE'S RECEIPT FOR LUMP SUM PAYMENT

Note: In no circumstances should this receipt be used for any payment other than the statutory redundancy lump sum or part thereof. This receipt will not be accepted as valid unless the sum paid is inserted.

WARNING: DO NOT SIGN THIS RECEIPT UNTIL YOU ACTUALLY RECEIVE PAYMENT OF THE SUM BEING ACKNOWLEDGED.

I acknowledge receipt of a lump sum redundancy payment
amounting to: £ ☐

Signature of Employee _____ | Day | Month | Year |

3. DECLARATION BY EMPLOYER

I declare that the employee was dismissed by reason of redundancy, that the employee is entitled to a lump sum of the amount set out in Part 1(v) of this certificate, and that the employee was paid a lump sum of _____

£ ☐

(If no payment made, please insert NIL)

Signature of Employer _____

Date ____

Position held in Company _____

GENERAL NOTE

The purpose of these Regulations is to require employers, when giving a redundancy certificate under the Redundancy Payments Acts, to use the amended form (RP2) provided by the Minister for this purpose and to furnish the appropriate declarations in the form. A penalty for failure to comply with the regulations is also specified.

REDUNDANCY (NOTICE OF DISMISSAL) REGULATIONS 1991

S.I. No. 348 of 1991

1. These Regulations may be cited as the Redundancy (Notice of Dismissal) Regulations 1991, and shall come into operation on the 30th day of December, 1991.

2. In these Regulations "the notice" means the notice required by section 17(1) of the Redundancy Payments Act 1967 (No. 21 of 1967), as amended by the Redundancy Payments Act 1971 (No. 20 of 1971).

3. The notice shall be given in the form set out in the Schedule to these Regulations, or in a form substantially to like effect, and shall contain the appropriate particulars referred to in that form.

4. A copy of the notice shall, at the same time as it is given to the employee concerned, be sent by the employer concerned to the Minister for [Enterprise and Employment] addressed to his office in Dublin.

5. An employer who fails to comply with these Regulations shall be guilty of an offence and shall be liable on summary conviction to a fine not exceeding £50.

6. The Redundancy (Notice of Dismissal) Regulations 1984 (S.I. No. 220 of 1984) are hereby revoked.

SCHEDULE

FORM RP1

NOTICE OF PROPOSED DISMISSAL FOR REDUNDANCY

REDUNDANCY PAYMENTS ACTS 1967 TO 1991

AN ROINN [FIONTAR agus FOSTAIOCHTA] – DEPARTMENT OF [ENTERPRISE AND EMPLOYMENT]

Note for Employer: On the date that this notice is given by an employer to the employee a copy of it must be sent to the Minister for [Enterprise and Employment] at Davitt House, 65A Adelaide Road, Dublin 2. Failure to do this may lead to a reduction in rebate payable.

PLEASE COMPLETE THIS FORM IN BLOCK CAPITALS

EMPLOYER'S PAYE REGISTERED NUMBER

BUSINESS NAME OF EMPLOYER

BUSINESS ADDRESS

GIVE DETAILS OF TYPE OF BUSINESS IN WHICH REDUNDANCY ARISES

For official use

NACE _____

Figures   Letters

EMPLOYEE'S REVENUE AND SOCIAL INSURANCE NUMBER

TO: SURNAME

FIRST NAME

ADDRESS

SOCIAL WELFARE INSURANCE NUMBER

SEX Male | Female

Tick Appropriate Box

DATE OF BIRTH OF EMPLOYEE Day | Month | Year

OCCUPATION _____

ADDRESS OF PLACE OF EMPLOYMENT
_____
_____
_____

For Office Use

MANCO

GIVE DETAILS OF THE REASON FOR REDUNDANCY
_____
_____
_____

AREA

REASON

Day   Month   Year

DATE OF COMMENCEMENT OF EMPLOYEE'S EMPLOYMENT

NUMBER OF HOURS NORMALLY EXPECTED TO WORK PER WEEK

It is necessary to terminate your employment by reason of redundancy. In accordance with the provisions of the Redundancy Payments Acts 1967 to 1991, I hereby give you notice that your employment will terminate on

Day | Month | Year

SIGNATURE OF EMPLOYER _____

POSITION HELD IN COMPANY _____

Day | Month | Year

DATE OF NOTICE

GENERAL NOTE

The purpose of these regulations is to require employers when giving notice of dismissal under the Redundancy Payments Acts to use the amended form (RP1) provided by the Minister for this purpose and to send a copy of the completed form to the Minister addressed to his office in Dublin. A penalty for failure to comply with the regulations is also specified.

106

(Obligatory Period)

LEAVING BEFORE REDUNDANCY NOTICE EXPIRES

It may be that when you get form RP1 — Notice of proposed dismissal for Redundancy — you might wish to leave your employment sooner than the date of termination notified to you, e.g., to take up alternative employment. If you decide to leave, there is a risk that you may lose any entitlement to redundancy payments unless you notify your employer in writing and also comply with the general conditions on the back of this form. You may use this form for writing to your employer.

If after receipt of this notice your employer objects to your leaving your employment and you leave notwithstanding, you may have to prove to the satisfaction of the Employment Appeals Tribunal that your grounds for leaving were reasonable.

PART 1:

NOTICE TO AN EMPLOYER BY AN EMPLOYEE TO TERMINATE EMPLOYMENT (SECTION 10 OF THE REDUNDANCY PAYMENTS ACT 1967 AS AMENDED BY SECTION 9 OF THE REDUNDANCY PAYMENTS ACT 1979)

To:_____(Name and address of Employer)

With reference to your Notice of Redundancy (RP 1) dated____proposing to terminate my employment on _____ (date of termination notified), I hereby give you notice of my intention to anticipate dismissal by leaving on _____ (insert date on which you propose to leave). Note that the date on which you give this notice and the date on which it expires must be within the obligatory period of notice. Your employer's consent may be necessary to ensure this, see Part 3 of this form).

Revenue & Social Insurance No:_____Signed:_____(Employee)

Social Welfare Insurance No:_____Date:_____

Part 2:

COUNTER NOTICE BY EMPLOYER

To:_____

Name of Employee

I request you to withdraw your notice and to continue in my employment until the date on which my notice expires. If you do not withdraw your notice I will contest any liability to pay you a redundancy payment. My reason for objection is_____

_____

Signed:_____(Employer)

Date:_____

PART 3:

CONSENT BY EMPLOYER TO ALTER DATE OF HIS DISMISSAL NOTICE SO AS TO BRING EMPLOYEE'S ANTICIPATORY NOTICE WITHIN THE OBLIGATORY PERIOD. (SECTION 9 OF THE REDUNDANCY PAYMENTS ACT 1979)

I agree that the date of termination notified on my notice of proposed dismissal (RP1) be altered to .... so that the giving of employee's notice to anticipate dismissal and the expiration date of his anticipating notice shall be within the obligatory period of notice.

Signed:_____(Employer)

Date:_____

EMPLOYEES PROPOSING TO ANTICIPATE THEIR REDUNDANCY NOTICE BY LEAVING SOONER THAN THE DATE OF TERMINATION NOTIFIED TO THEM ON FORM RP1 SHOULD READ THESE NOTES CAREFULLY BEFORE COMPLETING THE FORM OVERLEAF. *(This is not a statutory form and it is open to you to use an alternative means of communication with your employer, provided it is in writing).*

If you have been given Notice of proposed dismissal for Redundancy (Form RP1) and you wish to leave your job sooner than the date you are to become redundant *(as set out on the redundancy notice)* you should, if you want to preserve your entitlement to redundancy payment, fill in the form overleaf and send it or give it to your employer.

Thus must be done within (not before) your obligatory period of notice. Normally this period is the two weeks immediately before the date you are to become redundant but if you have been in the job for between 5 and 10 years, this period is extended to 4 weeks; if you have been in the job 10 to 15 years the period is 6 weeks and if you have been more than 15 years the period is 8 weeks. If your contract of employment lays down a longer period of notice, this longer period is the obligatory period of notice in your case.

You may leave your job before the date specified in your redundancy notice and still preserve your redundancy entitlement only if the dates on which you give notice and on which you leave are within your obligatory period of notice as set out in the previous paragraph. Furthermore if your employer gives you a counter-notice in form similar to the 'counter notice by employer' overleaf you will not be entitled to redundancy payment if you unreasonably refuse to comply with his request. *(Any disputes on this matter may be referred to the Appeals Tribunal).*

If the date on which you wish to give notice is outside the obligatory period your employer may bring it within that period by agreement in writing to an alteration of the date of termination shown on his notice of dismissal (RP1). Part 3 of this form may be used for this purpose. You should obtain written agreement to alteration of termination date on employer's notice prior to giving your anticipation notice, and if your employer refused to agree to such alteration you must wait until a date within the obligatory period before giving anticipatory notice.

NOTICE FOR EMPLOYERS

If an employee under notice of redundancy leaves by his own decision before the date set out in his notice (RP1) without complying with all of the conditions set out above, he may not be entitled to a lump sum under the Redundancy Payments Acts. Should you pay an employee a lump sum to which he is not entitled because he has not complied with the procedures outlined on this form, you will not get a rebate from the Department of Enterprise and Employment unless the Employment Appeals Tribunal decides otherwise.

If you agree to an employee leaving before the date set out in his notice of redundancy (RP1), though within his obligatory period of notice, you must attach completed form RP6, or whatever written notice you have received from him, to your claim for rebate, as evidence of compliance with these procedures, otherwise you will not be paid rebate.

If the date on which an employee wishes to give you anticipatory notice is outside the obligatory period you may (though you are not obliged to) bring it within such period by alteration of the termination date on your dismissal notice. Your agreement to do so must be in writing. Part 3 of this form may be used for this purpose.

If you do not agree to your employee's leaving before the date set out in his notice of redundancy (RP1), though within his obligatory period of notice, you should, before the expiration date of his anticipatory notice give him counter-notice in writing. Part 2 of this form may be used for that purpose.

The redundancy lump sum will be based on the period: date on which service commenced to date of actual termination.

Issued by the Department of Enterprise and Employment

AN ROINN FIONTAR AGUS FOSTAIOCHTA	DEPARTMENT OF ENTERPRISE AND EMPLOYMENT

LAY OFF AND SHORT TIME PROCEDURES

NOTES

An employer may use Part A overleaf of this form to notify an employee of temporary lay off or temporary short time (lay off and short time are defined at the end of this page).

An employee may use Part B overleaf of this form to notify his/her employer of intention to claim a redundancy lump sum payment in a lay off or short time situation.

An employer may use Part C overleaf of this form to give counter notice to an employee who claims payment of a redundancy lump sum in a lay off/short time situation.

EMPLOYER'S PAYE REGISTERED NUMBER

ADDRESS OF EMPLOYEE
_____

SEX (TICK APPROPRIATE BOX)
☐ Male   ☐ Female

DATE OF BIRTH OF EMPLOYEE
Day Month Year

DESCRIPTION OF BUSINESS IN WHICH REDUNDANCY ARISES

DATE OF COMMENCEMENT OF EMPLOYEE'S EMPLOYMENT
Day Month Year

FOR OFFICIAL USE ONLY – NACE CODE	ADDRESS OF PLACE OF EMPLOYMENT
EMPLOYEE'S REVENUE AND SOCIAL INSURANCE (R.S.I.) NUMBER Figures Letters ☐☐☐☐☐☐☐☐☐☐	_____ _____ _____
EMPLOYEE'S SURNAME	
EMPLOYEE'S FIRST NAME	FOR OFFICIAL USE ONLY — AREA CODE

DEFINITION OF LAY OFF AND SHORT TIME

A lay off situation exists when an employer suspends an employee's employment because there is no work available, when the employer expects the cessation of work to be temporary and when the employer notifies the employee to this effect.

A short time working situation exists when an employer, because he has less work available for an employee than is normal, reduces that employee's earnings to less than half the normal week's earnings or reduces the number of hours of work to less than half the normal weekly hours, when the employer expects this reduction to be temporary and when the employer notifies the employee to this effect.

PART A: Notification to employee of TEMPORARY LAY OFF or TEMPORARY SHORT TIME
Notification in respect of this part need not be in writing

It is necessary to place you on

☐ **TEMPORARY LAY OFF** ☐ **TEMPORARY SHORT TIME**
(Please tick)

as and from   ☐☐☐☐☐☐

by reason of _____

I expect the LAY OFF/SHORT TIME to be temporary.

Signature of Employer .... Date ....

PART B: Notice of intention to claim Redundancy Lump Sum Payment in a LAY OFF/SHORT TIME situation

An employee who wishes to claim a redundancy lump sum because of lay off/short time must service notice of intention to claim in writing within four weeks after the lay off/short time ceases. In order to become entitled to claim a redundancy lump sum on foot of a period of lay off, short time or a mixture of both, that period must be at least four consecutive weeks or a broken series of six weeks where all six fall within a thirteen-week period. An employee who wishes to terminate his contract of employment by reason of lay off or short time must give his employer the notice required by his contract or if none is required, at least one week's notice.

An employee who claims and receives redundancy payment in respect of lay off or short time is deemed to have voluntarily left his employment and therefore not entitled to notice under the Minimum Notice and Terms of Employment Act 1973.

To (Business Name of Employer): _____

I give you notice of my intention to claim a redundancy lump sum in respect of LAY OFF/SHORT TIME (Delete whichever does not apply)

	Day Month Year		Day Month Year
From		To	

Signature of Employee_____ Date_____

PART C: Counter Notice to Employee's Notice of Intention to claim a Redundancy Lump Sum

Notification in respect of this part must be in writing and must be given to the employee within seven days of service of the employee's notice.

I contest any liability to pay you a Redundancy Lump Sum on the grounds that it is reasonable to expect that within four weeks of the date of service of your notice, namely _____ (Date of Service), you will enter upon a period of employment of not less than thirteen weeks during which you will not be on lay off or short time any week.

Signature of Employer _____ **Date** _____

AN ROINN FIONTAR AGUS FOSTAIOCHTA	**DEPARTMENT OF ENTERPRISE AND EMPLOYMENT**

EMPLOYEE'S APPLICATION FOR LUMP SUM FROM THE SOCIAL INSURANCE FUND

NOTES FOR EMPLOYEE

This form is to be used when applying to the Minister for Enterprise and Employment for payment of a redundancy lump sum from the Social Insurance Fund. You should only use this form if you have applied in writing to your employer for payment (Form RP77 may be used) and he has failed to pay the redundancy lump sum.

This form must be accompanied by either a Redundancy Certificate or a favourable decision from the Employment Appeals Tribunal.

If you have applied in writing and your employer refuses to give you a Redundancy Certificate or ignores your application and you consider that you are entitled to a redundancy payment, you may appeal to the Employment Appeals Tribunal. If the Appeals Tribunal decides that you are entitled to a redundancy lump sum they will issue a decision which should be sent to the Minister for Enterprise and Employment with this form.

Please complete this form in BLOCK CAPITALS

Employer's PAYE Registered Number _____

(Available on Notice of Dismissal (RP1), Redundancy Certificate (RP2) and P45)

Business Name of Employer _____

Business Address _____

_____

_____

If the employer is deceased, give the name and address of his representative. If the business is in liquidation or receivership, please supply the name and address of the liquidator or receiver. If the business has ceased trading but has not gone into liquidation or receivership, and the employer is no longer available at the business address, please supply the address at which he may be contacted.

113

Name _____

Address _____

_____

_____

_____

Employee's Revenue and Social Insurance (R.S.I.) Number _____

Surname _____

First Name _____

Address* _____

_____

_____

NON PAYMENT BY MY EMPLOYER DUE TO	TICK
LIQUIDATION	
RECEIVERSHIP	
BANKRUPTCY	
CLAIMS INSOLVENCY	
EMPLOYER DECEASED	
REFUSES TO PAY	
IGNORES MY APPLICATION	
OTHER REASON (GIVE DETAILS)	

PLEASE ATTACH: Notice of Dismissal (RP1) and Redundancy Certificate (RP2), or state Employment Appeals Tribunal Case Number: _____
Decision Date: _____

I claim payment of a lump sum/part of a lump sum from the Social Insurance Fund by reason of default on the part of my employer. I applied in writing to my employer for payment on _____ (Date).

SIGNATURE OF EMPLOYEE _____ **DATE** _____

A person who fraudulently applies to the Minister for a lump sum shall be guilty of an offence and shall be liable on summary conviction to a fine of up to £300.

*Please ensure that the employee's correct address is given on this form as the cheque in respect of the lump sum entitlement shall be posted to that address. Any changes of address must be notified immediately to the Redundancy Payments Section of the Department of Enterprise and Employment.

REDUNDANCY PAYMENTS ACTS 1967 TO 1991

A claim by an employee against an employer for a lump sum or part of a lump sum.

An employee who is in doubt about whether he has a valid claim or not can check against an informational leaflet on the qualifications – (see the footnote overleaf).

To: _____

_____
_____

Name and Address of Employer

I claim a lump sum payment/balance of lump sum payment* from you in respect of my dismissal. My claim is based on the following grounds (tick whichever applies):

The grounds of my dismissal constitute redundancy but I have not received a redundancy notice/redundancy certificate* nor a lump sum payment. I request these. _____

I have received a redundancy notice/redundancy certificate* but no lump sum payment. _____

The lump sum which I received is incorrect. Particulars of the error are: _____

_____
_____
_____

I have received a favourable decision from the Appeals Tribunal in regard to my redundancy appeal and I now request you to pay the lump sum due to me. _____

Insurance No_____ Signed_____
Date:_____ Address_____

_____
_____
_____

*Strike out whichever is not applicable.

115

EXPLANATORY NOTE FOR EMPLOYEE WHEN APPLYING TO AN EMPLOYER FOR A LUMP SUM

This form may be used by an employee

A.   who considers that he is entitled to redundancy payments and his employer has not acknowledged his entitlement by giving him

(i)   Notice of proposed dismissal for Redundancy (Form RP1)

(ii) Redundancy Certificate (Form RP2)

(iii) Lump sum payment.

If an employee has received (i) and (ii), or (ii) only but not (iii), he should apply in writing to his employer for payment.

B.   who considers that he has received an incorrect lump sum.

C.   who has received a favourable decision from the Appeals Tribunal on his redundancy appeal and who wishes to pursue the matter of payment of the lump sum, or an unpaid part of it, with his employer's representative.

Should a payment or a balance of payment be refused or this application be ignored by an employer, the following options are open to the employee:

If he has not received a Redundancy Certificate (Form RP2): he may apply to the Appeals Tribunal for a declaration of redundancy or a declaration of the facts of redundancy. Form RP51A should be consulted and used for this purpose.

If he holds a Redundancy Certificate or alternatively has received a favourable decision from the Appeals Tribunal on his redundancy appeal: he may refer the matter to the Department of Enterprise and Employment for further attention. Form RP14 should be consulted and used for this purpose.

IMPORTANT

1.   Record the date on which you apply for payment to your employer.

2.   Allow a reasonable time, say 14 days, for the employer to deal with the matter before proceeding further.

3.   Do not use this Form for purposes other than applying to an employer for payment of a statutory Redundancy lump sum or balance of a lump sum.

4.   If dismissal arises in a lay-off or short-time situation consult Form RP9 in the first instance.

PROTECTION OF EMPLOYMENT ACT 1977

(1977 No. 7)

ARRANGEMENT OF SECTIONS

SECT.

An Act to provide for the implementation of the Directive of the Council of the European Communities done at Brussels on the 17th day of February, 1975, regarding the approximation of the laws of Member States of those communities relating to the collective redundancies, and to provide for other matters relating to that matter. [*5th April 1977*]

GENERAL NOTE

This Act is designed to satisfy Ireland's obligations under Council Directive 75/129/EEC on the approximation of the law of the Member States relating to collective redundancies (OJ L48/29, 22.2.1975), on which see further Freedland, "Employment Protection: Redundancy Provisions and the EEC" (1976) 5 I.L.J.

117

24; Hepple, "Community Measures for the Protection of Workers against Dismissals" (1977) 14 C.M.L. Rev. 489; Plas, "Droit Social European. Les Licenciements Collectifs" (1978) 50 *Revue de droit social* 305.

Freedland observed, *loc. cit.* at p. 34 that the Directive is primarily concerned with "the positive control of public authorities over the labour market" and less with strengthening the collective bargaining process. See further the decision of the Court of Justice in Case 91/81, *Commission v. Italy* [1982] E.C.R. 2133 where the Italian Republic was found to have failed in its obligations by not adopting within the prescribed period the measures needed to comply with the Directive. The Italian Republic was subsequently condemned for non-compliance with this judgment in Case 131/84, *Commission v. Italy* [1985] E.C.R. 3531.

Articles 2 and 3(2), however, lay down the principle that workers' representatives must be informed and consulted with regard to the details of projected collective redundancies and the possibility of reducing the numbers or effects of such redundancies and that those representatives must be in a position to submit any comments to the competent public authority (here the Department of Enterprise and Employment). Consequently the UK was condemned by the Court of Justice in Case-383/92, *Commission v. United Kingdom* [1994] E.C.R.I.–2479 for not providing a mechanism for the designation of workers' representatives in an undertaking where the employer refuses to recognise such representatives. Article 2, however, was not regarded by Blackburne J. in *Griffin v. South West Water Services Ltd* [1995] I.R.L.R. 15 as being sufficiently precise to be capable of direct enforcement.

Directive 75/129 has now been amended by Council Directive 92/56/EEC (OJ L 245/3, 26.8.1992), so the Act should have been amended by June 23, 1994 principally by ensuring that workers have at their disposal "administrative and/or judicial procedures in order to ensure that the obligations laid down in the Directives are fulfilled".

Citation

See section 1.

Commencement

The Act came into operation on May 10, 1977.

Statutory Instruments

Protection of Employment Act 1977 (Commencement) Order 1977 (S.I. No. 139 of 1977).
Protection of Employment Act 1977 (Notification of Proposed Collective Redundancies) Regulations 1977 (S.I. No. 140 of 1977).

Parliamentary Debates

295 *Dail Debates* Cols. 901–922 (Second Stage)
296 *Dail Debates* Cols. 1550–1569 (Second Stage resumed)
297 *Dail Debates* Cols. 668–688 (Committee Stage)
298 *Dail Debates* Cols. 338–349 (Report and Final Stages)
86 *Seanad Debates* Cols. 547–563 (Second Stage)
86 *Seanad Debates* Cols. 563–565 (Committee and Final Stages)

Be it enacted by the Oireachtas as follows:

PART 1

PRELIMINARY AND GENERAL

Short title and commencement

1.—(1) This Act may be cited as the Protection of Employment Act 1977.

(2) This Act shall come into operation on such day as may be appointed by order of the Minister.

GENERAL NOTE

The Protection of Employment Act 1977 (Commencement) Order 1977 (S.I. No. 139 of 1977) appointed May 10, 1977 to be the day on which the Act came into operation.

Interpretation

2.—(1) In this Act—

"authorised officer" means a person appointed by the Minister to be an authorised officer for the purposes of this Act;

"contract of employment" means a contract of service or of apprenticeship;

"employee" means a person who has entered into or works under (or, in the case of a contract which has been terminated, worked under) a contract of employment with an employer, whether the contract is for manual labour, clerical work or otherwise, is express or implied, oral or in writing, and "employer" and references to employment shall be construed accordingly;

"employees' representatives" means officials (including shop stewards) of a trade union or of a staff association with which it has been the practice of the employer to conduct collective bargaining negotiations;

"the Minister" means the [Minister for Enterprise and Employment];

"prescribed" means prescribed by regulations under this Act;

"staff associations" means a body of persons all the members of which are employed by the same employer and which carries on negotiations for the fixing of the wages or other conditions of employment of its own members only;

119

"trade union" means a trade union which is the holder of a negotiation licence granted under the Trade Union Acts 1941 [to 1990].

(2) In this Act a reference to a section is to a section of this Act unless it is indicated that reference to some other enactment is intended.

(3) In this Act a reference to a subsection is to the subsection of the section in which the reference occurs unless it is indicated that reference to some other section is intended.

GENERAL NOTE

"the Minister": the words in square brackets were substituted by virtue of the Labour (Transfer of Departmental Administration and Ministerial Functions) Order 1993 (S.I. No. 18 of 1993) and the Industry and Commerce (Alteration of Name of Department and Title of Minister) Order 1993 (S.I. No. 19 of 1993).

"employees' representatives": the question of whether it has been "the practice of the employer to conduct collective bargaining negotiations" has been considered on a number of occasions in Britain and the relevant law was laid down in *National Union of Gold, Silver and Allied Trades v. Albury Brothers Ltd* [1978] I.C.R. 62, 65, where it was stressed that recognition required "mutuality". See also *National Union of Tailors and Garment Workers v. Charles Ingram & Co. Ltd* [1977] I.C.R. 530 and *Union of Shop, Distributive and Allied Workers v. Sketchley Ltd* [1981] I.C.R. 644. It may be legitimately queried as to whether this definition satisfies the requirement of the Directive in respect of employers who refuse to recognise trade unions: see Case C–383/92, *Commission v. United Kingdom* [1994] E.C.R.I.–2479.

Regulations and Orders

3.—(1) The Minister may make regulations for the purpose of giving effect to this Act.

(2)(a) The Minister may by order amend any provision of this Act so as to comply with any international obligations relating to collective redundancies that the State has decided to assume.

(b) The Minister may by order amend or revoke an order under this section.

(3) Regulations under this section may contain such incidental, supplementary and consequential provisions as appear to the Minister to be necessary for the purposes of the regulations.

Laying of orders and regulations before Houses of Oireachtas

4.—(1) Every order and regulation under this Act (other than an order under section 3, section 6 or section 7(3)) shall be laid before each House of the Oireachtas as soon as possible after it is made and, if a resolution annulling the order or regulation is passed by either House within the next 21 days on which that House has sat after the order or regulation is laid before it, the order or regulation shall be annulled accordingly, but without prejudice to the validity of anything previously done under it.

(2) Where an order is proposed to be made under section 3, section 6 or section 7(3), a draft of the order shall be laid before both Houses of the Oireachtas and the order shall not be made until a resolution approving of the draft has been passed by each House.

Expenses

5. The expenses incurred in the administration of this Act shall, to such extent as may be sanctioned by the Minister for Finance, be paid out of moneys provided by the Oireachtas.

Meaning of collective redundancies

6.—(1) For the purpose of this Act, "collective redundancies" means dismissals which are effected for a reason specified in subsection (2) (other than a reason related to the individual employees dismissed) where in any period of 30 consecutive days the number of such dismissals is—

(a) at least five in an establishment normally employing more than 20 and less than 50 employees,

(b) at least ten in an establishment normally employing at least 50 but less than 100 employees,

(c) at least ten per cent. of the number of employees in an establishment normally employing at least 100 but less than 300 employees, and

(d) at least 30 in an establishment normally employing 300 or more employees.

(2) The reasons referred to in subsection (1) are—

(a) that the employer concerned has ceased, or intends to cease, to carry on the business for the purposes of which the employees concerned were employed by him, or has ceased, or intends to cease, to carry on that business in the place where those employees were so employed,

(b) that the requirements of the business for employees to carry out work of a particular kind in the place where the

121

employees concerned were so employed have ceased or diminished or are expected to cease or diminish,

(c) that the employer concerned has decided to carry on the business with fewer or no employees, whether by requiring the work for which the employees concerned had been employed (or had been doing before their dismissal) to be done by other employees or otherwise,

(d) that the employer concerned has decided that the work for which the employees concerned had been employed (or had been doing before their dismissal) should henceforward be done in a different manner for which those employees are not sufficiently qualified or trained,

(e) that the employer concerned has decided that the work for which the employees concerned had been employed (or had been doing before their dismissal) should henceforward be done by persons who are also capable of doing other work for which those employees are not sufficiently qualified or trained.

(3)(a) In this section "establishment" means—

(i) where an employer carries on business at a particular location, that location, or

(ii) where an employer carries on business at more than one location, each such location.

(b) For the purposes of the definition in paragraph (a) of this subsection, each workplace, factory, mine, quarry, dockyard, wharf, quay, warehouse, building site, engineering construction site, electricity station, gas works, water works, sewage disposal works, office, wholesale or retail shop, hotel, restaurant, cafe, farm, garden or forest plantation shall be taken to be a separate location.

(c) In ascertaining for the purposes of this section the total number of employees employed in an establishment, account shall be taken of those employees who are based at the establishment but who also perform some of their duties elsewhere.

(d) The Minister may, for the purpose of extending the provision of this section by order amend paragraph (a), (b) or (c) of this subsection and may be order amend or revoke such an order.

(4) For the purposes of this section, "business" includes a trade, industry, profession or undertaking, or any activity carried on by a person or body of persons, whether corporate or unincorporate, or

by a public or local authority or a Department of State, and the performance of its functions by a public or local authority or a Department of State.

GENERAL NOTE

The word "dismissals" is not defined in the Act but the Directive provides that collective redundancies mean dismissals "by an employer". So, in Case 284/83, *Dansk Metalarbejderforbund and Specialarbejforbund i Danmark v. Nielsen* [1985] E.C.R. 553, the Court of Justice held that there was no provision in the Directive capable of extending the scope of dismissal to terminations of employment by workers. In other words its scope does not extend to what are popularly known as "constructive dismissals". *Quaere* whether, by including in subsection (2) an exhaustive list of the circumstances in which "collective redundancies" are regarded as having taken place, the Act fails to adequately transpose the Directive (which applies to dismissals "for one or more reasons not related to the individual workers concerned").

Application and non-application of Act

7.—(1) Subject to subsection (2), this Act applies to all persons in employment on or after the commencement of this Act in an establishment normally employing more than 20 persons.

(2) This Act does not apply to—

(a) dismissals of employees engaged under a contract of employment for a fixed term or for a specified purpose (being a purpose of such a kind that the duration of the contract was limited but was, at the time of its making, incapable of precise ascertainment) where the dismissals occurred only because of the expiry of the term or the cesser of the purpose,

(b) a person employed by or under the State other than person standing designated for the time being under section 17 of the Industrial Relations act 1969,

(c) officers of a body which is a local authority within the meaning of the Local Government Act 1941,

(d) employment under an employment agreement pursuant to Part II or IV of the Merchant Shipping Act 1894,

(e) employees in an establishment the business carried on in which is being terminated following bankruptcy or winding-up proceedings or for any other reason as a result of a decision of a court of competent jurisdiction.

(3)(a) The Minister may by order declare this Act shall not apply to a class of employees specified in the order and from the commencement of the order this Act shall not apply to that class.

(b) The Minister may be order declare that this Act shall apply to a specified class of employee and from the commencement of the order this Act shall apply to that class.

(c) The Minister may by order amend or revoke an order under this subsection.

(4) Where a notice of dismissal by reason of redundancy which was given before the commencement of this Act expires after such commencement, sections 9, 10, 12 and 14 shall not apply to the dismissal concerned, but such a notice shall be in accordance with the Minimum Notice and Terms of Employment Act 1973, and with the relevant contract of employment.

(5) In this section "establishment" has the same meaning as in section 6.

GENERAL NOTE

The exclusions in subsection (2) follow closely the wording of Article 2 of the Directive, on which see Case 215/83, *Commission v. Belgium* [1985] E.C.R. 1039.

Calculation of normal number of employees

8. For the purposes of this Act, the number of employees normally employed in an establishment (within the meaning of section 6) shall be taken to be the average of the number so employed in each of the 12 months preceding the date on which the first dismissal takes effect.

PART II

CONSULTATION AND NOTIFICATION

Obligation on employer to consult employees' representatives

9.—(1) Where an employer proposes to create collective redundancies he shall, with a view to reaching an agreement, initiate consultations with employees' representatives representing the employees affected by the proposed redundancies.

(2) Consultations under this section shall include the following matters—

(a) the possibility of avoiding the proposed redundancies, reducing the number of employees affected by them or otherwise mitigating their consequences,

(b) the basis on which it will be decided which particular employees will be made redundant.

(3) Consultations under this section shall be initiated at the earliest opportunity and in any event at least 30 days before the first dismissal takes effect.

GENERAL NOTE

The question of precisely when can an employer be said to be proposing to create collective redundancies was considered by the English E.A.T. in *Hough v. Leyland DAF Ltd* [1991] I.R.L.R. 194. Knox J. said that this occurred when matters had reached a stage where a specific proposal had been formulated, which was a later stage than the diagnosis of a problem and the appreciation that at least one way of dealing with it would be by declaring redundancies. The matter was also considered by Glidewell L.J. in *R. v. British Coal Corporation, ex p. Vardy* [1993] I.R.L.R. 104 who drew attention to the fact that in the Directive consultation was to begin as soon as an employer contemplates redundancies (in the French language version "lorsque l'employeur envisage d'effectuer des licenciements collectifs") whereas under the similarly worded British legislation consultation need only begin when the employer proposes to dismiss as redundant an employee. Glidewell L.J. observed (at 116) that "the verb 'proposes' in its ordinary usage relates to a state of mind which is much more certain and further along the decision-making process than the verb 'contemplate'." Blackburne J., however, disagreed with this view in *Griffin v. South West Water Services Ltd* [1995] I.R.L.R. 15. He felt that the obligation to consult only arose when the employer's contemplation of redundancies had reached the point where it was able to identify the workers likely to be affected and could supply the required information. See also *Association of Patternmakers and Allied Craftsmen v. Kirvin Ltd* [1978] I.R.L.R. 318.

Obligation on employer to supply certain information

10.—(1) For the purpose of consultations under section 9, the employer concerned shall supply the employees' representatives with all relevant information relating to the proposed redundancies.

(2) Without prejudice to the generality of subsection (1), information supplied under this section shall include the following, of which details shall be given in writing—

(a) the reasons for the proposed redundancies,
(b) the number, and descriptions or categories, of employees whom it is proposed to make redundant,
(c) the number of employees normally employed, and
(d) the period during which it is proposed to effect the proposed redundancies.

(3) An employer shall as soon as possible supply the Minister with copies of all information supplied in writing under subsection (2).

GENERAL NOTE

The Act does not specify the degree of particularity as to the reasons for the proposed redundancies and all that can be usefully said is that there should be sufficient information to enable the employees' respresentatives to make constructive proposals: see *General and Municipal Workers Union v. British Uralite Ltd* [1979] I.R.L.R. 409, 412.

Penalty for contravention of section 9 or 10

11. An employer who fails to initiate consultations under section 9 or fails to comply with section 10 shall be guilty of an offence and shall be liable on summary ccnviction to a fine not exceeding £500.

GENERAL NOTE

It may be legitimately queried as to whether Ireland has failed to fulfil its obligations under Article 5 of the Treaty insofar as the sanctions provided in this section for failure on the part of an employer to comply with his obligations to inform and consult might not be considered a sufficient deterrent.

Obligation on employer to notify Minister of proposed redundancies

12.—(1) Where an employer proposes to create collective redundancies, he shall notify the Minister in writing of his proposals at the earliest opportunity and in any event at least 30 days before the first dismissal takes effect.

(2) The Minister may prescribe the particulars to be specified in a notification under this section.

(3) A copy of a notification under this section shall be supplied as soon as possible by the employer affected to the employees' representatives affected who may forward to the Minister in writing any observations they have relating to the notification.

GENERAL NOTE

The Protection of Employment Act 1977 (Notification of Proposed Collective Redundancies) Regulations 1977 (S.I. No. 140 of 1977), reproduced *infra* at p.131, prescribe the particulars to be specified by an employer in a notification under this section.

Penalty for contravention of section 12

13. An employer who contravenes section 12 shall be guilty of an offence and shall be liable on summary conviction to a fine not exceeding £500.

PART III

COMMENCEMENT OF COLLECTIVE REDUNDANCIES

Collective redundancies not to take effect for 30 days

14.—(1) Collective redundancies shall not take effect before the expiry of the period of 30 days beginning on the date of the relevant notification under section 12.

(2) Where collective redundancies are effected by an employer before the expiry of the 30-day period mentioned in subsection (1) the employer shall be guilty of an offence and shall be liable on conviction on indictment to a fine not exceeding £3,000.

GENERAL NOTE

Although the scope of subsection (1) has never been judicially explored, it would seem highly arguable that an injunction could be obtained to restrain a breach of the mandatory requirement therein. The section does not state, however, that any purported terminations of employment shall be void. See also the provisions of section 16.

Further consultations with Minister

15.—(1) For the purpose of seeking solutions to the problems caused by the proposed redundancies, the employer concerned shall, at the Minister's request, enter into consultations with him or an authorised officer.

(2) For the purpose of consultations under this section, an employer shall supply the Minister or an authorised officer with such information relating to the proposed redundancies as the Minister or the officer may reasonably require.

Saver for employees' rights to notice, etc.

16. Nothing in this Act shall effect the right of any employee to a period of notice of dismissal or to any other entitlement under any other Act or under his contract of employment.

Provisions relating to authorised officers.

17.—(1) An authorised officer may—

(a) enter at all reasonable times any premises or place where he has reasonable grounds for supposing that any employee is employed,

(b) there make any examination or enquiry necessary for ascertaining whether this Act has been or is being complied with,

(c) require an employer or his representative to produce any records which the employer is required by this Act to keep, and inspect and take copies of entries in the records,

(d) examine with regard to any matters under this Act any person whom he has reasonable cause to believe to be or to have been an employer or employee and require him to answer any questions (other than questions tending to incriminate him) which the officer may put relating to those matters and to sign a declaration of the truth of the answers.

(2) The powers conferred on an authorised officer by subsection (1) (a) shall not be exercisable in respect of a private dwelling house unless the Minister (or an officer of the Minister appointed by the Minister for the purpose) certifies that he has reasonable grounds for believing that an offence under this section in relation to an employee employed in the house has been committed by the employer, and the authorised officer in applying for admission to the house produces the certificate.

(3) Any person who—

(a) obstructs or impedes an authorised officer in the exercise of any power conferred by this section,

(b) refuses to produce any record which an authorised officer lawfully requires him to produce,

(c) produce, or causes to be produced or knowingly allows to be produced, to an authorised officer any record which is false in any material respect knowing it to be false,

(d) prevents or attempts to prevent any person from appearing before or being questioned by an authorised officer, or

(e) wilfully fails or refuses to comply with any lawful requirement of an authorised officer under subsection (1)(d) shall be guilty of an offence and shall be liable on summary conviction to a fine not exceeding £500.

(4) An authorised officer shall be furnished with a certificate of his appointment and, on applying for admission to any premises or place, shall, if so required, produce the certificate to the occupier and to any person being examined by him.

PART IV

MISCELLANEOUS

Records to be kept by employers

18.—(1) An employer shall keep such records as may be necessary to enable the Minister or an authorised officer to ascertain whether or not the provisions of this Act are being and have been complied with.

(2) Records kept under this section shall be retained by an employer for a period of not less than three years from the date on which they were made.

(3) An employer who contravenes subsection (1) or (2) shall be guilty of an offence and shall be liable on summary conviction to a fine not exceeding £500.

(4) Where an employer fails to keep or retain records under this section the onus of proving that he has complied or is complying with this Act shall lie on him.

Certain provisions to be null and void

19. Any provision in any agreement (whether a contract of employment or otherwise) purporting to exclude or limit the operation of any provision of this Act shall be null and void.

Notices, etc. to Minister

20. Any notice or other document which is required or authorised by this Act to be given by an employer to the Minister shall be in writing and shall be sent by registered post addressed to the head office of the Department of [Enterprise and Employment] or, where that is not practicable, shall be delivered to that office.

Proceedings under Act

21.—(1) An offence under this Act may be prosecuted by the Minister.

(2) Proceedings for an offence under this Act may be commenced within one year from the date of the offence.

(3) Where an offence under this Act committed by a body corporate is proved to have been committed with the consent or connivance of, or to be attributable to any neglect on the part of, any director, manager, secretary or other officer of the body corporate or any person who was purporting to act in any such capacity, he as well as the body corporate shall be guilty of that offence and shall be liable to be proceeded against and punished accordingly.

GENERAL NOTE

To date the only prosecution under the Act has been against Dunnes Stores (Newbridge) Ltd and fines totalling £300 were imposed on the company with two £50 fines imposed on a director: see *Industrial Relations News* No. 36 (September 24, 1992).

Mitigation of penalty for certain offences

22. Where an employer is convicted of an offence under section 11 or 14, he may plead in mitigation of the penalty for that offence that there were substantial reasons related to his business which made it impracticable for him to comply with the section under which the offence was committed.

GENERAL NOTE

The combination of "substantial reasons" and "impracticability" make it clear that employers who are going into the process of liquidation cannot avoid their responsibilities under the Act by being unreasonably late in coming to a decision: see *Armour v. Association of Scientific, Technical and Managerial Staffs* [1979] I.R.L.R. 24.

PROTECTION OF EMPLOYMENT ACT 1977 (NOTIFICATION OF PROPOSED COLLECTIVE REDUNDANCIES) REGULATIONS 1977

S.I. No. 140 of 1977

1. (1) These Regulations may be cited as the Protection of Employment Act 1977 (Notification of Proposed Collective Redundancies) Regulations 1977.

(2) These Regulations shall come into force on the 10th day of May, 1977.

2. The following particulars shall be specified by an employer in a notification under section 12 of the Protection of Employment Act 1977 (No. 7 of 1977)—

    (a) the name and address of the employer, indicating whether he is a sole trader, a partnership or a company;

    (b) the address of the establishment where the collective redundancies are proposed;

    (c) the total number of persons normally employed at that establishment;

    (d) the number and descriptions or categories of employees whom it is proposed to make redundant;

    (e) the period during which the collective redundancies are proposes to be affected, stating the dates on which the first and the final dismissals are expected to take effect;

    (f) the reasons for the proposed collective redundancies;

    (g) the names and addresses of the trade unions or staff associations representing employees affected by the proposed redundancies and with which it has been the practice of the employer to conduct collective bargaining negotiations;

    (h) the date on which consultations with each such trade union or staff association commenced and the progress achieved in those consultations to the date of the notification.

MINIMUM NOTICE AND TERMS OF EMPLOYMENT ACT 1973

(1973 No. 4)

ARRANGEMENT OF SECTIONS

SECT.

An Act to require a minimum period of notice to terminate the employment of those who have been employed for a qualifying period, to provide for matters connected with the giving of notice, and to require employers to give written particulars of the terms of employment, and to provide for other matters connected with the matters aforesaid. [9th May 1973]

GENERAL NOTE

According to the Minister for Labour, when introducing the Minimum Notice and Terms of Employment Bill to the Dail (263 *Dail Debates* Col. 873), this legislation would do "two simple things". It prescribed a minimum period of notice which must be given by an employer who wished to dispense with the services of an employee (or by an employee who wished to leave) and it gave an employee, who was in doubt about any of the more important terms of his employment, the right to have those terms confirmed in writing by his employer. He stressed that nothing would prevent an employer conceding better terms.

Disputes as to notice requirements were entrusted to what is now the Employment Appeals Tribunal and the bulk of its work, in numerical terms at least, is still provided by claims under this Act. In 1992 and 1993, for example, of the 12,218 claims referred to the Tribunal over those two years, 7,794 were referred under this Act out of which 7,489 were disposed of (25th and 26th Annual Reports of the Employment Appeals Tribunal).

The Act was amended by the Terms of Employment (Information) Act 1994 to comply with the provisions of Council Directive 91/533/EC on an Employer's Obligation to Inform Employees of the Conditions Applicable to the Contract or Employment Relationship (OJ L288/32, October 18, 1991) on which see further Clark and Hall, "The Cinderella Directive? Employee Rights to Information about Conditions Applicable to their Contract or Employment Relationship" (1992) 21 I.L.J. 106.

Originally the Act only applied to those employees who were normally expected to work 21 hours a week. This was reduced to 18 by the Protection of Employees (Employers' Insolvency) Act 1984 and, in the case of regular part-time employees, to eight by the Worker Protection (Regular Part-Time Employees) Act 1991.

Citation

See section 17.

Commencement

This Act came into operation on September 1, 1973.

Statutory Instruments

Minimum Notice and Terms of Employment Act 1973 (Commencement) Order 1973 (S.I. No. 242 of 1973).

Minimum Notice and Terms of Employment Act 1973 (Reference of Disputes) Regulations 1973 (S.I. No. 243 of 1973).

Parliamentary Debates

263 Dail Debates Cols. 872–887 (Second Stage)
264 Dail Debates Cols. 1248–1270 (Committee Stage)
264 Dail Debates Cols. 1270 (Report and Final Stages)
73 Seanad Debates Cols. 1365–1377 (Second Stage)
74 Seanad Debates Cols. 43–106 (Committee Stage)
74 Seanad Debates Cols. 282–318 (Report and Final Stages)
265 Dail Debates Col. 235 (Seanad Amendment)

Be it enacted by the Oireachtas as follows:

Interpretation

1.—In this Act—

"the Act of 1967" means the Redundancy Payments Act 1967;

"employee" means an individual who has entered into or works under a contract with an employer, whether the contract be for manual labour, clerical work or otherwise, whether it be expressed or implied, oral or in writing, and whether it be a contract of service or of apprenticeship or otherwise, and cognate expressions shall be construed accordingly;

"lay-off" has the meaning assigned to it by the Act of 1967;

"Minister" means the Minister for [Enterprise and Employment];

"prescribed" means prescribed by regulations made by the Minister under this Act;

"short-time" has the meaning assigned to it by the Act of 1967;

"strike" has the meaning assigned to it by Part II of the Act of 1967;

"the Tribunal" means the Tribunal established under the Act of 1967;

"week" means any period of seven consecutive days;

"year" means any period of fifty-two weeks.

GENERAL NOTE

The definition of "the Minister" was amended by virtue of the Labour (Transfer of Departmental Administration and Ministerial Functions) Order 1993 (S.I. No. 18 of 1993) and the Industry and Commerce (Alteration of Name of Department and Title of Minister) Order 1993 (S.I. No. 19 of 1993).

For the meaning of "lay-off", "short-time" and "strike" see pp. 18, 18–19 and 9 supra respectively. The Tribunal established under the Redundancy Payments Act 1967 is now known as the Employments Appeals Tribunal.

Commencement

2. This Act shall come into operation on such day as the Minister appoints by order.

GENERAL NOTE

By virtue of the Minimum Notice and Terms of Employment Act 1973 (Commencement) Order 1973 (S.I. No. 242 of 1973), September 1, 1973 was appointed as the day on which the Act came into operation.

Non-application of Act

3.—(1) This Act shall not apply to—

(a) employment of an employee who is normally expected to work for the same employer for less than [eighteen] hours in a week,

134

(b) employment by an employer of an employee who is the father, mother, grandfather, grandmother, stepfather, stepmother, son, daughter, grandson, granddaughter, stepson, stepdaughter, brother, sister, halfbrother or halfsister of the employer and who is a member of the employer's household and whose place of employment is a private dwellinghouse or a farm in or on which both the employee and the employer reside,

(c) employment in the Civil Service (other than in an unestablished position) within the meaning of the Civil Service Commissioners Act 1956,

(d) employment as a member of the Permanent Defence Forces (other then a temporary member of the Army Nursing Service),

(e) employment as a member of the Garda Siochana, and

(f) employment under an employment agreement pursuant to Part II or Part IV of the Merchant Shipping Act 1894.

(2) The Minister may by order declare that any provision of this Act shall not apply to a class or classes of employment specified in the order and from the commencement of the Order this Act shall not apply to that class or those classes.

(3) Notwithstanding subsection (1) or (2) of this section, the Minister may by order declare that any provision of this Act shall apply to a class or classes of employment specified in the order and from the commencement of the order this Act shall apply to that class or those classes.

(4) An order made by the Minister under this section may include such transitional and other supplemental and incidental provisions as appear to the Minister to be necessary or expedient.

(5) The Minister may by order amend or revoke an order made under this section, including this subsection.

GENERAL NOTE

The word in square brackets in subsection 1(a) was substituted by section 3 of the Protection of Employees (Employers' Insolvency) Act 1984. By virtue of the Worker Protection (Regular Part-Time Employees) Act 1991, "regular part-time employees" (i.e. those who have been in the continuous service of the employer for not less than 13 weeks and who are normally expected to work not less than eight hours a week for that employer) now enjoy the same protection under this Act as full-time employees.

On the exclusion in respect of employment under the Merchant Shipping Act 1894, see *Down v. B & I Line* M1426/1989 and *McAuley v. B & I Line* M976/1991.

Minimum period of notice

4.—(1) An employer shall, in order to terminate the contract of employment of an employee who has been in his continuous service for a period of thirteen weeks or more, give to that employee a minimum period of notice calculated in accordance with the provisions of subsection (2) of this section.

(2) The minimum notice to be given by an employer to terminate the contract of employment of his employee shall be—

    (a) if the employee has been in the continuous service of his employer for less than two years, one week,

    (b) if the employee has been in the continuous service of his employer for two years or more, but less than five years, two weeks,

    (c) if the employee has been in the continuous service of his employer for five years or more, but less than ten years, four weeks,

    (d) if the employee has been in the continuous service of his employer for ten years or more, but less than fifteen years, six weeks,

    (e) if the employee has been in the continuous service of his employer for fifteen years or more, eight weeks.

(3) The provisions of the First Schedule to this Act shall apply for the purposes of ascertaining the period of service of an employee and whether that service has been continuous.

(4) The Minister may by order vary the minimum period of notice specified in subsection (2) of this section.

(5) Any provision in a contract of employment, whether made before or after the commencement of this Act, which provides for a period of notice which is less than the period of notice specified in subsection (2) of this section, shall have the effect as if that contract provided for a period of notice in accordance with this section.

(6) The Minister may by order amend or revoke an order under this section including this subsection.

GENERAL NOTE

Following some uncertainty between different divisions of the Tribunal, Murphy J. in the High Court has confirmed that an employee who has been in his continuous "constructively dismissed" cannot claim under this Act: see *Halal Meat Packers (Ballyhaunis) Ltd v. Employment Appeals Tribunal* [1990] E.L.R. 49,59.

As is clear from the terms of subsection (1), the period of notice required by the Act is a minimum period of notice. Under the terms, express or implied, of the contract of employment an employee may be entitled to more. In *Jameson v. M.C.W. Ltd* M878/1983, for example, the employee was entitled under his contract of employment to four weeks notice. His statutory minimum entitlement, however, was only two weeks notice. The company gave him four weeks notice of termination but his employment came to an end when only a little over two weeks of contractual notice had expired. The question arose as to whether the company had complied with the Act. The Tribunal unanimously ruled that "the statutory notice period should occupy the last appropriate number of weeks of the contractual notice" and awarded the claimant 1.4 weeks compensation.

The Tribunal has frequently emphasised that notice must be certain and that it is not enough simply to notify an employee that his or her employment will be terminated at some future date. There must be precision of date and time.

The question of whether the employer must be treated as having re-employed the employee, if the employment does not actually end on the nominated date, was considered by the Supreme Court in *Bolands Ltd v. Ward* [1988] I.L.R.M. 382. The claimants were all formerly employed by the company and were in employment with it on August 3, 1984. On that date a receiver was appointed and one week later the receiver gave all the employees, including the claimants, notice of termination of employment. Each was given a period of notice calculated to expire on the day following the statutory period of notice to which he or she was entitled under the Act. During the months of August and September the receiver maintained the business of the company and continued the employment of the claimants for that purpose, As each period of notice expired the receiver purported to extend the notice for a further week. This was done by informing them in their pay packets that the notice they had been given had been extended for a further week. Ultimately the company ceased to carry on business on October 12, 1984, and the employment of the claimants terminated. The cessation of business would have been preceded by a final notice on October 5, advising the claimants that the notice which they had been given on August 10 had been extended for one further week, namely to October 12.

The position of the claimants could be summarised as follows. All at one time or another received a notice of termination of their employment for the period appropriate to the duration of their employment as of the month of August 1984 but, instead of their employment being terminated at the expiration of the minimum statutory period, those periods were extended from time to time so that the overall effect was that the claimants received a longer notice than that to which they were statutorily entitled. On the other hand the final actual period of notice was only one week—less than that to which they would have been entitled if that were the relevant notice. The Tribunal ruled that the claimants received only one week's notice and calculated their compensation by reference to the minimum period required under the Act less the week's notice actually given. The Tribunal, by a majority, ruled that the terms of the Act had not been complied with and stated:

> To comply with the Act, notice of termination of employment must be specific. The notice given by the respondent had expired when the employees' employment did not terminate as originally notified and accordingly further similar notice was required to comply with this Act. Each employee, however, was then retained on a week to week basis until termination and, the original notice having expired, the employees received one week's specific notice of the termination of the employment in compliance with the Minimum Notice and Terms of Employment Act 1973.

The company appealed to the High Court on a point of law contending that the original notices were still valid and that the extending of the notices in no way invalidated that original notice. Murphy J. said that he found the use of the word "specific" in the passage quoted above "somewhat puzzling". As a general statement of the law he did not think that it could be disputed that notice should be specific but he suspected that the word was used "not so much in relation to the terms of the notice" which was quite specific "but rather as to its effect". In his view the appeal raised two important points of law:

(i) whether notice of termination should be effective in its terms by specifying the date of the actual termination of the employment, and
(ii) whether the original notice given on August 10 was null and void and ceased to have any effect when the claimant's employment did not terminate on the date originally notified.

Murphy J. accepted that the purpose of the Act was to give to employees "a minimum but adequate period of time in which to find alternative employment on the expiration of their period of notice." What was intended was that the employees "should have a period of notice—varying with the length of their employment with a particular employer—as to when their employment will terminate." He continued (at 387):

> It well may be that in the present economic conditions many employees would welcome a 'stay of execution' in the form of an extension of the period of notice or otherwise. But the fact that it is so welcomed or even wholly or partly in their interest does not change the fact that looked at retrospectively the ultimate termination of their employment does not come at the end of a period of notice during which they knew, for the minimum period prescribed by law, not only their fate but when it would occur.

He ruled therefore that the statutory notice must nominate at the outset a date on which the employment is to terminate and if the employer does not, on the expiration of the notice, act thereon by bringing the employment to an end the employer must be treated as either having waived the original notice or re-employed the employee. The receiver appealed and the Supreme Court (Henchy, Hederman and McCarthy JJ.) unanimously allowed the appeal and held that the extended notices were a sufficient compliance with the Act.

The Supreme Court took a very pragmatic view of the situation. Each employee received a notice of termination which was longer than the period in the original notice. As Henchy J. put it (at 389–390):

> So far from seeking to shrink the minimum period laid down by the Act, the receiver accorded each employee a period of notice well in excess of the statutory entitlement . .There is nothing in the Act to suggest that the notice given should be stringently or technically construed as if it were analogous to a notice to quit. If the notice actually given—whether orally or in writing, in one document or in a number of documents—conveys to the employee that at the end of the period expressly or impliedly referred to in the notice or notices it is proposed to terminate his or her employment, the only question normally arising under the Act will be whether the period of notice is less than the statutory minimum.

138

Looked at from this perspective it was undeniable that the claimants received a *longer* notice than that to which they were statutorily entitled: in each case it was at least eight weeks longer than the statutory minimum.

Both Henchy and McCarthy JJ. stressed, however, that "quite different considerations" would apply if it could be shown that "an employer was improperly or fraudulently manipulating contracts of employment and, consequently, the Act itself, so as to evade the requirements of the Act, by a series of such postponements" (*per* McCarthy J. at 391) or if "a plurality of notices were used to mislead an employee or to subvert the proper operation of the Act" (*per* Henchy J. at 390). In this case it was conceded that the receiver acted in good faith in granting the extensions and it was clear that, from the time the first notice of termination of employment was given until employment actually ceased, "each employee knew that he or she was under notice and that he or she was benefiting from the repeated extensions of the period of notice."

That notice once given cannot be unilaterally withdrawn is illustrated by *Gallagher v. O'Mahoney* M20/1980 and *O'Looney v. Roderick Hogan & Associates* M2538/1987. See also *Brennan v. Lindley & Co. Ltd* [1974] I.R.L.R. 153.

Section 40(3) of the Maternity Protection Act 1994 provides that for the purposes of this Act the contract of employment of an employee to whom section 40 of that Act applies—*i.e.* an employee who is entitled to return to work but is not permitted so to do—shall be deemed to have been terminated on the expected date of return. See also section 30 of the Adoptive Leave 1995 which provides in similar terms for an "adopting parent".

Rights of employee during period of notice

5.—(1) The provisions of the Second Schedule to this Act shall have effect in relation to the liability of an employer during the period of notice required by this Act to be given—

(a) by an employer to terminate the contract of employment of an employee who has been in his continuous service for thirteen weeks or more, and

(b) by an employee who has been in such continuous service to terminate his contract of employment with that employer.

(2) This section shall not apply in any case where an employee gives notice to terminate his contract of employment in response to a notice of lay-off or short-time given by his employer.

(3) Any provision in a contract which purports to exclude or limit the obligation imposed on an employer by this section shall be void.

GENERAL NOTE

Where any employee is temporarily "laid-off" and whilst on lay-off is given notice of redundancy, is that employee entitled to be paid during that period of notice? This question arose in *Foley v. Irish Leathers Ltd* M1024/1984 where the company contended that, because the claimant was on lay-off, he was not in a position to suffer "loss" and was therefore not entitled under the Act to, in his case, six weeks pay. This argument was not accepted by the Tribunal and the company appealed to the High Court; the judgment of Barrington J. being reported at [1986] I.R. 177 (*sub nom. Irish Leathers Ltd v. Minister for Labour*).

Section 5 deals with the rights of an employee during the period of notice and provides that the provisions of the Second Schedule shall apply. Paragraph 2(a)(1) of this Schedule provides:

> An employee shall be paid by his employer in respect of any time during his normal working hours when he is ready and willing to work but no work is provided for him by his employer.

Section 12(1)(b) provides that, if an employer fails to comply with the provisions of section 5, the employee may refer the matter to the Tribunal for arbitration and the Tribunal may award "compensation for any loss sustained" by the employee by reason of his employer's default. The employer's contention was that, as the employee was on lay-off, he would not have been earning and therefore no "loss" was occasioned to him. Like the Tribunal, Barrington J. did not accept this and his reasoning was as follows. Although lay-off is not defined in the Act, it is defined in the Redundancy Payments Act 1967 in terms of a temporary cessation of employment (see section 11). This was undoubtedly the position when the claimant was laid-off initially. Subsequently, the employer accepted that there was no chance of re-employing him and served notice of dismissal for redundancy. Once such notice was served it appeared to Barrington J. that "the employee was no longer 'laid-off' but was an employee under notice of dismissal". As Barrington J. put it: "the contract of employment, the operation of which had been suspended, had been reinstated for the purpose of terminating it." Once this happened, it seemed to him that the rights of the parties were governed by the provisions of the 1973 Act and among the rights which the employee had under these circumstances was the right to be paid by his employer in respect of any time during his normal working hours when he was ready and willing to work but no work was provided for him by his employer. That was the position so far as the claimant was concerned. He was ready and willing to work and, therefore, had a statutory right to be paid the sum indicated in the Schedule and his loss under section 12 of this Act was the amount of money to which he was entitled by statute to receive and which he did not receive.

Right of employer to notice

6. An employer shall, subject to the right of an employee to give counter-notice under section 10 of the Act of 1967 or to give notice of intention to claim redundancy payment in respect of lay-off or short-time under section 12 of that Act, be entitled to not less than one week's notice from an employee who has been in his continuous employment for thirteen weeks or more of that employee's intention to terminate his contract of employment.

Right to waive notice

7.—(1) Nothing in this Act shall operate to prevent an employee or an employer from waiving his right to notice on any occasion or from accepting payment in lieu of notice.

(2) In any case where an employee accepts payment in lieu of notice, the date of termination of that person's employment shall, for the purposes of the Act of 1967, be deemed to be the date on which notice, if given, would have expired.

GENERAL NOTE

It is unclear whether the employee has a right to refuse to accept wages in lieu. The section, it should be noted, does not speak of a right to give wages in lieu of notice.

Right to terminate contract of employment without notice

8. Nothing in this Act shall affect the right of any employer or employee to terminate a contract of employment without notice because of misconduct by the other party.

GENERAL NOTE

No definition of "misconduct" is provided in the Act. In interpreting it, however, the Tribunal has taken a restrictive view of the types of misconduct which justify dismissal without notice or payment in lieu of notice: see *Lennon v. Bredin* M160/ 1978 (reproduced in Madden and Kerr, *Unfair Dismissal: Cases and Commentary* (1990) p. 209) where the Tribunal said that the section 8 "exemption" applied only "to cases of very bad behaviour of such a kind that no reasonable employer could be expected to tolerate the continuance of the relationship for a minute longer" and *Creed v. K.M.P. Co-op Society Ltd* UD 187/1990 (reported at [1991] E.L.R. 140). See, further, the decision of Hamilton J. in *Brewster v. Burke* High Court, February 8, 1978 (reported at (1985) 4 J.I.S.L.L.98).

The Canadian case of *Jim Pattison Industries Ltd v. Page* (1984) 10 D.L.R. (4th) 430 dealt with the question of whether an employee whose employment is summarily terminated for just cause is entitled to some notice because of his previous exemplary work record. The Saskatchewan Court of Appeal answered this in the negative, saying that there was no room for any middle ground between the case where there was cause for summary dismissal and the case where there was not.

Written statement of terms of employment

9. [*Repealed by section 13 of the Terms of Employment (Information Act 1994*]

Failure of employer to furnish statement

10. [*Repealed by section 13 of the Terms of Employment (Information) Act 1994*]

Reference of disputes to Tribunal

11.—(1) Any dispute arising on any matter under this Act (other than a dispute arising on any matter under section 9 of this Act) shall be referred in the prescribed manner to the Tribunal.

(2) The decision of the Tribunal on any matter referred to it under this section shall be final and conclusive, save that any person dissatisfied with the decision may appeal therefrom to the High Court on a question of law.

(3) The Minister may, on the request of the Tribunal, refer any question of law for the decision of the High Court.

GENERAL NOTE

The manner in which disputes under this Act should be referred to the Tribunal is prescribed by the Minimum Notice and Terms of Employment (Reference of Disputes) Regulations 1973 (S.I. No. 243 of 1973), reproduced *infra* at p.151.

The manner in which appeals should be brought to the High Court is regulated by R.S.C. 1986 Order 105; rule 1 of which provides that such appeals shall be brought by special summons. The summons should be entitled in the matter of the Minimum Notice and Terms of Employment Act 1973 on the application of the person bringing the appeal and should state the decision of the Tribunal appealed against and the grounds of appeal (rule 2). The summons should be served on the Minister for Enterprise and Employment and on all parties to the decision of the Tribunal (rule 3). The summons should be issued within 21 days of the date on which notice of the decision of the Tribunal was given to the party appealing, provided that the time within which the summons may be issued may be extended on application *ex parte* at any time within six weeks from the date on which notice of the decision was given to the party making the appeal (rule 4).

As regards any question of law referred to the High Court by the Minister, R.S.C. 1986 Order 105, rule 5 provides that such questions should also be brought be special summons entitled in the matter of the Minimum Notice and Terms of Employment Act 1973 on the application of the Minister. The summons should state "concisely" the question referred for the decision of the Court and should be served on all parties to the application to the Tribunal.

Finally rule 6 provides that no costs shall be allowed of any proceedings under Order 105 "unless the Court shall by special order allow such costs".

The appropriate procedure for appealing a question of law was considered by the Supreme Court in *Bates v. Model Bakery Ltd* [1993] 1 I.R. 359. Finlay C.J., with whom Hederman, McCarthy and O'Flaherty JJ. agreed (Egan J. expressing no view on this point), said that the summons should state the decision being appealed against, the question of law which it is suggested is in error and the grounds of the appeal. It should be supported by an affidavit which *only* exhibits the determination of the Tribunal including any findings of fact or recital of evidence made by it and identifying the parties and the grounds on which the aggrieved party seeks a determination on a question of law. The Chief Justice said, at 365, that there did not appear to be any room in the procedure "for repeating and, in particular, for adding to or supplementing evidence which was given before the Employment Appeals Tribunal concerning the circumstances of the dispute which had been referred to that Tribunal."

Rights of employee on default of employer

12.—(1) If an employer—

(a) fails to give to an employee the notice required by section 4(2) of this Act, or

142

(b) fails to comply with the provisions of section 5 of this Act in relation to the rights of the employee during the period of notice,

the employee may refer the matter to the Tribunal for arbitration and the Tribunal may award to the employee compensation for any loss sustained by him by reason of the default of the employer.

(2) The amount of any compensation awarded by the Tribunal under subsection (1) of this section shall be recoverable by the employee from his employer as a simple contract debt in a court of competent jurisdiction.

(3) Proceedings for the recovery of any sum due by way of compensation awarded by the Tribunal under subsection (1) of this section may be instituted and maintained on behalf of the employee by the Minister or by that employee's trade union.

GENERAL NOTE

The loss sustained must be due to the employer's default. In the main the Tribunal has held that if notice had been given and the employee could not have worked out that notice because he or she was sick (see, for instance, *McLoughlin v. D.N.U. Ltd* M744/1987, *Lehane v. Feeney* UD 868/1987 and *McIntyre v. Hendrik Haulage Ltd* M2623/1992) there is no loss due to the employer's default; the loss is due instead to the employee's inability to earn. Similar decisions have been given where the employee secures employment elsewhere immediately (see, for instance, *Hogan v. Van Hool McArdle* M315/1979 and *Hislop v. Klingner* M392/1979). In such cases the Tribunal appears to have taken the view (unlike the position in Britain and Northern Ireland) that the statutory entitlement to notice, or compensation in lieu, is not something to which the employee is automatically entitled irrespective of any other payments which are received or due. This approach is supported by the decision of Lardner J. in the High Court in *Irish Shipping Ltd v. Byrne* [1987] I.R.468.

This was an appeal by the liquidator of Irish Shipping Ltd against a Tribunal decision to award sums of compensation to Captain Byrne, the Master of the *Irish Ceder*, and certain shore based employees under the Act. The claimants' employment had been terminated as a result of a winding up order and it was not disputed that there was a failure to give the claimants the notice required under section 4. However, for a continuous period of more than eight weeks after termination, each of the claimants was re-employed by the liquidator on a day-to-day basis at the same wages as his original employment. The liquidator therefore contended that, since the claimants had been re-employed immediately on the determination of their respective contracts of employment on similar terms and conditions for periods longer than the periods of notice of termination which should have been given, their loss had been fully mitigated. On behalf of the employees it was argued that the Act conferred a statutory entitlement to the payment of wages in lieu of notice irrespective of whether during the period of such notice any employee had been in receipt of wages or had suffered loss.

Lardner J. agreed with the liquidator. The intention behind section 12 (which authorises the award of compensation for any loss sustained by reason of the employer's default), he said, was to enable the Tribunal to deal with real and

143

actual loss sustained by loss of wages or for other reasons relating to the breach of contract or failure to comply with the obligation to give due notice. He continued:

> Actual loss must be established, and where as here there is no evidence of any actual loss because the respondents were all re-employed by the liquidator and paid their full wages for a period longer than the prescribed period notice, the Tribunal should have taken that fact into consideration. In the circumstances I think the Tribunal's decision in these cases was erroneous.

This decision sits uneasily alongside the earlier judgment (which is not referred to by Lardner J.) of Barrington J. in *Irish Leathers Ltd v. Minister for Labour* [1986] I.R. 177 to the effect that compensation should not be reduced by any social welfare payments the claimant might have received during the period of notice. Barrington J. was of the view that, looking at the matter from first principles, the employee's right was "to receive from his employer a fixed sum of money determined in a manner set out by statute." It appeared to him that the employer's duty to pay this sum was "antecedent to the State's obligation, in certain circumstances, to pay unemployment benefit." To decide otherwise, he concluded, "would be to hold that the State in effect would be obliged to subsidise employers who fail to fulfil their statutory duties." Lardner J.'s decision in *Byrne* also casts doubts on the Tribunal's practice of assessing compensation on gross earnings without reference to the income tax that would have been payable on those earnings.

The position as to whether the employer is entitled to offset the claimant's minimum notice against his holiday entitlement is somewhat confused. Some decisions have held that the employer is so entitled (see *Kelly v. Michael Amber Ltd* M409/1979, *Buckley v. D. & E. Fitzgibbon Ltd* M808/1986 and *McQuinn v. Kennedy* UD 548/1988); whereas others have held to the contrary (see *Maher v. Ashton Tinbox Ireland Ltd* M4720/1986 and *Roche v. United Yeast Co. Ltd* UD 822/1987). In *Maher* the claimant was entitled under the Act to eight weeks notice. He was dismissed on the day he was due to take two weeks holiday. The Tribunal held that the employer was not entitled to fuse the minimum notice and holiday entitlements. The Tribunal said that holiday entitlement, if not given in days off prior to dismissal, was described by section 5 of the Holidays (Employees) Act 1973 as "compensation" on cesser of employment.

> Compensation under this Act is not therefore pay in respect of a future time but rather a sum of money paid for a statutory entitlement and places no restriction on the employee as to when he should take holidays or how he should allocate the compensation paid. It therefore in no manner affects his right to notice or in this case his pay in lieu of notice upon waiver.

There have also been conflicting decisions as to whether the Tribunal can only award compensation in respect of the minimum statutory period. In *Foley v. Labtech Ltd* M259/1978 the Tribunal ruled that its jurisdiction was limited to what was prescribed by the statute. If the employee was contractually entitled to more, he or she had to go elsewhere for a remedy (then the District Court or Circuit Court, depending on the amount claimed; now also a Rights Commissioner under the Payment of Wages Act 1991). In *Benson v. Switzers Ltd* M850/1984, however, the claimant was entitled under the Act to two weeks notice. The Tribunal decided that she was contractually entitled to three months notice and, in awarding her compensation under the Act, awarded her the equivalent of three months salary.

Provisions relating to winding up and bankruptcy

13.—(1) There shall be included among the debts which, under section 285 of the Companies Act 1963, [as amended by section 10 of the Companies (Amendment) Act 1982 and section 134 of the Companies Act 1990] are, in the distribution of the assets of a company being wound up, to be paid in priority to all other debts, all compensation payable under section 12 of this Act by the company to an employee, and that Act shall have effect accordingly, and formal proof of the debts to which priority is given under this subsection shall not be required except in cases where it may otherwise be provided by rules made under that Act.

(2) There shall be included among the debts which, under [section 81 of the Bankruptcy Act 1988], are in the distribution of the property of a bankrupt or arranging debtor, to be paid in priority to all other debts, all compensation payable under section 12 of this Act by the bankrupt or arranging debtor, as the case may be, to an employee, and that Act shall have effect accordingly, and formal proof of the debts to which priority is given under this subsection shall not be required except in cases where it may otherwise be provided by general orders made under the said Act.

GENERAL NOTE

See, further, the Protection of Employers (Employers' Insolvency) Acts 1984 to 1991, under which employees are entitled to apply to the Minister for Enterprise and Employment for payment of the whole or part of those debts set out in section 6 of the 1984 Act (which include compensation payable under section 12 of this Act) which have remained unpaid because the employer became insolvent on or after October 22, 1983.

Regulations

14. The Minister may make regulations in relation to any matter referred to in this Act as prescribed.

Laying of Regulations and certain draft orders before Houses of Oireachtas

15.—(1) Whenever an order is proposed to be made under section 3, 4 or 9 of this Act, a draft of the proposed order shall be laid before each House of the Oireachtas and the order shall not be made until a resolution approving of the draft had been passed by both Houses of the Oireachtas.

(2) Every regulation made under this Act shall be laid before each House of the Oireachtas as soon as may be after it is made and, if a resolution annulling the regulation is passed by either such House within the next twenty-one days on which that House has sat after the regulation is laid before it, the regulation shall be annulled accordingly but without prejudice to the validity of anything previously done thereunder.

Expenses of Minister

16. Any expenses incurred by the Minister in the administration of this Act shall, to such extent as may be sanctioned by the Minister for Finance, be paid out of moneys provided by the Oireachtas.

Short title

17. This Act may be cited as the Minimum Notice and Terms of Employment Act 1973.

GENERAL NOTE

Section 18(3) of the Protection of Employees (Employers' Insolvency) Act 1984 provides that section 13 of that Act and this Act may be cited together as the Minimum Notice and Terms of Employment Acts 1973 and 1984.

Section 8(3) of the Worker Protection (Regular Part-Time Employees) Act 1991 provides that, in so far as it relates to the Minimum Notice and Terms of Employment Acts 1973 and 1984, that Act and these Acts shall be construed together and may be cited together as the Minimum Notice and Terms of Employment Acts 1973 to 1991.

FIRST SCHEDULE

COMPUTATION OF CONTINUOUS SERVICE

CONTINUITY OF SERVICE

1. The service of an employee in his employment shall be deemed to be continuous unless that service is terminated by—

(a) the dismissal of the employee by his employer, or
(b) the employee voluntarily leaving his employment.

2. A lock-out shall not amount to a dismissal of the employee by his employer.

3. A lay-off shall not amount to the termination by an employer of his employee's service.

4. A strike by an employee shall not amount to that employee's voluntarily leaving his employment.

[5. An employee who claims and receives redundancy payment in respect of lay-off or short time shall be deemed to have voluntarily left his employment.]

6. The continuous service of an employee in his employment shall not be broken by the dismissal of the employee by his employer followed by the immediate re-employment of the employee.

[7. Where the whole or part of a trade, business or undertaking was or is transferred to another person either before or after the passing of this Act, the service of an employee before the transfer in the trade, business or undertaking; or the part thereof so transferred—

    (a) shall be reckoned as part of the service of the employee with the transferee, and
    (b) the transfer shall not operate to break the continuity of the service of the employee,

unless the employee received and retained redundancy payment from the transferor at the time of and by reason of the transfer.]

Computable service

8. Any week in which an employee is not normally expected to work for at least [18] hours or more will not count in computing a period of service.

9. If any employee is absent from his employment by reason of service in the Reserve Defence Force, such period of absence shall count as a period of service.

10. If an employee is absent from his employment for not more than twenty-six weeks between consecutive periods of employment because of—

    (a) a lay-off,
    (b) sickness or injury, or
    (c) by agreement with his employer,

such period shall count as a period of service.

11. If, in any week or part of a week, an employee is absent from his employment because he was taking part in a strike in relation to

the trade or business in which he is employed, that week shall not count as a period of service.

12. If, in any week or part of a week, an employee was, for the whole or any part of the week, absent from work because of a lockout by his employer, that week shall count as a period of service.

13. If, in any week or part of a week, an employee is absent from his employment by reason of a strike or lock-out in a trade or business other than that in which he is employed, that week shall count as a period of service.

GENERAL NOTE

Paragraph 5 was substituted by virtue of section 20 of the Unfair Dismissals Act 1977.

Paragraph 6 provides that continuity is not broken by the dismissal of an employee followed by their "immediate re-employment". The Tribunal has had some difficulty with this issue and the cases generally turn on their particular facts rather than through the application of legal principle. In *Howard v. Breton Ltd* UD 486/1984, a dismissal followed by re-employment on new conditions a week later was considered sufficiently immediate to preserve continuity. In *Mulhall & Sons Builders v. Dunphy* UD 710/1981, however, a breach of similar length during which the claimant sought work elsewhere was held to break continuity. More recently the point arose in *Myles v. O'Kane* UD 354/1990 (reported at [1991] E.L.R. 181) and the Tribunal ruled that "two periods of employment, with a break of four months between them, must be regarded as separate periods of employment". See also *Ennis v. Toyota (Ireland) Ltd* UD 597/1983.

Paragraph 7 was substituted by virtue of section 15 of the Unfair Dismissals (Amendment) Act 1993.

The question of whether there has been a transfer within the meaning of paragraph 7 was considered by Barron J. in *Nova Colour Graphic Supplies Ltd v. Employment Appeals Tribunal* [1987] I.R. 426, who said that there was "no hard and fast rule" as to what constitutes a transfer. In some cases the question was whether the effect of the transaction was to put the transferee in possession of a going concern. In others the question was whether the employees had continued to work as if no change of ownership had occurred. Essentially it was a question of fact for the Tribunal to decide. See, for example, *Allen v. Adhmaid Thior Theas Teo.* UD 771/1987 and *O'Donnell v. Maoin Na Farriage Teo.* UD 331/1988, which emphasise the important distinction between business transfers and transfers of assets.

Paragraph 7 must be read in conjunction with the European Communities (Safeguarding of Employees' Rights on Transfer of Undertakings) Regulations 1980 (S.I. No. 306 of 1980) which implement Council Directive 77/187/EEC and ensure that, in any transfer of a business or undertaking or part thereof, the employment of the existing workers is preserved or, if their employment terminates by reason of the transfer, that their rights arising out of that termination are effectively safeguarded. In so far as paragraph 7 purports to allow for a break in continuity of service if the employee receives and retains a redundancy payment from the transferor, the Tribunal (in *Brett v. Niall Collins Ltd* UD929/1994) were of the view that it appears to run contrary to the provisions of the Directive.

148

Note that section 2(1) of the Worker Protection (Regular Part-Time Employees) Act 1991 provides that, for the purpose of calculating the 13 weeks continuous service with an employer referred to in the definition of "regular part-time", the provisions of this Schedule shall apply as if;

   (a) references to employer and employee were to be construed in accordance with section 1(2) of the 1991 Act, and reference to employment and cognate words were construed accordingly, and

   (b) the reference to "18 hours" in paragraph 8 of this Schedule were a reference to "eight hours".

The use of the phrase "normally expected to" in paragraph 8 causes problems for employees whose hours regularly alternate above and below the threshold.

Paragraph 10 is straightforward in that absences for not more than twenty six weeks because of lay off, sickness, injury or by agreement count as periods of service. The converse situation, namely periods of absence in excess of twenty six weeks, is not explicitly dealt with. It would seem to follow that they are not computable but the question still remains as to whether the whole of the period is to be discounted or only that which is in excess of twenty six weeks. The better view is that it is only the excess which is discounted but in *O'Flaherty v. Rowntree Mackintosh (Ireland) Ltd* M4140/1987 the claimant's redundancy entitlement was calculated on the basis that none of the period of lay off which was almost two years in duration, was to be counted. In this context, it should be noted that continuity of employment is preserved even in those situations where service is not computable.

Second Schedule

Rights Of Employee During Period Of Notice

1. Subject to the provisions of this Schedule, an employee shall, during the period of notice, be paid by his employer in accordance with the terms of his contract of employment and shall have the same rights to sick pay or holidays with pay as he would have if notice of termination of his contract of employment had not been given.

Employments for which there are normal working hours

  2. (a)(i) An employee shall be paid by his employer in respect of any time during his normal working hours when he is ready and willing to work but no work is provided for him by his employer.

       (ii) In this subparagraph "normal working hours" in the case of an employee who is normally expected to work overtime, include the hours during which such overtime is usually worked.

    (b) In any case where an employee's pay is not wholly calculated by reference to time, the pay which his employer is bound to pay him under sub-paragraph (a) shall be calculated by reference to the average rate of pay earned by the employee in respect of any time worked during the thirteen weeks next preceding the giving of notice.

EMPLOYMENTS FOR WHICH THERE ARE NO NORMAL WORKING HOURS

3. Subject to paragraph 4 of this Schedule, an employer shall pay to an employee, if there are no normal working hours for that employee under the contract of employment in force in the period of notice, in respect of each week in the period of notice, a sum not less than the average weekly earnings of the employee in the thirteen weeks next preceding the giving of notice.

4. An employer shall not be liable to pay to his employee any sum under paragraph 3 of this Schedule unless the employee is ready and willing to do work of a reasonable nature and amount to earn remuneration at the rate mentioned in the said paragraph 3.

MINIMUM NOTICE AND TERMS OF EMPLOYMENT (REFERENCE OF DISPUTES) REGULATIONS 1973

S.I. No. 243 of 1973

GENERAL

1. (1) These Regulations may be cited as the Minimum Notice and Terms of Employment (Reference of Disputes) Regulations 1973.

(2) These Regulations shall come into force on the 1st day of September, 1973.

2. In these Regulations—

"the Act" means the Minimum Notice and Terms of Employment Act 1973 (No. 4 of 1973);

"appellant" has the meaning assigned to it by Regulation 3 of these Regulations;

"dispute", save where the context otherwise requires, means a dispute referred under section 11 of the Act to the Tribunal;

"the Minister" means the Minister for [Enterprise and Employment];

"respondent" has the meaning assigned to it by Regulation 6 of these Regulations.

ORIGINATING APPLICATION

3. Where a person (in these Regulations referred to as the appellant) desires to have a dispute referred under section 11 of the Act to the Tribunal, he shall give written notice to the Secretary, [Employment] Appeals Tribunal, Dublin.

4. The notice referred to in Regulation 3 of these Regulations shall be given on the form provided by the Minister for the purpose and shall be accompanied by a statement of the facts and contentions on which the appellant intends to reply.

151

WITHDRAWAL OF REFERENCES

5. An appellant may withdraw a reference of a dispute to the Tribunal by sending notice of withdrawal to the Secretary, [Employment] Appeals Tribunal, Dublin.

FORWARDING OF REFERENCES

6. On receipt of a notice referred to in Regulation 3 of these Regulations, the Secretary of the Tribunal shall forward to the employer concerned (in these regulations referred to as the respondent) a copy of the statement received by him and required by Regulation 4 hereof.

APPEARANCE BY RESPONDENT

7. (1) A respondent shall within 14 days of receiving a copy of the appropriate notice enter an appearance to the proceedings by sending to the Secretary, [Employment] Appeals Tribunal, Dublin, a statement indicating whether he intends to contest the reference and, if so, to what extent the facts and contentions advanced by the appellant are admitted or disputed.

(2) Subject to paragraph (3) of this regulation, a respondent who has not entered an appearance as required by paragraph (1) hereof shall not be entitled to take any part in the reference proceedings or to be represented thereat.

(3) A respondent may apply within the 14-day period mentioned in the said paragraph (1) for an extension of the time in which to enter an appearance.

(4) When the Secretary of the Tribunal receives a notice of appearance from a respondent, he shall forthwith send a copy thereof to the relevant appellant.

REGISTER OF REFERENCES

8. (1) A decision of the Tribunal on a dispute shall be entered in a Register of References and a copy of the decision shall be sent to the appellant and to any other person concerned.

(2) The Register of References shall be open to inspection by any person without charge during normal business hours.

(3) In case the chairman of the Tribunal by certificate under his hand corrects a clerical mistake, error or omission in a decision of the Tribunal on a dispute, the correction shall be duly entered in the Register of Reference and a copy of the corrected decision shall be sent to the appellant and to any other person concerned.

NOTICES

9. (1) Any notice required by these Regulations shall be in writing, and all notices and documents required or authorised by these Regulations to be sent or given to any person may be deemed to have been duly sent if sent by registered post and directed—

- (i) in the case of the Secretary of the Tribunal, to the Secretary, [Employment] Appeals Tribunal, Dublin.
- (ii) in the case of an appellant, to the address specified in the notice given by him pursuant to Regulation 3 of these Regulations.
- (iii) in the case of any other person, to his usual or last-known address or his place of business,
- (iv) in the case of a body corporate, to its registered office.

(2) Any such notice or document if sent or given to the authorised representative of a person shall be deemed to have been sent or given to that person.

(3) A party to a dispute may at any time by notice to the Tribunal and to any other party or parties concerned in the dispute change his address for service under these Regulations.

APPLICATION AND NON-APPLICATION OF CERTAIN OTHER REGULATIONS

10. (1) Regulations 10, 11, 13, 14, 16, 17(1), 17(2), 19 and 24 of the Regulations of 1968 shall apply to a dispute as they apply to references to the Tribunal under section 39 of the Redundancy Payments Act 1967 (No. 21 of 1967), and any reference to an appeal in the regulations hereinbefore specified shall be construed as including a reference to a dispute.

(2) Regulations 20(2) and 20A(3) (inserted by Regulation 2 of the [Redundancy (Employment Appeals Tribunal) Regulations 1979 (S.I. No. 114 of 1979)]) of the Regulations of 1968 shall not apply to a dispute.

(3) In this Regulation "the Regulations of 1968" means the Redundancy (Redundancy Appeals Tribunal) Regulations 1968 (S.I. No. 24 of 1968).

GENERAL NOTE

Regulation 10(2), as originally drafted, referred to the Redundancy (Redundancy Appeals Tribunal) (Amendment) Regulations 1969 (S.I. No. 26 of 1969), which Regulations were revoked and replaced by the 1979 Regulations. The 1968 Regulations as amended are reproduced *supra* at p.88. The form used for making a claim under the Act is form RP51A which is reproduced *infra* at p.275.

UNFAIR DISMISSALS ACT 1977

(1977 No. 10)

Arrangement of Sections

Sect.

An Act to provide for redress for employees unfairly dismissed from their employment, to provide for the determination of claims for such redress by rights commissioners and by the Tribunal established, for the purpose of determining certain appeals, by the Redundancy Payments Act 1967, to provide that the Tribunal shall be known as the Employment Appeals Tribunal, to make provision for other matters connected with the matters aforesaid and to amend the Minimum Notice and Terms of Employment Act 1973. [6th April 1977]

154

GENERAL NOTE

In his address to the Irish Society for Labour Law on "The Impact of the Unfair Dismissals Act in Workplace Industrial Relations" (published (1987) 6 J.I.S.L.L. 36) Tom Murphy concluded that the Unfair Dismissals Act 1977 had made "a major impact on the practices of employers and trade unions at workplace level leading to an improved ability on their parts to resolve dismissal issues without resort to industrial action." Indeed the Minister for Labour, when introducing the Bill in 1976 (293 *Dail Debates* Col. 1076), expressed the hope that the legislation would lessen the necessity for employees to engage in industrial action over dismissals. He said that in the years 1972–1975 there were 187 recorded disputes classified as relating to "engagement or dismissal, redundancies, *etc.*" in which 26,299 people were involved. These disputes alone accounted for over a quarter of a million days lost in industry.

But, as Dr. Redmond has pointed out in *Dismissal Law in the Republic of Ireland* (1982) pp. 116–119, international influences were also at play. ILO recommendation No. 119 on Termination of Employment (1963) required that dismissals not take place unless there were valid reasons for such termination of employment connected with the capacity or conduct of the worker or based on the employer's operational requirements. Certain reasons were stated as not constituting valid reasons for dismissal such as trade union membership, race, colour, sex, marital status, religion, political opinion, national extraction or social origin.

The primary purpose of the 1977 Act, according to the Minister for Labour (*ibid.*), is "to limit the area of arbitrary behaviour in industrial relations" and provide employees with forms of redress in the event of unwarranted termination by employers of the employment relationship. Before the 1977 Act the common law provided minimal safeguards against arbitrary or unwarranted termination. As long as the appropriate contractual notice, or wages in lieu, was given an employers was free to dismiss an employee for whatever reason. The 1977 Act, in contrast, provides in essence that a dismissal is unfair unless there are substantial grounds justifying that dismissal and also establishes mechanisms whereby claims of unfair dismissal could be investigated impartially, cheaply and relatively informally.

The 1977 Act does not permit a high degree of intrusion into managerial decision making and the Tribunal has consistently held that the question of whether the employer has demonstrated that there were substantial grounds justifying the dismissal was to be answered by applying the objective standard of the way in which a reasonable employer, in those circumstances and in that line of business, would have behaved: see, for example, *Bunyan v. United Dominions Trust (Ireland) Ltd* UD 66/1980 (reported at [1982] I.L.R.M. 404) and *Looney & Co. Ltd v. Looney* UD 843/1984 (reproduced in Madden and Kerr, *Unfair Dismissal: Cases and Commentary* (1990) p. 235).

Citation

See section 22. The collective citation is now the Unfair Dismissals Acts 1977 to 1993.

Commencement

This Act came into operation on May 9, 1977.

Statutory Instruments

Unfair Dismissals Act 1977 (Commencement) Order 1977 (S.I. No. 138 of 1977)

Unfair Dismissals (Claims and Appeals) Regulations 1977 (S.I. No. 286 of 1977)

Unfair Dismissals (Calculation of Weekly Remuneration) Regulations 1977 (S.I. No. 287 of 1977).

Parliamentary Debates

293 *Dail Debates* Cols. 1075–11 (Second Stage)
294 *Dail Debates* Cols. 473–529 (Committee Stage)
295 *Dail Debates* Cols. 172–189 (Committee Stage resumed)
296 *Dail Debates* Cols. 50–131 (Committee Stage resumed)
297 *Dail Debates* Cols. 583–602 (Report Stage)
297 *Dail Debates* Cols. 642–668 (Report Stage resumed and Final Stage)
86 *Seanad Debates* Cols. 509–542 (Second Stage)
86 *Seanad Debates* Cols. 566–614 (Committee and Final Stages)
298 *Dail Debates* Cols. 836–846 (Seanad amendments).

Be it enacted by the Oireachtas as follows:

Definitions

1. [(1)] In this Act—

["adopting parent" means an employee who is an employed adopting mother, an adopting father or sole male adopter within the meaning of section 2(1) of the Adoptive Leave Act 1995;]

"contract of employment" means a contract of service or of apprenticeship, whether it is express or implied and (if it is express) whether it is oral or in writing;

"date of dismissal" means—

(a) where prior notice of the termination of the contract of employment is given and it complies with the provisions of that contract and of the Minimum Notice and Terms of Employment [Acts 1973 to 1991], the date on which that notice expires.

(b) where either prior notice of such termination is not given or the notice given does not comply with the provisions of the contract of employment or the Minimum Notice and Terms of Employment [Acts 1973 to 1991], the date on which such a notice would have expired, if it had been given on the date of such termination and had been expressed to expire on the later of the following dates—

156

     (i) the earliest date that would be in compliance with the provisions of the contract of employment.

    (ii) the earliest date that would be in compliance with the provisions of the Minimum Notice and Terms of Employment [Acts 1973 to 1991].

(c) where a contract of employment for a fixed term expires without its being renewed under the same contract or, in the case of a contract for a specified purpose (being a purpose of such a kind that the duration of the contract was limited, but was, at the time of its making, incapable of precise ascertainment), there is a cesser of the purpose, the date of the expiry or cesser;

"dismissal", in relation to an employee, means—

(a) the termination by his employer of the employee's contract of employment with the employer, whether prior notice of the termination was or was not given to the employee.

(b) the termination by the employee of his contract of employment with his employer, whether prior notice of the termination was or was not given to the employer, in circumstances in which, because of the conduct of the employer, the employee was or would have been entitled, or it was or would have been reasonable for the employee, to terminate the contract of employment without giving prior notice of the termination to the employer, or

(c) the expiration of a contract of employment for a fixed term without its being renewed under the same contract or, in the case of a contract for a specified purpose (being a purpose of such a kind that the duration of the contract was limited but was, at the time of its making, incapable of precise ascertainment), the cesser of the purpose;

"employee" means an individual who has entered into or works under (or, where the employment has ceased, worked under) a contract of employment and, in relation to redress for a dismissal under this Act, includes, in the case of the death of the employee concerned at any time following the dismissal, his personal representative;

"employer", in relation to an employee, means the person by whom the employee is (or, in a case where the employment has ceased, was) employed under a contract of employment and an individual in the service of a local authority for the purposes of the Local Government Act 1941, shall be deemed to be employed by the local authority;

"industrial action" means lawful action taken by any number or body of employees acting in combination or under a common understanding, in consequence of a dispute, as a means of compelling their employers or any employee or body of employees, or to aid other employees in compelling their employer or any employee or body of employees, to accept or not to accept terms or conditions of or affecting employment;

"the Minister" means the Minister for [Enterprise and Employment];

"redundancy" means any of the matters referred to in paragraphs (a) to (e) of section 7(2) of the Redundancy Payments Act 1967, as amended by the Redundancy Payments Act 1971;

"statutory apprenticeship" means an apprenticeship in a designated industrial activity within the meaning of the Industrial Training Act 1967, and includes any apprenticeship in a trade to which an order, rule or notice referred to in paragraph (a) or (b) of section 49(1) of that Act applies;

"strike" means the cessation of work by any number or body of employees acting in combination or a concerted refusal or a refusal under a common understanding of any number of employees to continue to work for an employer, in consequence of a dispute, done as a means of compelling their employer or any employee or body of employees, or to aid other employees in compelling their employer or any employee or body of employees, to accept or not to accept terms or conditions of or affecting employment;

["trade union" means a trade union which is the holder of a negotiation licence under Part II of the Trade Union Act 1941];

["the Tribunal" means the Tribunal established by section 39 of the Redundancy Payments Act 1967 and known, by virtue of section 18 of this Act, as the Employment Appeals Tribunal].

[(2) Where on the date of an award to an employee or reinstatement under this Act—

(a) the terms or conditions on which are employed other employees of the same employer who occupy positions similar to that from which the employee was dismissed, or

(b) if there are no such employees, the terms or conditions on which are employed employees generally of the same employer,

are more favourable to the employees concerned than they were at the date of the dismissal, then, the references in sections 5(4) and 7(1)(a) of this Act to the terms and conditions on which an employee was employed immediately before his dismissal shall, in the case of the first-mentioned employee, be construed as references to terms and conditions corresponding to those on which the other employees concerned are employed on the date of the award.

(3) In this Act a reference to any enactment shall, unless the context otherwise requires, be construed as a reference to that enactment as amended, adapted or extended by or under any subsequent enactment including this Act.]

GENERAL NOTE

The definitions of "trade union" and "the Tribunal", in what is now subsection (1), were substituted by virtue of section 2 of the Unfair Dismissals (Amendment) Act 1993. Subsections (2) and (3) were likewise inserted by virtue of the said section 2 of the 1993 Act. The definition of "adopting parent" in what is now subsection (1) was inserted by virtue of section 22 of the Adoptive Leave Act 1995. Section 2(1) of that Act defines "employed adopting mother" as "a female employee in whose care a child (of whom she is not the natural mother) has been placed or is to be placed with a view to the making of an adoption order, or to the effecting of a foreign adoption or following any such adoption". The subsection also defines "adopting father" and "sole male adopter" as, respectively, "a male employee in whose care a child has been placed or is to be placed with a view to the making of an adoption order, or to the effecting of a foreign adoption or following any such adoption, where the adopting mother has died" and "a male employee who is not an adoption father within the meaning of this Act and in whose sole care a child has been placed or is to be placed with a view to the making of an adoption order, or to the effecting of a foreign adoption or following any such adoption".

"contract of employment" and "employee": in order to bring a valid claim, the claimant must establish that he or she is an employee: see *O'Friel v. The Trustees of St. Michael's Hospital* [1982] I.L.R.M. 260; *O Riain v. Independent Newspapers Ltd* UD 134/1978 (reproduced in Madden and Kerr, *Unfair Dismissal: Cases and Commentary* (1990) at p. 45); *Kelly v. Irish Press Ltd* UD 23/1985 and Circuit Court, November 19, 1985 (reproduced in Madden and Kerr, *op. cit.* at p.46); *Young v. Bounty Services (Ireland) Ltd* [1993] E.L.R. 224. Note that section 13 of the 1993 Amendment Act extends the scope of the legislation to include persons employed through employment agencies.

"date of dismissal": in cases of "constructive dismissal" notice entitlement is not taken into account in assessing the date of dismissal: see *Stamp v. McGrath* UD

159

1243/1983 (reproduced in Madden and Kerr, *op. cit.* at p. 5). Nor will the claimant's entitlement under the Holidays (Employees) Act 1973 be added on: *Maher v. B & I Line* UD 271/1978 (reproduced in Madden and Kerr, *op. cit.* at p.7). The Tribunal has also held that, where payment of wages is made in lieu of notice, it should be treated as a "no notice" case falling within paragraph (b): see *O'Reilly v. Pullman Kellog Ltd* UD 340/1979 (reproduced in Madden and Kerr, *op. cit.* at p.6).

"dismissal": paragraph (b) refers to what is commonly described as "constructive dismissal". Paragraph (c) refers to the expiry of fixed-term and fixed purpose contracts but it should be noted that it is possible to exclude the application of the legislation by strictly complying with the requirements set out in section 2(2)(b) of the 1977 Act.

"employer": the fact that the employer has died before the hearing will not deprive the Tribunal of jurisdiction: *Hutton v. Philippi* [1982] I.L.R.M. 578.

"the Minister": this definition was amended by virtue of the Labour (Transfer of Departmental Administration and Ministerial Functions) Order 1993 (S.I. No. 18 of 1993) and the Industry and Commerce (Alteration of Name of Department and Title of Minister) Order 1993 (S.I. No. 19 of 1993).

"statutory apprenticeship": the industrial activities designated under the Industrial Training Act 1967 are the activities specified in the following Orders:

The Industrial Training (Textiles Industry) Order 1968 (S.I. No. 278 of 1968);

The Industrial Training (Engineering Industry) Order 1969 (S.I. No. 40 of 1969);

The Industrial Training (Clothing and Footwear Industry) Order 1969 (S.I. No. 44 of 1969);

The Industrial Training (Construction Industry) Order 1969 (S.I. No. 47 of 1969);

The Industrial Training (Food Drink & Tobacco Industry) Order 1969 (S.I. No. 260 of 1969);

The Industrial Training (Printing and Paper Industry) Order 1970 (S.I. No. 21 of 1970);

The Industrial Training (Chemical and Allied Products Industry) Order 1972 (S.I. No. 181 of 1972);

The Industrial Training Order 1978 (S.I. No. 312 of 1978).

Exclusions

2. (1) [Except in so far as any provision of this Act otherwise provides] this Act shall not apply in relation to any of the following persons:

(a) an employee (other than a person referred to in section 4 of this Act) who is dismissed, who, at the date of his dismissal, had less than one year's continuous service with the employer who dismissed him [...],

(b) an employee who is dismissed and who, on or before the date of his dismissal, had reached the normal retiring age

for employees of the same employer in similar employment or who on that date was a person to whom by
reason of his age the Redundancy Payments Acts 1967 to
[1991], did not apply,

(c) a person who is employed by his spouse, father, mother,
grandfather, grandmother, step-father, step-mother, son,
daughter, grandson, granddaughter, step-son, stepdaughter, brother, sister, half-brother or half-sister, is a
member of his employer's household and whose place of
employment is a private dwellinghouse or a farm in or on
which both the employee and the employer reside,

(d) a person in employment as a member of the Defence Forces, the Judge Advocate-General, the chairman of the
Army Pensions Board or the ordinary member thereof
who is not an officer of the Medical Corps of the Defence
Forces,

(e) a member of the Garda Siochana,

(f) a person (other than a person employed under a contract
of employment) who is receiving a training allowance from
or undergoing instruction by [An Foras Aiseanna Saothair]
or is receiving a training allowance from and undergoing
instruction by that body,

(g) a person who is employed by [An Foras Aiseanna Saot-
hair] under a contract of apprenticeship,

(h) a person employed by or under the State other than persons standing designated for the time being under section
17 of the Industrial Relations Act 1969,

(i) officers of a local authority for the purposes of the Local
Government Act 1941,

[(j) officers of a health board (other than temporary officers)
or a vocational education committee established by the
Vocational Education Act 1930.]

(2) This Act shall not apply in relation to—

(a) dismissal where the employment was under a contract of
employment for a fixed term made before the 16th day of
September, 1976, and the dismissal consisted only of the
expiry of the term without its being renewed under the
same contract, or

(b) dismissal where the employment was under a contract of
employment for a fixed term or for a specified purpose
(being a purpose of such a kind that the duration of the

161

contract was limited but was, at the time its making, incapable of precise ascertainment) and the dismissal consisted only of the expiry of the term without its being renewed under the said contract or the cesser of the purpose and the contract is in writing, was signed by or on behalf of the employer and by the employee and provides that this Act shall not apply to a dismissal consisting only of the expiry or cesser aforesaid.

[Provided that where, following dismissal consisting only of the expiry of the term of a contract of employment such as aforesaid ('the prior contract') without the term being renewed under the contract or the cesser of the purpose of the contract—

(i) the employee concerned is re-employed by the employer concerned within 3 months of the dismissal under a contract of employment such as aforesaid made between the employer and the employee ('the subsequent contract') and the nature of the employment is the same as or similar to that of the employment under the prior contract,

(ii) the employee is dismissed from the employment,

(iii) the dismissal consisted only of the expiry of the term of the subsequent contract without the term being renewed under the contract or the cesser of the purpose of the contract,

(iv) in the opinion of the rights commissioner, the Tribunal or the Circuit Court, as the case may be, the entry by the employer into the subsequent contract was wholly or partly for or was connected with the purpose of the avoidance of liability under this Act—

then—

(I) this Act shall, subject to the other provisions thereof, apply to the dismissal, and

(II) the term of the prior contract and of any antecedent contracts shall be added to that of the subsequent contract for the purpose of the ascertainment under this Act of the period of service of the employee with the employer and the period so ascertained shall be deemed for those purposes to be one of continuous service.

In this proviso "antecedent contract", in relation to a prior contract, means—

(A) a contract of employment such as aforesaid the term
of which expired not more than 3 months before the
commencement of the prior contract, or
(B) each of a series of contracts the term of the last of
which expired not more than 3 months before the
commencement of that of the prior contract and the
term of the other or of each of the other contracts in
the series expired not more than 3 months before the
commencement of that of the other, or the next, contract in the series,
being a contract or contracts made between the employer
and the employee who were parties to the prior contract and
the nature of the employment under which was the same as or
similar to that of the employment under the prior contract.]

or

[(c) dismissal where the employee's employer at the commencement of the employment informs the employee in
writing that the employment will terminate on the return to
work with that employer of another employee who is
absent from her work while on protective leave or natal
care absence, within the meaning of Part IV of the Maternity Protection Act 1994, and the dismissal of the first
mentioned employee duly occurs for the purpose of facilitating the return to work of that other employee.]

or

[(d) dismissal where the employee's employer at the commencement of the employment informs the employee in
writing that the employment will terminate on the return to
work with that employer of an adopting parent who is
absent from work while on adoptive leave or additional
adoptive leave under the Adoptive Leave Act 1995 and
the dismissal of the employee duly occurs for the purpose
of facilitating the return to work of the adopting parent.]

(3)(a) This Act shall not apply in relation to the dismissal of an
employee who, under the relevant contract of employment, ordinarily worked outside the State unless—
(i) he was ordinarily resident in the State during the term
of the contract or,
(ii) he was domiciled in the State during the term of the
contract, and the employer—

163

    (I) in case the employer was an individual, was ordi-
    narily resident in the State, during the term of the
    contract, or

    (II) in case the employer was a body corporate or an
    unincorporated body of persons, had its principal
    place of business in the State during the term of the
    contract.

  (b) In this subsection "term of the contract" means the whole
of the period from the time of the commencement of work
under the contract to the time of the relevant dismissal.

(4) The First Schedule to the Minimum Notice and Terms of
Employment Act 1973, as amended by section 20 of this Act [, the
Protection of Employees (Employers' Insolvency) Act 1984 and the
Worker Protection (Regular Part-Time Employees) Act 1991], shall
apply for the purpose of ascertaining for the purposes of this Act
the period of service of an employee and whether that service has
been continuous.

[(5) Notwithstanding subsection (4) of this section, the dismissal
(not being a dismissal referred to in the proviso (inserted by the
Unfair Dismissals (Amendment) Act 1993) to subsection (2) of this
section) of an employee followed by his re-employment by the
same employer not later than 26 weeks after the dismissal shall not
operate to break the continuity of service of the employee with the
employer if the dismissal was wholly or partly for or was connected
with the purposes of the avoidance of liability under this Act.]

GENERAL NOTE

The words in square brackets at the beginning of subsection (1) were inserted by
virtue of section 38(1) of the Maternity Protection Act 1994, which subsection also
provided for the deletion of the words in square brackets in paragraph (a) of that
subsection.

  Paragraph (j) in subsection (1) was substituted by virtue of section 3(a) of the
Unfair Dismissals (Amendment) Act 1993. The proviso to subsection (2) was inserted by virtue of section 3(b) of the 1993 Act and allows for the examination of any
second or subsequent fixed term or fixed purpose contracts to ascertain whether
the fixed nature of the contract was wholly or partly for or connected with the
avoidance of liability under the legislation. Subsection (5) was inserted by virtue of
section 3(c) of the 1993 Act and provides to similar effect in the case of open-
ended contracts. Paragraph (c) in subsection (2) was inserted by virtue of section
38(2) of the Maternity Protection Act 1994. "Protective leave" is defined in section 21(1) of the 1994 Act as meaning maternity leave, additional maternity leave,
leave to which a father is entitled under section 16(1) or (4), or leave on health
and safety grounds granted under section 18. Paragraph (d) in subsection (2) was
inserted by virtue of section 23 of the Adoptive Leave Act 1995.

Subsection (1)

Paragraph (a): there are two significant exceptions to the rule that dismissed employees are precluded from bringing a claim if they have less than one year's continuous service with the employer who dismissed them—employees dismissed for trade union membership or activity (section 14 of the 1993 Amendment Act) and employees dismissed for pregnancy or matters connected therewith (section 6(2A) inserted by section 38(5) of the Maternity Protection Act 1994). The rules of computing length of service and continuity are set out in the First Schedule to the Minimum Notice and Terms of Employment Act 1973 (as amended), reproduced *supra* at pp.146–148.

Paragraph (b): this paragraph creates two important disqualifications. Where there is no "normal retiring age" any employee who has reached the age of 66 before dismissal is excluded. Where there is a "normal retiring age" any employee who has reached that age before dismissal is also excluded. Note that section 14 of the 1993 Amendment Act provides that this paragraph does not apply if the dismissal resulted wholly or mainly from the employee's trade union membership or activity.

Paragraph (h): the persons designated under the 1969 Act comprise State industrial employees and civilian employees serving with the Defence Forces. In *Hayes and Caffrey v. B & I Line* UD 193 and 192/1979 (reproduced in Madden and Kerr, *Unfair Dismissal: Cases and Commentary* (1990) p. 7), the Tribunal rejected the argument that because the respondent company was wholly owned by the Minister of Finance, the claimants were persons employed by or under the State.

Subsection (2)

This subsection permits an employer to avail of a fixed term or specified purpose contracts and ensure that the Acts do not apply when the term expires or the purpose ceases. Paragraph (b) provides, however, that four conditions must be satisfied. The contract must

(1) be in writing;
(2) be signed by or on behalf of the employer;
(3) be signed by the employee;
(4) must provide that the Unfair Dismissals Act 1977 shall not apply to a dismissal consisting only of the expiry of the fixed term or the cesser of the specified purpose.

These conditions must be completely satisfied: *Sheehan v. Dublin Tribune Ltd* UD 914/1991 (reported at [1992] E.L.R. 239), and *O'Connor v. Kilnamanagh Family Recreation Centre Ltd* UD 1102/1993. Provided the employee has the requisite service, this provision would not prevent a claim being made in respect of a dismissal during the continuance of the fixed term.

It was felt by the Department of Labour that the use of fixed term contracts was being abused particularly by the use of a series of such contracts for less than one year and to combat this the 1993 Amendment Act amended subsection (2) by inserting a proviso that where the dismissal consists only of the expiry of a fixed term contract and the employee concerned is re-employed within three months under another fixed term contract and the employee is then dismissed by reason of the expiry of the second or subsequent fixed term contract, the terms of the various contracts can be added together and will be deemed to be continuous service. The proviso's operation, however, is conditional on it being found that the entry into the second or subsequent contract was wholly or partly for or was connected with the purpose of the avoidance of liability under the Act.

It is unclear as to whether the proviso applies to the expiry of the last of a series of "back-to-back" fixed term contracts, all of which have been drawn up in accordance with the provisions of subsection (2)(b). It would seem to be anomalous for the Tribunal to condemn an employer for seeking to avoid liability under the Acts by availing of a facility, statutorily provided, for the exclusion of certain fixed term contracts. In any event, even if the proviso applies, the employer may still be able to show that there were substantial grounds justifying the dismissal.

In *Fitzgerald v. St. Patrick's College Maynooth* UD 244/1978 (reproduced in Madden and Kerr, *op. cit.* at p. 86), the Tribunal held that the mere expiry of a fixed term contract was not in itself a substantial ground for the non-renewal of the claimant's employment. In Britain it has been held (*Terry v. East Sussex County Council* [1978] I.C.R. 536) that whether the expiry and non-renewal of a fixed term contract constitutes a substantial reason for dismissal depends upon whether "the case is a genuine one where an employee has to his knowledge been employed for a particular period ... on a temporary basis". A balance has to be drawn between the need for protection for employers who have a genuine need for fixed term employment, which can be seen from the outset not to be ongoing, and "the need for protection for employees against being deprived of their rights through ordinary employments being dressed up in the form of temporary fixed term contracts".

As to what is meant by a "contract of employment for a fixed term" and particularly as to whether a contract for a stated period, which is determinable by either party giving to the other a specified period of notice, is such a contract see the contrasting decisions of the English Court of Appeal in *BBC v. Ioannou* [1975] I.C.R. 267 and *Dixon v. BBC* [1979] I.C.R. 281.

Subsection (3)

As to whether a claimant is ordinarily resident in Ireland see *Roche v. Sealink Stena Line Ltd* [1993] E.L.R. 89. In *Davis v. Sealink Stena Line Ltd* UD 874/1993, however, the Tribunal decided that the mere fact that a person was ordinarily resident in the State during the term of his contract of employment did not entitle him to bring a claim under the Act where the contract was performed outside the State and the proper law governing the contract was a foreign law.

Dismissal during probation or training

3.—[Except in so far as any provision of this Act otherwise provides]

(1) This Act shall not apply in relation to the dismissal of an employee during a period starting with the commencement of the employment when he is on probation or undergoing training—

    (a) if his contract of employment is in writing, the duration of the probation or training is 1 year or less and is specified in the contract, or

    (b) if his contract of employment was made before the commencement of this Act and was not in writing and the duration of the probation or training is 1 year or less.

(2) This Act shall not apply in relation to the dismissal of an employee during a period starting with the commencement of the employment when he is undergoing training for the purpose of becoming qualified or registered, as the case may be, as a nurse, pharmacist, health inspector, medical laboratory technician, occupational therapist, physiotherapist, speech therapist, radiographer or social worker.

GENERAL NOTE

The words in square brackets were inserted by virtue of section 38(3) of the Maternity Protection Act 1994.

The first exclusion appears to have originated in an attempt to meet the claims of managers of secondary schools that a period of probation should be built into the Act (see 295 *Dail Debates* Cols. 178–181). It is, however, of general application.

The second exclusion originated in representations made by the Department of Health to the effect that the Tribunal's judgment should not be substituted in relation to what were considered to be necessary professional standards for certain paramedical personnel (see 297 *Dail Debates* Cols. 596–597).

Note that section 14 of the Unfair Dismissals (Amendment) Act 1993 provides that section 3 shall not apply to a person who is dismissed for trade union membership or activity and that section 6(2A) of this Act (inserted by virtue of section 38(5) of the Maternity Protection Act 1994) provides that section 3 does not apply to a case falling within section 6(2)(f) or (g).

Dismissal during apprenticeship

4. [Except in so far as any provision of this Act otherwise provides] this Act shall not apply in relation to the dismissal of a person who is or was employed under a statutory apprenticeship if the dismissal takes place within 6 months after the commencement of the apprenticeship or within 1 month after the completion of the apprenticeship.

GENERAL NOTE

The words in square brackets were inserted by virtue of section 38(3) of the Maternity Protection Act 1994.

Section 14 of the Unfair Dismissals (Amendment) Act 1993 provides that section 4 shall not apply to a person who is dismissed for trade union membership or activity. Section 6(2A) of this Act (inserted by virtue of section 38(5) of the Maternity Protection Act 1994) also provides that section 4 does not apply to a case falling within section 6(2)(f) or (g).

Section 27(5)(c) of the Industrial Training Act 1967 provides that where apprenticeship rules have been made "a person shall neither dismiss nor suspend a person employed by him as an apprentice . . . save in accordance with the rules". The Labour Services Act Apprenticeship Rules 1993 (S.I. No. 236 of 1993) provide in rule 7 that:

(1) Subject to 7(2), no employer shall dismiss any apprentice save in strict accordance with the provisions of the Unfair Dismissals Act 1977, the Minimum Notice and Terms of Employment Act 1973, and the Redundancy Payments Acts 1967 to 1990.

(2) Where it is no longer possible for reasons of redundancy for an employer to continue an apprenticeship the employer shall give written prior notice to An Foras accordingly and shall take all reasonable steps to have his/her obligations under the contract of apprenticeship transferred to another employer.

Dismissal by way of lock-out or for taking part in strike

5.—[(1) For the purposes of this Act (other than section 2(4)), the lock-out of an employee shall be deemed to be a dismissal and the dismissal shall be deemed to be an unfair dismissal if, after the termination of the lock-out—

    (a) the employee was not permitted to resume his employment on terms and conditions at least as favourable to the employee as those specified in paragraph (a) or (b) of subsection (1) of section 7 of this Act, and

    (b) one or more other employees in the same employment were so permitted.

(2) The dismissal of an employee for taking part in a strike or other industrial action shall be deemed for the purposes of this Act to be an unfair dismissal if—

    (a) one or more employees of the same employer who took part in the strike or other industrial action were not dismissed for so taking part, or

    (b) one or more of such employees who were dismissed for so taking part were subsequently permitted to resume their employment on terms and conditions at least as favourable to the employees as those specified in the said paragraph (a) or (b) and the employee was not.

(3) The said section 7 shall be construed in relation to an unfair dismissal specified in subsection (1) or (2) of this section as if it contained a requirement that the terms or conditions on which the person the subject of the unfair dismissal is, if appropriate, to be re-instated under paragraph (a) of subsection (1) of that section or re-engaged under paragraph (b) of that subsection included a term that the re-instatement or re-engagement should be deemed to

have commenced on such day as is agreed upon by the employer concerned and by or on behalf of the employees or, in the absence of such agreement, on the earliest date from which re-instatement or re-engagement, as the case may be, was offered to a majority of the other employees of the same employer who were the subject of the lock-out concerned or took part in the strike or other industrial action concerned.]

(4) In this section a reference to an offer of re-instatement or re-engagement, in relation to an employee, is a reference to an offer (made either by the original employer or by a successor of that employer or by an associated employer) to re-instate that employee in the position which he held immediately before his dismissal on the terms and conditions on which he was employed immediately before his dismissal together with a term that the re-instatement shall be deemed to have commenced on the day of the dismissal, or to re-engage him, either in the position which he held immediately before his dismissal or in a different position which would be reasonably suitable for him, on such terms and conditions as are reasonable having regard to all the circumstances.

(5) In this section—

"lock-out" means an action which, in contemplation or furtherance of a trade dispute (within the meaning of the Industrial Relations [Acts 1946–1990]), is taken by one or more employers, whether parties to the dispute or not, and which consists of the exclusion of one or more employees from one or more factories, offices or other places of work or of the suspension of work in one or more such places or of the collective, simultaneous or otherwise connected termination or suspension of employment of a group of employees;

"the original employer" means, in relation to the employee, the employer who dismissed the employee.

GENERAL NOTE

Subsections (1), (2) and (3) were substituted by virtue of section 4 of the Unfair Dismissals (Amendment) Act 1993.

This section, whilst effecting a conclusive presumption that selective dismissals for taking part in a strike or other industrial action are unfair, does not deem non-selective dismissals to be fair. Such dismissals are subject to the general presumption of unfairness established by section 6(1) of the 1977 Act.

Unfair dismissal

6.—(1) Subject to the provisions of this section, the dismissal of an employee shall be deemed, for the purposes of this Act, to be an unfair dismissal unless, having regard to all the circumstances, there were substantial grounds justifying the dismissal.

(2) Without prejudice to the generality of subsection (1) of this section, the dismissal of an employee shall be deemed, for the purposes of this Act, to be an unfair dismissal if it results wholly or mainly from one or more of the following:

(a) the employee's membership, or proposal that he or another person become a member, of, or his engaging in activities on behalf of, a trade union or excepted body under the Trade Union Acts 1941 and 1971 [as amended by the Industrial Relations Act 1990], where the times at which he engages in such activities are outside his hours of work or are times during his hours of work in which he is permitted pursuant to the contract of employment between him and his employer so to engage,

(b) the religious or political opinions of the employee,

(c) civil proceedings whether actual, threatened or proposed against the employer to which the employee is or will be a party or in which the employee was or is likely to be a witness,

(d) criminal proceedings against the employer, whether actual, threatened or proposed, in relation to which the employee has made, proposed or threatened to make a complaint or statement to the prosecuting authority or to any other authority connected with or involved in the prosecution of the proceedings or in which the employee was or is likely to be a witness,

[(e) the race, colour or sexual orientation of the employee,

(ee) the age of the employee,

(eee) the employee's membership of the travelling community,]

[(f) the employee's pregnancy, giving birth or breastfeeding or any matters connected therewith,]

[(g) the exercise or proposed exercise by the employee of a right under the Maternity Protection Act 1994 to any form of protective leave or natal care absence, within the meaning of Part IV of that Act,]

[(h) the exercise or contemplated exercise by an adopting parent of her right under the Adoptive Leave Act 1995 to adoptive leave or additional adoptive leave or additional adoptive leave.]

170

[(2A) Sections 3 and 4 do not apply to a case falling within paragraph (f) or (g) of subsection (2) and, for the purposes of those paragraphs, "employee" and "adopting parent" include a person who would otherwise be excluded from this Act by paragraph (a), (c), (f) or (g) of section 2(1).]

(3) Without prejudice to the generality of subsection (1) of this section, if an employee was dismissed due to redundancy but the circumstances constituting the redundancy applied equally to one or more other employees in similar employment with the same employer who have not been dismissed, and either—

(a) the selection of that employee for dismissal resulted wholly or mainly from one or more of the matters specified in subsection (2) of this section or another matter that would not be a ground justifying dismissal, or

(b) he was selected for dismissal in contravention of a procedure (being a procedure that has been agreed upon by or on behalf of the employer and by the employee or a trade union, or an excepted body under the Trade Union Acts 1941 and 1971 [as amended by the Industrial Relations Act 1990], representing him or has been established by the custom and practice of the employment concerned) relating to redundancy and there were no special reasons justifying a departure from that procedure, then the dismissal shall be deemed, for the purposes of this Act, to be an unfair dismissal.

(4) Without prejudice to the generality of subsection (1) of this section, the dismissal of an employee shall be deemed, for the purposes of this Act, not to be an unfair dismissal, if it results wholly or mainly from one or more of the following:

(a) the capability, competence or qualifications of the employee for performing work of the kind which he was employed to do,

(b) the conduct of the employee,

(c) the redundancy of the employee, and

(d) the employee being unable to work or continue to work in the position which he held without contravention (by him or by his employer) of a duty or restriction imposed by or under any status or instrument made under statute.

(5)(a) Without prejudice to the generality of subsection (1) of this section, the dismissal by the Minister for Defence of a civilian employed with the Defence Forces under section

171

30(1)(g) of the Defence Act 1954 shall be deemed for the purposes of this Act not to be an unfair dismissal if it is shown that the dismissal was for the purpose of safeguarding national security.

(b) A certificate purporting to be signed by the Minister for Defence and stating that a dismissal by the Minister for Defence of a civilian named in the certificate from employment with the Defence Forces under section 30(1)(g) of the Defence Act 1954 was for the purpose of safeguarding national security shall be evidence, for the purposes of this Act, of the facts stated in the certificate without further proof.

(6) In determining for the purposes of this Act whether the dismissal of an employee was an unfair dismissal or not, it shall be for the employer to show that the dismissal resulted wholly or mainly from one or more of the matters specified in subsection (4) of this section or that there were other substantial grounds justifying the dismissal.

[(7) Without prejudice to the generality of subsection (1) of this section, in determining if a dismissal is an unfair dismissal, regard may be had, if the rights commissioner, the Tribunal or the Circuit Court, as the case may be, considers it appropriate to do so—

(a) to the reasonableness or otherwise of the conduct (whether by act or omission) of the employer in relation to the dismissal, and

(b) to the extent (if any) of the compliance or failure to comply by the employer, in relation to the employee, with the procedure referred to in section 14(1) of this Act or with the provisions of any code of practice referred to in paragraph (d) (inserted by the Unfair Dismissals (Amendment) Act 1993) of section 7(2) of this Act.]

GENERAL NOTE

Paragraphs (e), (ee) and (eee) of subsection (2) were substituted by virtue of section 5(a) of the Unfair Dismissals (Amendment) Act 1993. Paragraphs (f) and (g) of subsection (2) were substituted by virtue of section 38(4) of the Maternity Protection Act 1994. Paragraph (h) of subsection (2) was inserted by virtue of section 24 of the Adoptive Leave Act 1995. Subsection (2A), which was inserted by the Maternity Protection Act 1994, was then substituted by virtue of section 25 of the Adoptive Leave Act 1995. Subsection (7) was substituted by virtue of section 5(b) of the 1993 Amendment Act.

Subsection (1) contains the general overriding proposition that the dismissal of an employee is deemed to be unfair unless, having regard to all the circumstances, there were substantial grounds justifying dismissal. Subsection (6) further provides that, in determining whether the dismissal was unfair or not, it will be for the employer to show that there were substantial grounds justifying the dismissal. The burden of proof is thus, in this respect, firmly on the employer. Neither subsection (1) nor subsection (6), by virtue of section 14 of the 1993 Amendment Act, apply to a person referred to in section 2(1)(a) and (b), 3 or 4 if the dismissal results wholly or mainly from the claimant's trade union membership or activity. It would appear from this peculiarly worded provision that the onus of proving the real reason for the dismissal lies on the claimant, even where he or she had more than one year's continuous service: see *Reid v. Oxx* (1986) 4 I.L.T. (*n.s.*) 207.

Subsection (2) provides that dismissals for certain specified reasons are deemed to be unfair, likewise subsections (4) and (5) provide that dismissals for certain specified reasons are deemed to be fair. The use of the concept of deeming dismissals to be fair or unfair is problematic in that it would seem to suggest that, once it is established that the dismissal resulted wholly or mainly from one or more of the matters therein set out, then the dismissal is automatically fair or unfair. This, however, is not the case as the Tribunal has taken the view that subsection (4) merely sets out potentially fair reasons. The Tribunal put it well in *Durnin v. Building & Engineering Co. Ltd* UD 159/1978:

> In our opinion, reasons which might justify a dismissal are set out in section 6(4), with a more general area of "justification" in a form of "other substantial grounds" provided for in section 6(6). In any area of "justification" even where clearly provided for in section 6(4), there is at best only, a *prima facie* "justification" and the substance of such "justification" may be enquired into by the Tribunal which attaches the question of fairness to same.

Subsection (2) sets out a series of what might be described as inadmissible reasons for dismissal. Paragraph (a) does not apply to employees who have been dismissed because they refuse to join a trade union. Such employees, assuming they had the requisite service requirements, could rely, however, on the general terms of subsection (1). In this context the Tribunal must bear in mind that one of the rights guaranteed by Article 40.6.1 of the Constitution is the right to form associations and unions and that the Supreme Court has ruled, in cases such as *Meskell v. Coras Iompair Eireann* [1973] I.R. 121, that this guarantee embraces the right to dissociate. The impact of the Constitution is vividly illustrated by *White v. Aluset Ltd* UD 9/1988 (reproduced in Madden and Kerr, *Unfair Dismissal: Cases and Commentary* (1990) p. 162) where the claimant was found to have been unfairly dismissed following his refusal to transfer union membership.

As regards paragraphs (f) and (g), the decision of the Court of Justice in Case C–32/93, *Webb v. EMO Air Cargo (UK) Ltd* [1994] I.R.L.R. 482 should be noted.

This case concerned Council Directive 76/207/EEC (the Equal Treatment Directive) and the Court of Justice held that dismissal of a pregnant woman recruited for an indefinite period could not be justified on grounds relating to her inability on a temporary basis to fulfil a fundamental condition of her employment contract, namely to perform the work for which she had been engaged. The Court stressed that the protection afforded by Community law to a woman during pregnancy could not be dependent on whether her presence at work during maternity was essential to the proper functioning of the undertaking in which she was employed.

See further, however, *Fox v. National Council for the Blind of Ireland* EE18/1994 which concerned the withdrawal of an offer of a fixed term contract for which training was essential because the claimant would have been due to take maternity leave at the time this training was scheduled to take place. The Equality Officer distinguished *Webb* and held that the Council had not discriminated against the claimant on the basis of her sex.

Section 40 of the Maternity Protection Act 1994, which applies to an employee who, having duly complied with section 28 of that Act is entitled to return to work following absence on "protective leave" but is not permitted to do so by the relevant employer, provides in subsection (4) that, for the purposes of this Act,

(a) an employee to whom section 40 applies who is also an employee to whom this Act applies shall be deemed to have been dismissed on the "expected date of return"; and

(b) the dismissal shall be deemed to be an unfair dismissal unless, having regard to all the circumstances, there were substantial grounds justifying the dismissal.

Section 26 of the Adoptive Leave Act 1995, which applies to an "adopting parent" who, having duly compiled with section 20 of that Act, is entitled to return to work but is not permitted to do so by the relevant employer, provides in similar terms that, for the purposes of this Act, the adopting parent shall be deemed to have been dismissed on the date he or she expected to return to work and that the dismissal shall be deemed to be an unfair dismissal unless, having regard to all the circumstances, there were substantial grounds justifying the dismissal.

Subsection (3) provides that a dismissal due to redundancy is deemed to be an unfair dismissal if the claimant has been unfairly selected for redundancy. Two things must be established: first, that the circumstances constituting the redundancy applied equally to one or more other employees in similar employment with the same employer who have not been dismissed; and, second, that the selection was either for one of the reasons set out in subsection (2) or was unjustifiably in contravention of a procedure relating to redundancy. For an example of an unfair selection resulting from a matter that would not be a ground justifying dismissal, see *Lynch v. Baily* UD 837/1994. The burden of proving that the circumstances described in this subsection apply falls on the employer: *Caladom Ltd v. Hoard and Kelly* Circuit Court (Judge Clarke) November 8, 1985 (reproduced in Madden and Kerr, *Unfair Dismissal: Cases and Commentary* (1990), p. 281).

Where there is no procedure relating to redundancy within the meaning of this subsection, divisions of the Tribunal have differed as to whether "redundancy" is an automatically fair reason for dismissal or whether the Tribunal can consider the fairness of the assessment used in selecting employees for redundancy: contrast *Roche v. Sealink Stena Line Ltd* UD 187/1992 (reported at [1993] E.L.R. 89), *Phillips v. International Health Benefits (Irl) Ltd* UD 331/1993, *Long v. Woodside Engineering Ltd* UD 983/1993 and *Naughton v. Radio Limerick One Ltd* UD 1115/1993 on the one hand and *Boucher v. Irish Productivity Centre* UD 882/1992, *Kelly v. Langarth Properties Ltd* UD 742/1993 and *Clancy v. Maysteel C.M.E. Teo* UD 1029/1993 on the other.

As noted above, the Tribunal takes the view that subsection (4) (although *quaere* redundancy) merely sets out potentially fair reasons for dismissal. The Tribunal also takes the view that it is not the function of the Tribunal to establish whether the employee, for example, is in fact incompetent or incapable. If an employee is dismissed for one of those reasons it is sufficient that the employer honestly believes on reasonable grounds that the employee is incompetent or incapable. The requirements were succinctly stated by Lardner J. in *Bolger v. Showrings (Ireland) Ltd* [1990] E.L.R. 184 as follows:

In this case it was the ill-health of the plaintiff which the company claimed rendered him incapable of performing his duties as a forklift driver. For the employer to show that the dismissal was fair, he must show that:

(1) It was the ill-health which was the reason for the dismissal;
(2) That this was substantial reason;
(3) That the employee received fair notice that the question of his dismissal for incapacity was being considered; and
(4) That the employee was afforded an opportunity of being heard.

Consequently an employer, before dismissal, should first tell the employee of the respects in which he or she is failing to do the job adequately, warn the employee of the possibility of dismissal on this ground and give the employee an opportunity of improving performance. The Tribunal has ruled that there is an obligation on the employer, where the competence of an employee is in question, to update itself on that employee's performance before taking the decision to dismiss: *O'Brien v. Professional Contract Cleaners Ltd* UD 184/1990 (reported at [1991] E.L.R. 143).

The general approach of the Tribunal to cases of dismissals for "conduct" was set out in *Hennessy v. Read & Write Shop Ltd* UD 192/1978 (reproduced in Madden and Kerr, *Unfair Dismissal: Cases and Commentary* (1990), p. 211):

> In deciding whether or not the dismissal of the claimant was unfair we apply a test of reasonableness to
>
> 1. the nature and extent of the enquiry carried out by the respondent prior to the decision to dismiss the claimant, and
> 2. the conclusion arrived at by the respondent that, on the basis of the information resulting from such enquiry, the claimant should be dismissed.

This requires the Tribunal to consider whether the employee was made aware of all allegations and complaints that formed the basis of the proposed dismissal, whether the employee had adequate opportunity to deny the allegations or explain the circumstances before the decision to dismiss was taken, whether the employer believed that the employee had conducted himself or herself as alleged, whether the employer had reasonable grounds to sustain that belief and, if so, whether the penalty of dismissal was proportionate to the alleged misconduct.

The insertion of a new subsection (7) into this section reinforces the concept of procedural fairness which the Tribunal had developed since the Act's enactment and which requires that the employer establish not only that it had substantial grounds justifying dismissal but also that it followed fair and proper procedures before dismissal.

Redress for unfair dismissal

7.—(1) Where an employee is dismissed and the dismissal is an unfair dismissal, the employee shall be entitled to redress consisting of whichever of the following the rights commissioner, the Tribunal or the Circuit Court, as the case may be, considers appropriate having regard to all the circumstances:

    (a) re-instatement by the employer of the employee in the position which he held immediately before his dismissal on the terms and conditions on which he was employed immediately before his dismissal together with a term that the re-instatement shall be deemed to have commenced on the day of the dismissal, or

    (b) re-engagement by the employer of the employee either in the position which he held immediately before his dismissal or in a different position which would be reasonably suitable for him on such terms and conditions as are reasonable having regard to all the circumstances, or

    [(c)(i) if the employee incurred any financial loss attributable to the dismissal, payment to him by the employer of such compensation in respect of the loss (not exceeding in amount 104 weeks remuneration in respect of the employment from which he was dismissed calculated in accordance with regulations under section 17 of this Act) as is just and equitable having regard to all the circumstances, or

    (ii) if the employee incurred no such financial loss, payment to the employee by the employer of such compensation (if any, but not exceeding in amount 4 weeks remuneration in respect of the employment from which he was dismissed calculated as aforesaid) as is just and equitable having regard to all the circumstances,

and the reference in the foregoing paragraphs to an employer shall be construed, in a case where the ownership of the business of the employer changes after the dismissal, as references to the person who, by virtue of the change, becomes entitled to such ownership.]

(2) Without prejudice to the generality of subsection (1) of this section, in determining the amount of compensation payable under that subsection regard shall be had to—

    (a) the extent (if any) to which the financial loss referred to in that subsection was attributable to an act, omission or conduct by or on behalf of the employer,

    (b) the extent (if any) to which the said financial loss attributable to an action, omission or conduct by or on behalf of the employee,

(c) the measure (if any) adopted by the employee or, as the case may be, his failure to adopt measures, to mitigate the loss aforesaid,

[(d) the extent (if any) of the compliance or failure to comply by the employer, in relation to the employee, with the procedure referred to in subsection (1) of section 14 of this Act or with the provisions of any code of practice relating to procedures regarding dismissal approved of by the Minister,

(e) the extent (if any) of the compliance or failure to comply by the employer, in relation to the employee, with the said section 14, and

(f) the extent (if any) to which the conduct of the employee (whether by act or omission) contributed to the dismissal.]

[(2A) In calculating financial loss for the purposes of subsection (1), payments to the employee—

(a) under the [Social Welfare (Consolidation) Act 1993] in respect of any period following the dismissal concerned, or

(b) under the Income Tax Acts arising by reason of the dismissal,

shall be disregarded.]

(3) In this section—

"financial loss", in relation to the dismissal of an employee, includes any actual loss and any estimated prospective loss of income attributable to the dismissal and the value of any loss or diminution, attributable to the dismissal, of the rights of the employee under the Redundancy Payments Acts 1967 to [1991], or in relation to superannuation;

"remuneration" includes allowances in the nature of pay and benefits in lieu of or in addition to pay.

GENERAL NOTE

Paragraph (c) in subsection (1) was substituted by virtue of section 6(a) of the Unfair Dismissals (Amendment) Act 1993. Paragraphs (d), (e) and (f) in subsection (2) were substituted by virtue of section 6(b) of the 1993 Amendment Act. Subsection (2A) was inserted by virtue of section 6(c) of the 1993 Amendment Act. The first of these amendments provides for a new basic financial award in cases where no financial loss has been incurred by the employee. Such an award, however, is not mandatory. Secondly, the considerations that are required to be taken into account in calculating the amount of compensation payable to an employee who has been unfairly dismissed are clarified. Thirdly, payments to an employee under the social welfare and income tax legislation are to be disregarded in calculating the claimant's financial loss.

The Tribunal has an absolute discretion to choose which remedy to award "having regard to all the circumstances", although it is now obliged by virtue of section 8(1A) to set out, where a specified redress is awarded, a statement of the reasons why either of the other forms of redress was not awarded. It was established by the Supreme Court in *State (Irish Pharmaceutical Union) v. Employment Appeals Tribunal* [1987] I.L.R.M. 36 that the views of the parties should be sought on the issue of redress before the decision on choice of remedy is taken. Most successful claims for unfair dismissal result in awards of compensation. In assessing the extent of that compensation the Tribunal is limited to a maximum award of 104 weeks remuneration.

In 1993 the average award was £4,929. The calculation is based on net figures.

Determination of claims for unfair dismissal

8.—(1) A claim by an employee against an employer for redress under this Act for unfair dismissal may be brought by the employee before a rights commissioner or the Tribunal and the commissioner or Tribunal shall hear the parties and any evidence relevant to the claim tendered by them and, in the case of a rights commissioner, shall make a recommendation in relation to the claim, and, in the case of the Tribunal, shall make a determination in relation to the claim.

[(1A) There shall be included in—

(a) a recommendation of a rights commissioner under subsection (1) of this section,

(b) a determination of the Tribunal under the said subsection (1), and

(c) an order of the Circuit Court, under section 11 of the Unfair Dismissals (Amendment) Act 1993,

under which specified redress under this Act is awarded to an employee a statement of the reasons why either of the other forms of redress specified in section 7(1) of this Act was not awarded to the employee.

(2) A claim for redress under this Act shall be initiated by giving a notice in writing (containing such particulars (if any) as may be specified in regulations under section 17 of this Act made for the purposes of subsection (8) of this section) to a rights commissioner or the Tribunal, as the case may be—

(a) within the period of 6 months beginning on the date of the relevant dismissal, or

(b) if the rights commissioner or the Tribunal, as the case may be, is satisfied that exceptional circumstances prevented the giving of the notice within the period aforesaid, then, within such period not exceeding 12 months from the date aforesaid as the rights commissioner or the Tribunal, as the case may be, considers reasonable,

and a copy of the notice shall be given by the rights commissioner or the Tribunal, as the case may be, to the employer concerned as soon as may be after the receipt of the notice by the rights commissioner or the Tribunal.

(3) A rights commissioner shall not hear a claim for redress under this Act if—

(a) the Tribunal has made a determination in relation to the claim, or

(b) any party concerned notifies the rights commissioner in writing, within 21 days of the giving to the employer pursuant to subsection (2) of this section of the copy of the notice concerned referred to in that subsection and relating to the claim, that he objects to the claim being heard by a rights commissioner.

(4)(a) Where a recommendation of a rights commissioner in relation to a claim for redress under this Act has not been carried out by the employer concerned in accordance with its terms, the time for bringing an appeal against the recommendation has expired and no such appeal has been brought, the employee concerned may bring the claim before the Tribunal and the Tribunal shall, notwithstanding subsection (5) of this section, without hearing the employer concerned or any evidence (other than in relation to the matters aforesaid), make a determination to the like effect as the recommendation.

(b) The bringing of a claim before the Tribunal by virtue of this subsection shall be effected by giving to the Tribunal a notice in writing containing such particulars (if any) as may be specified in regulations under section 17 of this Act made for the purposes of subsection (8) of this section.]

(5) [...] The Tribunal shall not hear a claim for redress under this Act (except by way of appeal from a recommendation of a rights commissioner)—

(a) if a rights commissioner has made a recommendation in relation to the claim, or

[(b) unless, before the commencement of the hearing of the claim, one of the parties concerned notifies in writing—

    (i) in a case where the claim has been initiated before a rights commissioner, or

    (ii) in any other case, the Tribunal, that he objects to the claim being heard by a rights commissioner.]

(6) Proceedings under this section before a rights commissioner shall be conducted otherwise than in public.

(7) A rights commissioner shall notify the Tribunal of any recommendation he makes under this section.

(8) Regulations under section 17 of this Act may provide for all or any of the following matters and for anything consequential thereon or incidental or ancillary thereto—

(a) the procedure to be followed regarding the bringing of claims under this section or appeals under section 9 of this Act before the Tribunal,

(b) the times and places of hearings by the Tribunal,

(c) the representation of parties attending hearings by the Tribunal,

(d) procedure regarding the hearing of such claims and appeals as aforesaid by the Tribunal,

(e) publication and notification of determinations of the Tribunal,

(f) the particulars to be contained in the notices referred to in subsections (2) and (4) of this section and section 9 of this Act,

(g) the award by the Tribunal of costs and expenses in relation to such claims and appeals as aforesaid and the payment thereof.

(9) Section 21(2) of the Industrial Relations Act 1946 shall apply in relation to all proceedings before the Tribunal as if the references in that section to the Labour Court were references to the Tribunal and subsection (17) of section 39 of the Redundancy Payments Act 1967 shall apply in relation to proceedings before the Tribunal under this Act as it applies to matters referred to it under the said section 39 [with the substitution in paragraph (e) of the said subsection (17) of "a fine not exceeding £1,000" for "a fine not exceeding twenty pounds"].

[(10) (a) A dispute in relation to a dismissal as respects which a recommendation has been made by a rights commissioner under this Act or a hearing by the Tribunal under this Act has commenced shall not be referred, under the Industrial Relations Acts 1946 to 1990, to a rights commissioner or the Labour Court.

(b) Where, in relation to a dismissal, a recommendation has been made by a rights commissioner, or a hearing by the Labour Court under the said Acts has commenced, the employee concerned shall not be entitled to redress under this Act in respect of the dismissal.

(11) Where the dismissal of an employee is an unfair dismissal and a term or condition of the contract of employment contravened any provision of or made under the Income Tax Acts or the [Social Welfare (Consolidation) Act 1993], the employee shall, notwithstanding the contravention, be entitled to redress under this Act, in respect of the dismissal.

(12) Where, in proceedings under this Act, it is shown that a term or condition of a contract of employment contravened any such provision as aforesaid, the rights commissioner, the Tribunal or the Circuit Court, as the case may be, shall notify the Revenue Commissioners or the Minister for Social Welfare, as may be appropriate, of the matter.]

GENERAL NOTE

Subsections (1A), (2), (3) and (4) were inserted and substituted by virtue of section 7(c) of the Unfair Dismissals (Amendment) Act 1993. The words in square brackets at the outset of subsection (5) were deleted by virtue of section 7(b)(i) of the 1993 Amendment Act and subsection 5(b) was substituted by virtue of section 7(b)(ii) of the 1993 Amendment Act. The words in square brackets in subsection (9) were inserted by virtue of section 7(c) of the 1993 Amendment Act. Subsections (10), (11) and (12) were substituted by virtue of section 7(d) of the 1993 Amendment Act.

The regulations referred to in subsections (2), (4) and (8) are the Unfair Dismissals (Claims and Appeals) Regulations 1977 (S.I. No. 286 of 1977), reproduced *infra* at p.197.

The Tribunal had oft bemoaned the rigidity of the old section 8(2) of the 1977 Act, having ruled in *Cherubini v. Joseph Downes & Son Ltd* UD 22/1978 (reproduced in Madden and Kerr, *Unfair Dismissal: Cases and Commentary* (1990) p. 20) that it had no inherent jurisdiction to alter either by abridgement or by extension, any provision made by the legislature fixing a time limit for the taking of any step. The amendment to subsection (2) will permit the extension of the time limit for lodging a claim to twelve months in cases where "exceptional circumstances" prevented the lodgement of the claim within the normal time-limit of six months. This amendment also removes the mandatory requirement of service of notice on the employer within the six month period.

Concern had also been expressed by the Tribunal as to the approach it should adopt when hearing a claim for implementation of a rights commissioner's recommendation where the employer had not appealed. Subsection (4) has now been amended to allow the Tribunal issue a determination confirming a recommendation "without hearing the employer concerned". Problems had also arisen (see *Sutcliffe v. McCarthy* [1993] 2 I.R. 48) with cases that had been processed both under the 1977 Act and the Industrial Relations Acts 1946 to 1990. A new subsection (10) prohibits explicitly the processing of a claim under both pieces of legislation.

The most controversial amendment is the insertion of a new subsection (11) which provides that, in the case of a contact tainted with illegality, the employee shall nonetheless be entitled to redress for unfair dismissal and a new subsection (12) makes it mandatory on the Tribunal to refer the matter to the Revenue Commissioners or the Department of Social Welfare where it is shown that a term or condition of a contract of employment contravened any provision of or made under the Income Tax or Social Welfare Acts. That such contracts are unenforceable at common law was confirmed by Barron J. in *Hayden v. Sean Quinn Properties Ltd* [1994] E.L.R. 45. The amendments, however, do not address the question of the effect of illegality on continuity of employment: see *Hyland v. J. Barker (North West) Ltd* [1985] I.C.R. 861.

The application, by subsection (9), of the provisions of section 21(2) of the Industrial Relations Act 1946 to proceedings before the Tribunal means that a witness will be entitled to the same immunities and privileges as if he or she were a witness before the High Court.

The European Communities (Safeguarding of Employees' Rights on Transfer of Undertakings) Regulations 1980 (S.I. No. 306 of 1980) provide in regulation 5 that the transfer of an undertaking, business or part of a business shall not in itself constitute grounds for dismissal by the transferor or the transferee and go on to state that "a dismissal, the grounds for which are such a transfer, by a transferor or a transferee is hereby prohibited". Although there is no mention in the Regulations of the 1977 Act, the High Court has held, in *Mythen v. Employment Appeals Tribunal* [1990] 1 I.R. 98, that the Tribunal (or, presumably, a Rights Commissioner if neither party objects) must hear and determine claims brought by employees of the transferor who had not been employed by the transferee. See further *Morris v. Smart Bros. Ltd* UD 699/1933 and *Gray v. Irish Society for the Prevention of Cruelty to Animals* UD 509/1994. On whether there has been a transfer, see *Bannon v. Employment Appeals Tribunal* [1993] 1 I.R. 500; Case C–29/91, *Dr Sophie Redmond Stichting v. Bartol* [1992] E.C.R. 1–3189; and Case C–392/92, *Schmidt v. Spar- und Leihkasse der Frueheren Amter Bordesholm, Kiel und Cronshagen* [1994] E.C.R. 1–1311.

Appeal from recommendation of rights commissioner

9.—(1) A party concerned may appeal to the Tribunal from a recommendation of a rights commissioner in relation to a claim for redress under this Act and the Tribunal shall hear the parties and any evidence relevant to the appeal tendered by them and shall make a determination in relation to the appeal.

(2) An appeal under this section shall be initiated by a party by giving, within 6 weeks of the date on which the recommendation to

which it relates was given to the parties concerned, a notice in writing (containing such particulars (if any) as may be specified in regulations under section 17 of this Act for the purposes of section 8(8) thereof) to the Tribunal and stating the intention of the party concerned to appeal against the recommendation and a copy of the notice shall be given to the other party concerned [by the Tribunal as soon as may be after the receipt by it of the notice].

GENERAL NOTE

The words in square brackets in subsection (2) were substituted by virtue of section 8 of the Unfair Dismissals (Amendment) Act 1993.

This section provides for an appeal from a rights commissioner's recommendation and subsection (2) provides that such an appeal should be initiated by notice in writing within six weeks of the recommendation being given. It has been held that merely writing to the rights commissioner, advising him that the company rejected his findings and that it intended to appeal, does not constitute a valid appeal: *Geraghty v. Moracrete Ltd* UD 335/1984 (reproduced in Madden and Kerr, *Unfair Dismissal: Cases and Commentary* (1990), p.19). The subsection formerly provided that a copy of the appeal notice should be given to the other party within the said six week period. It now provides that the responsibility for serving the copy notice of appeal falls on the Tribunal and that this should be done as soon as may be after the receipt by it of the notice. The Tribunal, however, has no power to extend the time for appeal beyond the six weeks: *Cherubini v. Joseph Downes & Son Ltd* UD 22/1978 (reproduced in Madden and Kerr, *op. cit.*, at p. 20).

Proceedings in Circuit Court for redress under Act

10. [*Repealed by section 16 of the Unfair Dismissals (Amendment) Act 1993*]

Service of documents on bodies

11. Any summons or other document required to be served for the purpose or in the course of any proceedings under this Act on a body corporate or an unincorporated body of persons may be served by leaving it at or sending it by post to the registered office for the purpose of the Companies Act 1963 of that body or, if there is no such office, by leaving it at or sending it by post to any place in the State at which that body conducts its business.

Provisions relating to winding up and bankruptcy

12.—(1) There shall be included among the debts which, under section 285 of the Companies Act 1963 [as amended by section 10 of the Companies (Amendment) Act 1982 and by section 134 of the Companies Act 1990], are, in the distribution of the assets of a company being wound up, to be paid in priority to all other debts, all compensation payable under this Act by the company to an employee, and that Act shall have effect accordingly, and formal proof of the debts to which priority is given under this subsection shall not be required except in cases where it may otherwise be provided by rules made under the Act.

(2) There shall be included among the debts which, under [section 81 of the Bankruptcy Act 1988] are in the distribution of the property of a bankrupt or arranging debtor, to be paid in priority to all other debts, all compensation payable under this Act by the bankrupt or arranging debtor, as the case may be, to an employee, and that Act shall have effect accordingly, and formal proof of the debts to which priority is given under this subsection shall not be required except in cases where it may otherwise be provided by general orders made under the said Act.

Voidance of certain provisions in agreements

13. A provision in an agreement (whether a contract of employment or not and whether made before or after the commencement of this Act) shall be void in so far as it purports to exclude or limit the application of, or is inconsistent with, any provision of this Act.

GENERAL NOTE

The scope of this provision has not been extensively explored although it has been held by the Tribunal, in *Hegarty v. Agra Ltd* UD 822/1984 (reproduced in Madden and Kerr, *Unfair Dismissal: Cases and Commentary* (1990), p.168), that any provision in an agreement is void insofar as it purports to exclude or limit the application of the Act or insofar as it is inconsistent with any of its provisions, including the provisions on trade union membership activities. Its operation occasionally arises where the claimant has signed an agreement settling or compromising any claim he or she might have under the Act: see *McGrane v. Avery Label Ltd* UD 573/1988 and *Gaffney v. Fannin Ltd* UD 1/1989 (reproduced in Madden and Kerr, *op. cit.* at pp. 30 and 29 respectively).

Notice to employees of procedure for, and grounds of, dismissal

14.—(1) An employer shall, not later than 28 days after he enters into a contract of employment with an employee, give to the employee a notice in writing setting out the procedure which the employer will observe before and for the purpose of dismissing the employee.

(2) Where there is an alteration in the procedure referred to in subsection (1) of this section, the employer concerned shall, within 28 days after the alteration takes effect, give to any employee concerned a notice in writing setting out the procedure as so altered.

[(3) The reference in subsection (1) of this section to a procedure is a reference to a procedure that has been agreed upon by or on behalf of the employer concerned and by the employee concerned or a trade union or an excepted body within the meaning of the Trade Union Act 1941, representing him or has been established by the custom and practice of the employment concerned and the reference in subsection (2) of this section to an alteration in the said procedure are references to an alteration that has been agreed upon by the employer concerned or a person representing him and by the employee concerned or a trade union, or an excepted body, within the meaning aforesaid, representing him.

(4) Where an employee is dismissed, the employer shall, if so requested, furnish to the employee within 14 days of the request, particulars in writing of the principal grounds for dismissal, but, in determining for the purposes of this Act whether, in accordance with the provisions of this Act, the dismissal was an unfair dismissal, there may be taken into account any other grounds which, subject to the provisions of this Act and having regard to all the circumstances, are substantial grounds justifying the dismissal.]

GENERAL NOTE

Subsections (3) and (4) were substituted by virtue of section 9 of the Unfair Dismissals (Amendment) Act 1993. The section imposes various obligations on employers but, curiously, provides no remedies or redress in the event that the employer does not comply with the particular obligation. It should be noted that the section does not impose an obligation to provide a dismissal procedure.

Alternative remedies of employee

15.—(1) Nothing in this Act, apart from this section, shall prejudice the right of a person to recover damages at common law for wrongful dismissal.

[(2) Where a recommendation has been made by a rights commissioner in respect of a claim by an employer for redress under this Act or the hearing of a claim by the Tribunal has commenced, the employee shall not be entitled to recover damages at common law for wrongful dismissal in respect of the dismissal concerned.

(3) Where the hearing by a court of proceedings for damages at common law for wrongful dismissal of an employee has commenced, the employee shall not be entitled to redress under this Act in respect of the dismissal to which the proceedings relate.]

(4) A person who accepts redress awarded under section 9 or 10 of the Anti-Discrimination (Pay) Act 1974, in respect of any dismissal shall not be entitled to accept redress awarded under section 7 of this Act in respect of that dismissal and a person who accepts redress awarded under the said section 7 in respect of any dismissal shall not be entitled to accept redress awarded under the said section 9 or 10 in respect of that dismissal.

GENERAL NOTE

Subsections (2) and (3) were substituted by virtue of section 10 of the Unfair Dismissals (Amendment) Act 1993, thus permitting some flexibility to an employee changing a claim as between redress at common law or under the Acts. The two subsections only apply where the common law proceedings are for damages for wrongful dismissal: see *Tammemagi v. Employment Appeals Tribunal* High Court (Blayney J.), November 27, 1987 (noted at (1988) 6 I.L.T. (n.s.) 26).

Sections 9 and 10 of the Anti-Discrimination (Pay) Act 1974 concern dismissals because of an equal pay claim and provide that such dismissals constitute a criminal offence as well as conferring jurisdiction on the Labour Court to award compensation and reinstatement.

Amendment of Act by order of Minister

16.—(1) The Minister may by order amend section 2(1) of this Act so as to extend the application of the Act to any class of employee specified in that section or part (defined in such manner and by reference to such matters as the Minister considers appropriate) of any such class.

(2) The Minister may by order amend paragraph (c) of section 7(1) of this Act so as to vary the maximum amount of compensation referred to in the said paragraph (c).

(3) The Minister may by order amend section 2(2), 3 or 4 of this Act so as to vary—

(a) the application of this Act in relation to dismissals where the employment was under a contract of employment for a fixed term or a specified purpose,
(b) the period of 1 year specified in the said section 3, or
(c) the periods of 6 months and 1 month specified in the said section 4 or either of them.

(4) The Minister may, by order, made with the consent of the Minister for Health, amend subsection (2) of section 3 of this Act so

186

as to extend the application of the subsection to other employments connected with medicine or health.

(5) The Minister may by order amend any provision of this Act so as to comply with any international obligations in relation to dismissals that the State has decided to assume.

(6) An order under this section may contain such supplementary and ancillary provisions as the Minister considers necessary or expedient.

(7) The Minister may by order revoke or amend an order under this section including an order under this subsection.

(8) Where an order is proposed to be made under this section, a draft thereof shall be laid before both Houses of the Oireachtas and the order shall not be made until a resolution approving of the draft has been passed by each such House.

Regulations

17.—(1) The Minister may make regulations for the purposes of sections 7(1)(c) and 8(8) of this Act and for the purpose of enabling any other provisions of this Act to have full effect.

(2) Regulations under this section may contain such incidental, supplementary and consequential provisions as appear to the Minister to be necessary for the purposes of the regulations.

(3) Every regulation made under this section shall be laid before each House of the Oireachtas as soon as may be after it is made, and if a resolution annulling the regulation is passed by either such House within the next 21 days on which that House has sat after the regulation is laid before it, the regulation shall be annulled accordingly, but without prejudice to the validity of anything previously done thereunder.

GENERAL NOTE

The following regulations have been made under this section:

Unfair Dismissals (Claims and Appeals) Regulations 1977 (S.I. No. 286 of 1977)

Unfair Dismissals (Calculation of Weekly Remuneration) Regulations 1977 (S.I. No. 287 of 1977).

Employment Appeals Tribunal

18. The Tribunal established by section 39 of the Redundancy Payments Act 1967 shall be known as the Employment Appeals Tribunal and references in that Act and any other Act of the Oireachtas and any instrument made under any Act of the Oireachtas to the Redundancy Appeals Tribunal shall be construed as references to the Employment Appeals Tribunal.

Repayment of moneys paid under Redundancy Payments Acts 1967 [to 1991]

19. Where an employee is re-instated or re-engaged by an employer in pursuance of a determination or order under this Act in relation to the dismissal of the employee by the employer, any payments made under the Redundancy Payments Acts 1967 to [1991], in relation to the dismissal shall be repaid by the person to whom they were made to the person by whom they were made and may be recovered by the latter from the former as a simple contract debt in any court of competent jurisdiction and any moneys due and owing to any person under those Acts in relation to the dismissal shall cease to be due or owing.

Amendment of First Schedule to Minimum Notice and Terms of Employment Act 1973

20. [...]

Expenses

21. The expenses incurred by the Minister in the administration of this Act shall, to such extent as may be sanctioned by the Minister for Finance, be paid out of moneys provided by the Oireachtas.

Short title and commencement

22.—(1) This Act may be cited as the Unfair Dismissals Act 1977.

(2) This Act shall come into operation on such day as the Minister may appoint by order.

GENERAL NOTE

The collective citation is now the Unfair Dismissals Acts 1977 to 1993.

The Act came into operation on May 9, 1977: Unfair Dismissals Act 1977 (Commencement) Order 1977 (S.I. No. 138 of 1977).

UNFAIR DISMISSALS (AMENDMENT) ACT 1993

(1993 No. 22)

ARRANGEMENT OF SECTIONS

SECT.

An Act to amend and extend the Unfair Dismissals Act 1977 and 1991 and to provide for related matters. [*14th July 1993*].

GENERAL NOTE

As experience was gained of the 1977 Act, certain criticisms were made of its operation in practice and various options for reform were considered in the Department of Labour's *Discussion Document* published in November 1987. Following consultation and discussion with the Social Partners the government, in line with the commitment in the *Programme for Economic and Social Progress* and the undertaking in the *Programme for Partnership Government 1993–1997* to amend and improve the working of the 1977 Act, introduced an amending Bill in the Seanad in March 1993.

The Act does not purport to effect any fundamental alterations to the broad purpose and intent of the 1977 Act. It does address, however, a number of important issues of substance and also effects a range of technical and administrative amendments. For an analysis of the Act see Byrne, (1990–93) 9 J.I.S.L.L. 100.

Citation

See section 17 which provides that this Act and the Unfair Dismissals Act 1977 and 1991 may be cited together as the Unfair Dismissals Acts 1977 to 1993.

Commencement

This Act came into operation on October 1, 1993 : see section 17.

Parliamentary Debates

135 *Seanad Debates* Cols. 523–580 (Second Stage)
135 *Seanad Debates* Cols. 1187–1229 (Second Stage resumed)
136 *Seanad Debates* Cols. 202–266 (Committee Stage)
136 *Seanad Debates* Cols. 434–475 (Committee Stage resumed)
136 *Seanad Debates* Cols. 544–570 (Committee Stage resumed)
136 *Seanad Debates* Cols. 584–612 (Report and Final Stages)
431 *Dail Debates* Cols. 913–973 (Second Stage)
431 *Dail Debates* Cols. 1043–1101 (Second Stage resumed)
432 *Dail Debates* Cols. 1558–1597 (Committee Stage)
432 *Dail Debates* Cols. 2129–2144 (Committee Stage)
137 *Seanad Debates* Cols. 637–648 [Seanad Bill amended by the Dail] (Report and Final Stages)

Be it enacted by the Oireachtas as follows:

Interpretation

1.—(1) In this Act "the Principal Act" means the Unfair Dismissals Act 1977.

(2) In this Act, a reference to any enactment shall, unless the context otherwise requires, be construed as a reference to that enactment as amended, adapted or extended by or under any subsequent enactment including this Act.

Amendment of section 1 of Principal Act

2. [...]

Amendment of section 2 of Principal Act

3. [...]

Amendment of section 5 of Principal Act

4. [...]

Amendment of section 6 of Principal Act
5. [...]

Amendment of section 7 of Principal Act
6. [...]

Amendment of section 8 of Principal Act
7. [...]

Amendment of section 9 of Principal Act
8. [...]

Amendment of section 14 of Principal Act
9. [...]

Amendment of section 15 of Principal Act
10. [...]

Appeals from, and enforcement of determinations of, Tribunal

11.—(1) A party concerned may appeal to the Circuit Court from a determination of the Tribunal in relation to a claim for redress under the Principal Act within 6 weeks from the date on which the determination is communicated to the parties.

(2)(a) Where, in proceedings under this section, the Circuit Court finds that an employee is entitled to redress under the Principal Act, it shall order the employer concerned to make to the employee the appropriate redress.

(b) If an employer fails to comply with an order of the Circuit Court under paragraph (a) of this subsection ("the former order"), the Circuit Court shall, on application to it in that behalf by—

(i) the employee concerned, or

(ii) if he considers it appropriate to make the application having regard to all the circumstances, the Minister,

make—

(I) such order for the enforcement of the former order as it considers appropriate having regard to all the circumstances, or

(II) if the former order directed the re-instatement or re-engagement of the employee concerned and that

191

Court considers it appropriate to do so having regard to all the circumstances, in lieu of making an order under subparagraph (I), make an order directing the employer, in lieu of re-instating or re-engaging the employee to pay compensation to him under section 7(1)(c) of the Principal Act and giving such directions for the enforcement of the latter order as it considers appropriate having regard to all the circumstances.

(3)(a) If an employer fails to carry out in accordance with its terms a determination of the Tribunal in relation to a claim for redress under the Principal Act within 6 weeks from the date on which the determination is communicated to the parties, the Circuit Court shall, on application to it in that behalf by—

(i) the employee concerned, or

(ii) if he considers it appropriate to make the application having regard to all the circumstances, the Minister,

without hearing the employer or any evidence (other than in relation to the matters aforesaid) make—

(I) an order directing the employer to carry out the determination in accordance with its terms, or

(II) if the determination directed the re-instatement or re-engagement of the employee concerned and that Court considers it appropriate to do so having regard to all the circumstances, in lieu of making an order under subparagraph (I), make an order directing the employer, in lieu of re-instating or re-engaging the employee, to pay compensation to him under section 7(1)(c) of the Principal Act and giving such directions for the enforcement of the latter order as it considers appropriate having regard to all the circumstances.

(b) In paragraph (a) of this subsection the reference to a determination of the Tribunal is a reference to such a determination in relation to which, at the expiration of the time for bringing an appeal against it, no such appeal has been brought, or if such an appeal has been brought it has been abandoned and the reference to the date on which the determination is communicated to the parties shall, in a case where such an appeal is abandoned, be construed as a reference to the date of such abandonment.

(4) The Circuit Court may, in an order under this section, if in all the circumstances it considers it appropriate to do so—

192

(a) in case the order relates to the payment of compensation, direct the employer concerned to pay to the employee concerned interest on the compensation at the rate referred to in section 22 of the Courts Act 1981 in respect of the whole or any part of the period beginning 6 weeks after the date on which the determination of the Tribunal is communicated to the parties and ending on the date of the order, and

(b) in case the order relates to re-instatement or re-engagement, direct the employer to pay to the employee compensation of such amount as it considers reasonable in respect of the loss of wages suffered by the employee by reason of the failure of the employer to comply with the determination aforesaid.

(5) Proceedings under this section shall be heard in the county where the employer concerned ordinarily resides or carries on any profession, business or occupation.

GENERAL NOTE

This section replaces section 10 of the 1977 Act, itself repealed by section 16 of this Act, which had proven to be extremely unsatisfactory in practice. Doubtless due to fears as to the constitutional validity of the Tribunal (as not being a body exercising limited judicial powers and functions), Tribunal determinations are not in themselves enforceable (contrast the position under the Payment of Wages Act 1991 where a Tribunal decision can be enforced as if it were a Circuit Court decision). The 1977 Act established a procedure whereby the Minister might institute and carry on, if he thought it appropriate, proceedings in the Circuit Court where an employer had failed to carry out in accordance with its terms a determination of the Tribunal. This procedure proved problematical especially in the case of claimants whose employer had gone into "informal insolvency". Unable to claim against the Social Insurance Fund (under the Protection of Employees (Employers' Insolvency) Act 1984), many claimants had found that the Chief State Solicitor's Office was reluctant to proceed against their former employer. This section ameliorates some of these difficulties by permitting the employee (but not his or her trade union) to appeal and by providing that the Circuit Court shall dispose of the matter "without hearing the employer" (thus overruling *Minister for Labour v. We Frame It Ltd* (1987) 5 I.L.T. (n.s.) 185).

This section also empowers the Circuit Court to award interest and to change the nature of an award from re-engagement or re-instatement to financial compensation. Welcome as these changes may be, the section does not address the position of the High Court, to which a full appeal still lies: *McCabe v. Lisney & Sons* [1981] I.L.R.M. 289, *Western Health Board v. Quigley* [1982] I.L.R.M. 390 and *Commissioners of Irish Lights v. Sugg* [1994] E.L.R. 97.

In *Walsh v. H.R. Holfield (Hydraulics) Ltd* (Circuit Court, April 25, 1985) (reproduced in Madden and Kerr, *Unfair Dismissals: Cases and Commentary* (1990), p. 26) Judge Clarke took the opportunity of stating that time for appealing begins to run from the date the written determination of the Tribunal is communicated to the parties, not from when the decision was verbally communicated. The Supreme

Court has also confirmed in *McIlwraith v. Fawsitt* [1990] 1 I.R. 343 that the Circuit Court has no jurisdiction to extend the time provided for appeal.

Evidence of failure to attend before or give evidence or produce documents to Tribunal

12.—A document purporting to be signed by the chairman or a vice-chairman of the Tribunal stating that

    (a) a person named in the document was, by a notice under paragraph (c) of section 39(17) of the Redundancy Payments Act 1967, required to attend before the Tribunal on a day and at a time and place specified in the document, to give evidence or produce a document.

    (b) a sitting of the Tribunal was held on that day and at that time and place, and

    (c) the person did not attend before the Tribunal in pursuance of the notice or, as the case may be, having so attended, refused to give evidence or refused or failed to produce the document,

shall, in a prosecution of the person under paragraph (e) of the said section 39(17), be evidence of the matters so stated without further proof.

Employment Agencies

13.—Where, whether before, on or after the commencement of this Act, an individual agrees with another person, who is carrying on the business of an employment agency within the meaning of the Employment Agency Act 1971, and is acting in the course of that business, to do or perform personally any work or service for a third person (whether or not the third person is a party to the contract and whether or not the third person pays the wages or salary of the individual in respect of the work or service), then, for the purposes of the Principal Act, as respects a dismissal occurring after such commencement—

    (a) the individual shall be deemed to be an employee employed by the third person under a contract of employment,

    (b) if the contract was made before such commencement, it shall be deemed to have been upon such commencement, and

(c) any redress under the Principal Act for unfair dismissal of the individual under the contract shall be awarded against the third person.

GENERAL NOTE

This section extends the scope of the 1977 Act to include persons employed through employment agencies. Essentially the person hiring the individual from the employment agency is deemed to be the employer, thus overruling *Cervi v. Atlas Staff Bureau* UD 616/1985 (reproduced in Madden and Kerr, *Unfair Dismissal: Cases and Commentary* (1990), p. 42).

Dismissal of persons during apprenticeship, training, etc. or during first year of service, for trade union membership or activities

14. Sections 2(1), 3 and 4 and subsections (1) and (6) of section 6 of the Principal Act shall not apply to a person referred to in paragraph (a) or (b) of the said section 2(1) or the said section 3 or 4 who is dismissed if the dismissal results wholly or mainly from one or more of the matters referred to in subsection (2)(a) of the said section 6.

GENERAL NOTE

The purpose of this section is to confirm the application of the protection of the 1977 Act to employees dismissed for trade union membership or activity who would otherwise not be covered because of their failure to satisfy the minimum one year service requirement or because of certain exclusions relating to training, probation and apprenticeship. It would appear from this peculiarly worded provision that the onus of proving the real reason for the dismissal lies on the claimant, even where he or she has more than one year's continuous service: see *Reid v. Oxx* (1986) 4 I.L.T. (*n.s.*) 207.

Amendment of First Schedule to Minimum Notice and Terms of Employment Act 1973

15. [...]

Repeal

16. Section 10 of the Principal Act is hereby repealed.

Short title, collective citation, construction, commencement and application

17.—(1) This Act may be cited as the Unfair Dismissals (Amendment) Act 1993.

(2) The Unfair Dismissals Acts 1977 and 1991 and this Act may be cited together as the Unfair Dismissals Acts 1977 to 1993.

(3) The Unfair Dismissals Acts 1977 and 1991 and this Act shall be construed together as one.

(4) This Act shall come into operation on the 1st day of October, 1993.

(5) This Act shall have effect as respects dismissals occurring after the commencement of this Act.

UNFAIR DISMISSALS (CLAIMS AND APPEALS) REGULATIONS 1977

S.I. No. 286 of 1977

1. (1) These Regulations may be cited as the Unfair Dismissals (Claims and Appeals) Regulations 1977.

(2) These Regulations shall come into operation on the 14th day of September 1977.

2. In these Regulations—

"the Act" means the Unfair Dismissals Act 1977 (No. 10 of 1977);

"appeal" means an appeal under section 9 of the Act;

"claim" means a claim under section 8(1) or section 8(4)(a) of the Act;

"the Minister" means the Minister for [Enterprise and Employment];

"the Tribunal" means the Employment Appeals Tribunal established by the Redundancy Payments Act 1967.

3. A notice under subsection (2) of section 8 of the Act to the Tribunal or under subsection (4) of the said section 8 or section 9(2) of the Act shall specify—

(a) the name and address of the person bringing the claim or appeal,

(b) the name and address of the employer or the employee as the case may be, concerned,

(c) the date of the commencement of the employment to which the notice relates,

(d) the date of the dismissal to which the notice relates, and

(e) the amount claimed by the said person to be the weekly remuneration of the said person in respect of the said employment calculated in accordance with regulations under section 17 of the Act.

4. A claim or appeal may be withdrawn by sending a notification in writing signifying such withdrawal to the Tribunal.

5. (1) A party to a claim or appeal who receives notice thereof under section 8 or 9, as the case may be, of the Act and who intends to oppose the claim or appeal shall enter an appearance to the claim or appeal by giving to the Tribunal, within 14 days of the receipt by him of the said notice, a notice in writing stating that he intends to oppose the claim or appeal, as the case may be, and containing the facts and contentions on which he will ground such opposition.

(2) A party to a claim or appeal who does not enter an appearance to the claim or appeal in pursuance of this Regulation shall not be entitled to take part in or be present or represented at any proceedings before the Tribunal in relation to the claim or appeal [unless the Tribunal at its discretion otherwise decides].

(3) A party to a claim or appeal may, before the expiration of the period referred to in paragraph (1) of this Regulation, apply, by giving to the Tribunal a notice in writing containing the facts and contentions on which he grounds the application, for an extension of the said period and the Tribunal may make such order in relation to the application as it thinks just.

6. On receipt by the Tribunal of a notice referred to in Regulation 3 or 5 of these Regulations or a notification under Regulation 4 of these Regulations, the Tribunal shall cause a copy of the notice or notification, as the case may be, to be given to the other party concerned.

7. The chairman of the Tribunal may, by certificate under his hand, correct any mistake (including an omission) of a verbal or formal nature in a determination of the Tribunal.

8. (1) The Tribunal shall maintain a register, to be known as the Register of Unfair Dismissals Determinations (referred to subsequently in this Regulation as "the Register"), and shall cause to be entered in the Register particulars of every determination by the Tribunal under section 8 or 9 of the Act.

(2) The Register may be inspected free of charge by any person during normal office hours.

(3) Where the chairman of the Tribunal makes a correction, pursuant to Regulation 7 of these Regulations, particulars thereof shall be entered in the Register.

(4) A copy of an entry in the Register shall be sent to the parties concerned.

9. (1) A notice required by subsection (2) or (4) of section 8 or section 9(2) of the Act or by these Regulations to be given to the Tribunal may be sent by registered post addressed to the Secretary, Employment Appeals Tribunal, Dublin [2], and a document required by these Regulations to be given to a party to proceedings

before the Tribunal may be sent by registered post addressed to the party—

(a) in case his address is specified in a notice referred to in Regulation 3 of these Regulations, at that address, and

(b) in the case of a body corporate (being a case to which paragraph (a) of this Regulation does not apply) at its registered office, and

(c) in any other case, at his known place of residence or at a place where he works or carries on business.

(2) Any such notice or notification as aforesaid that is sent or given to a person authorised to receive it by the person to whom it is required by these Regulations to be given shall be deemed to have been sent to the latter person.

10. Regulations 10 to 17(2), 19, 20, 20A (inserted by the [Redundancy (Employment Appeals Tribunal) Regulations 1979 (S.I. No. 114 of 1979)]), 23 and 24 of the Redundancy (Redundancy Appeals Tribunal) Regulations 1968 (S.I. No. 24 of 1968), shall, with any necessary modifications, and in the case of the said Regulations 20 and 20A, with the modification that a sum awarded by the Tribunal under either such Regulation shall, in lieu of being paid out of the fund referred to therein, be paid by the Minister for [Enterprise and Employment] with the consent of the Minister of Finance, apply in relation to a claim under section 8 of the Act, an appeal under section 9 of the Act and proceedings in relation to such a claim or appeal as they apply in relation to appeals provided for by section 39 of the Redundancy Payments Act 1967 (No. 21 of 1967).

GENERAL NOTE

These regulations prescribe the procedure to be followed in relation to the submission and hearing of claims and appeals before the Employment Appeals Tribunal under the Unfair Dismissals Act 1977.

The words in square brackets in Regulation 5(2) were inserted by virtue of regulation 15 of the Maternity Protection (Disputes and Appeals) Regulations 1981 (S.I. No. 357 of 1981). Given what the Supreme Court had to say in *Halal Meat Packers (Ballyhaunis) Ltd v. Employment Appeals Tribunal* [1990] E.L.R. 49, 60–64 it seems unlikely that there will be many cases in which the Tribunal would be justified in not hearing the employer. Regulation 10, as originally drafted, referred to the Redundancy (Redundancy Appeal Tribunal) (Amendment) Regulations 1969 (S.I. No. 26 of 1969), which Regulations were revoked and replaced by the 1979 Regulations. The 1968 Regulations are reproduced *supra* at p.88.

The form used for making a claim under the Acts is Form RP51A which is reproduced *infra* at p.275.

UNFAIR DISMISSALS (CALCULATION OF WEEKLY REMUNERATION) REGULATIONS 1977

S.I. No. 287 of 1977

1. (1) These Regulations may be cited as the Unfair Dismissals (Calculation of Weekly Remuneration Regulations 1977.

(2) These Regulations shall come into operation on the 14th day of September 1977.

2. In these Regulations—

"the Act" means the Unfair Dismissals Act 1977 (No. 10 of 1977);

"date of dismissal" has the meaning assigned to it by section 1 of the Act, and "date", in relation to a dismissal, shall be construed accordingly;

"relevant employment", in relation to an employee, means the employment in respect of which the weekly remuneration of the employee is calculated for the purposes of section 7(1)(c) of the Act;

"week", in relation to an employee whose remuneration is calculated by reference to a week ending on a day other than a Saturday, means a week ending on that other day and, in relation to any other employee, means a week ending on a Saturday, and "weekly" shall be construed accordingly.

3. (a) A week's remuneration of an employee in respect of an employment shall be calculated for the purposes of section 7(1)(c) of the Act in accordance with these Regulations.

(b) Where, at the date of his dismissal from an employment, an employee had less than 52 weeks' continuous service in the employment, a week's remuneration of the employee in respect of the employment shall be calculated, for the purposes of the said section 7(1)(c), in the manner that in the opinion of the Tribunal corresponds most closely with that specified in these Regulations.

4. In the case of an employee who is wholly remunerated in respect of the relevant employment at an hourly time rate or by a fixed wage or salary, and in the case of any other employee whose remuneration in respect of the relevant employment does not vary by reference to the amount of work done by him, his weekly remuneration in respect of the relevant employment shall be his earnings in respect of that employment (including any regular bonus or allowance which does not vary having regard to the amount of work done and any payment in kind) in the latest week before the date of the relevant dismissal in which he worked for the number of hours that was normal for the employment together with, if he was normally required to work overtime in the relevant employment, his average weekly overtime earnings in the relevant employment as determined in accordance with Regulation 5 of these Regulations.

5. For the purpose of Regulation 4 of these Regulations, the average weekly overtime earnings of an employee in the relevant employment shall be the amount obtained by dividing by 26 the total amount of his overtime earnings in that employment in the period of 26 weeks ending 13 weeks before the date of the dismissal of the employee.

6. For the purpose of Regulations 5 and 7(b) of these Regulations, any week during which the employee concerned did not work shall be disregarded and the latest week before the period of 26 weeks mentioned in the said Regulation 5 or 7(b), as the case may be, of these Regulations or before a week taken into account under this Regulation, as may be appropriate, shall be taken into account instead of a week during which the employee did not work as aforesaid.

7. (a) In the case of an employee who is paid remuneration in respect of the relevant employment wholly or partly at piece rates, or whose remuneration includes commissions (being piece rates or commissions related directly to his output at work) or bonuses, and in the case of any other employee whose remuneration in respect of the relevant employment varies in relation to the amount of work done by him, his weekly remuneration shall be the amount obtained by dividing the amount of the remuneration to be taken into account in accordance with paragraph (b) of this Regulation by the number of hours worked in the period of 26 weeks mentioned in the said paragraph (b) and multiplying the resulting amount by the normal number of hours for which, at the date of the dismissal of the

employee, an employee in the relevant employment was required to work in each week.

(b) The remuneration to be taken into account for the purposes of paragraph (a) of this Regulation shall be the total remuneration paid to the employee concerned in respect of the employment concerned for all the hours worked by the employee in the employment in the period of 26 weeks that ended 13 weeks before the date on which the employee was dismissed, adjusted in respect of any variations in the rates of pay which became operative during the period of 13 weeks ending on the date of dismissal of the employee.

(c) For the purposes of paragraph (b) of this Regulation, any week worked in another employment shall be taken into account if it would not have operated, for the purposes of the First Schedule to the Minimum Notice and Terms of Employment Act 1973 (No. 4 of 1973), to break the continuity of service of the employee concerned in the employment from which he was dismissed.

8. (1) Where, under his contract of employment, an employee is required to work for more hours than the number of hours that is normal for the employment, the hours for which he is so required to work shall be taken, for the purposes of Regulations 4 and 7(b) of these Regulations, to be, in the case of that employee, the number of hours that is normal for the employment.

(2) Where, under his contract of employment, an employee is entitled to additional remuneration for working for more than a specified number of hours per week—

(a) in case the employee is required under the said contract to work for more than the said specified number of hours per week, the number of hours per week for which he is so required to work shall, for the purposes of Regulations 4 and 7(b) of these Regulations, be taken to be, in his case, the number of hours of work per week that is normal for the employment, and

(b) in any other case, the specified number of hours shall be taken, for the purposes of the said Regulations 4 and 7(b), to be, in the case of that employee, the number of hours of work per week that is normal for the employment.

9. Where, in a particular week, an employee qualifies for a payment of a bonus, pay allowance or commission which relates to

work the whole or part of which was not done in that particular week, the whole or the appropriate proportionate part of the payment as the case may be, shall, for the purposes of Regulations 4 and 7(b) of these Regulations, be disregarded in relation to that particular week and shall for those purposes, be taken into account in relation to any week in which any of the work was done.

10. An employee who is normally employed on a shift cycle and whose remuneration in respect of the employment varies having regard to the particular shift on which he is employed, and an employee whose remuneration for working for the number of hours that is normal for the employment varies having regard to the days of the week or the times of the day on or at which he works, shall each be taken, for the purposes of these Regulations, to be an employee who is paid wholly or partly by piece rates.

11. Where, in respect of the relevant employment, there is no number of hours for which employees work in each week that is normal for the employment, the weekly remuneration of each such employee shall be taken, for the purposes of these Regulations, to be the average amount of the remuneration paid to each such employee in the 52 weeks in each of which he was working in the employment immediately before the date of the relevant dismissal.

12. Where under these Regulations account is to be taken of remuneration paid in a period which does not coincide with the periods for which the remuneration is calculated, the remuneration shall be apportioned in such manner as may be just.

13. For the purposes of Regulations 4 and 7 of these Regulations, account shall not be taken of any sums paid to an employee by way of recoupment of expenses incurred by him in the discharge of the duties of his employment.

GENERAL NOTE

These Regulations prescribe the method of calculating weekly remuneration for the purpose of redress in the form of compensation under the Unfair Dismissals Act 1977. In *O'Meara v. A.I.B.P. (Nenagh) Ltd* UD 1099/1993 the claimant had been on certified sick leave since October 15, 1992 when he was dismissed on October 4, 1993. The Tribunal held that, by virtue of regulation 4, it was to have regard to the remuneration that the claimant received in the last week in which he worked.

CIRCUIT COURT RULES 1950

Order 63

Rule 1 Definition

1. In this Order, "the Acts" mean the Unfair Dismissals Acts 1977--1993 (No. 10 of 1977, No. 5 of 1991 and No. 22 of 1993), "the Tribunal" means the Employment Appeals Tribunal, and "the Minister" means the Minister for Enterprise and Employment.

Rule 2 Transitional

2. All applications served or proceedings taken before these Rules shall have come into operation but which are in accordance with the existing Rules and practice of the Court shall have the same validity as applications made or proceedings taken in accordance with these Rules.

Rule 3 Forms

3. All applications under section 10 of the 1977 Act or under section 11 or the 1993 Act whether by way of claim for redress by the Minister or by way of claim for enforcement by the Minister or by the employee concerned or by way of appeal from the Tribunal shall be brought in accordance with the forms in the Schedule of Forms annexed hereto, or such modifications thereof as may be appropriate.

Rule 4 Venue

4. Applications shall be brought in the County where the employer concerned ordinarily resides or carries on any profession, business or occupation.

Rule 5 Service

5. All applications shall be served before filing, either in accordance with the provisions as to service of Civil Bills and other documents contained in Order 10 of the Circuit Court Rules 1950, as amended, or, alternatively, where applicable, in accordance with section 11 of the 1977 Act, or section 7 of the Courts Act 1964, or by being delivered to or served upon the Solicitor who is on record before the Tribunal as acting for the person named as the

Respondent before the Court; and service of an application or any other document upon such Solicitor, or delivery of the same at his office, or sending the same to him by prepaid post to such office shall be deemed to be good service upon the party for whom such Solicitor acts upon the day when the same is so delivered or served, or upon which in the ordinary course of postage it would be delivered.

Rule 6 Date of Hearing (outside Dublin) 6. This Rule shall not apply to Dublin. Every application shall state the date of commencement of the Sittings at which it is intended that the application shall be listed for hearing, and shall be filed at the Office of the County Registrar by the applicant not later than twenty-one days before the commencement of such sittings.

Rule 7 Date of Hearing (Dublin) 7. This Rule shall apply only to the Dublin Circuit. Every application shall state the date on which it is desired that the application shall be listed for hearing and shall be filed by the applicant at the Office of the County Registrar not later than twenty-one days before such date.

Rule 8 Notice to Tribunal 8. Notice of every application shall be given to the Tribunal. Such notice shall be effected before the filing of the application by the delivery of a copy of the application at, or by sending same by prepaid registered post to the Office of the Secretary of the Tribunal.

Rule 9 Filing 9. The application shall be filed within seven days of service thereof on the Respondent, or, if there be more than one Respondent, within seven days of service on the Respondent last served. There shall be filed with the application copies of the documents referred to in the following rule. In default of such filing, a Respondent may himself file the same and thereupon or at any time thereafter, the Judge may make such Order as to him shall seem right.

Rule 10 Documents to be filed 10. The following documents shall be filed with the application—

205

(a) a copy of the original Notice of Appeal

to the Tribunal;
(b) a copy of the Notice of Appearance;
(c) a copy of the determination of the Tribunal;
(d) the original letter from the Tribunal notifying the making of communication of the said determination; and
(e) a copy of any particulars provided by either party to the Tribunal.

Rule 11

11. Every application made by way of an appeal from a determination of the Tribunal shall contain a statement of the grounds upon which the Applicant intends to rely. If the Applicant wishes to appeal against part only of a determination of the Tribunal, the application shall clearly identify that part against which it is intended to appeal.

Rule 12 Signatures to Application

12. All applications shall be dated, and bear the name, address and description of the Applicant and shall be signed by his Solicitor, if any, or if none, by himself.

Rule 13 Further Particulars. Copies of documents

13. Upon the application on notice of any party the Judge may order any other party to deliver full and better particulars of any matters stated in the application, or to deliver copies of any documents referred to therein.

Rule 14 Oral evidence

14. Save by special leave of the Court or save as otherwise provided by the Acts, all applications under the Acts shall be heard upon oral evidence.

Rule 15 Costs

15. The Court may make such Order as to costs as may be appropriate, having regard to the provisions of section 10 of the 1977 Act.

Rule 16 Access to Information

16. The Secretary of the Tribunal shall have the right of access to all the information contained on the file kept in the Office of the County Registrar in respect of each application and shall be entitled upon request to receive a copy of any written Judgment delivered by the Judge relating thereto.

SCHEDULE
Form One

_____CIRCUIT   COUNTY OF_____

UNFAIR DISMISSALS ACT 1977, S.10(1)
or
UNFAIR DISMISSALS (AMENDMENT) ACT 1993, S.11(2)(b) or (c)
(Delete as appropriate)

BETWEEN/
> THE MINISTER FOR ENTERPRISE AND EMPLOYMENT
>
>   Applicant

AND

> _____
>
>   Respondent

TAKE NOTICE that the Minister for Enterprise and Employment having his office at _____ in the County of _____ hereby applies to the Court sitting at _____ in the County of _____ pursuant to the provisions of [insert appropriate Act and section] on behalf of [insert name of employee] for redress under the Act and for the costs of the Application.

AND TAKE NOTICE that the Minister will rely upon the following matters in support of the application:

(1)   The said [insert name of employee] is the employee of the Respondent for the purposes of the said Act.

(2)   The Employment Appeals Tribunal/Circuit Court on the _____ day of _____ 19_____ has determined/ordered that the said employee be entitled to redress under the said Acts and accordingly ordered the Respondent to reinstate/re-engage/compensate [delete as appropriate] the said employee as by [insert brief details of the determination].

(3)   The Respondent has failed to carry out the terms of the said determination/ Order, which was communicated to the parties on the _____ day of _____19_____.

AND TAKE NOTICE that the application will be listed for hearing by the Court on the _____ day of _____ 19_____ or on the first available day thereafter. (The words 'or on the first available day thereafter' should be omitted where the application is made in Dublin.)

                Dated the _____ day of _____ 19_____

SIGNED   _____

                Solicitor for the Applicant

                (Address)

To: _____

        _____

        _____

The above named Respondent/Solicitor for Respondent and

The Secretary, Employment Appeals Tribunal, Department of Enterprise and Employment, 65A Adelaide Road, Dublin 2.

Form Two

_____CIRCUIT   COUNTY OF_____

UNFAIR DISMISSALS (AMENDMENT) ACT 1993,
S.11(2)(b) or (c)
(Delete as appropriate)

BETWEEN/

_____ Applicant

AND

_____ Respondent

TAKE NOTICE that the above-named Applicant of _____ in the County of _____ hereby applies to the Court sitting at _____ in the County of _____ pursuant to the provisions of [insert appropriate Act and section] for redress under the Act and for the costs of the Application.

AND TAKE NOTICE that the Applicant will rely upon the following matters in support of the application:

(1)   The said [insert name of Applicant] is the employee of the Respondent for the purposes of the said Act.

(2)   The Employment Appeals Tribunal/Circuit Court on the _____ day of _____ 19_____ has determined/ordered that the Applicant be entitled to redress under the said Act and accordingly ordered the Respondent to re-instate/re-engage/compensate [delete as appropriate] the Applicant as by [insert brief details of the determination].

(3)   The Respondent has failed to carry out the terms of the said determination/ Order, which was communicated to the parties on the _____ day of _____ 19_____.

AND TAKE NOTICE that the application will be listed for hearing by the Court on the _____ day of _____ 19_____ or on the first available day thereafter. (The words 'or on the first available day thereafter' should be omitted where the application is made in Dublin).

Dated the _____ day of _____ 19_____

SIGNED   _____

Solicitor for the Applicant

(Address)

To: _____

_____

_____

The above named Respondent/Solicitor for Respondent
and
The Secretary, Employment Appeals Tribunal, Department of Enterprise and Employment, 65A Adelaide Road, Dublin 2.

Form Three

_____CIRCUIT   COUNTY OF_____

UNFAIR DISMISSALS (AMENDMENT) ACT 1993, S.10(4)
or
UNFAIR DISMISSALS (AMENDMENT) ACT 1993
S. 11(1)
(Delete as appropriate)

BETWEEN/

_____ Applicant

AND

_____ Respondent

TAKE NOTICE that the above-named Applicant of _____ in the County of _____ hereby applies to the Court sitting at _____ in the County of _____ pursuant to the provisions of [insert appropriate Act and section] by way of Appeal against the determination of the Employment Appeals Tribunal dated the _____ day of _____ 19_____ granting/refusing [delete as appropriate] the claim of the Appellant/Respondent [delete where appropriate] for redress under the said Act and for an Order providing for the costs of this application. The said determination of the Employment Appeals Tribunal was communicated to the Appellant on the _____ day of _____ 19_____.

AND TAKE NOTICE that the Appellant will rely upon the following matters in support of his Appeal: (Here insert grounds relied upon. If appeal is against part only of the determination, clearly identify that part against which an appeal is sought).

AND TAKE NOTICE that the application will be listed for hearing by the Court on the _____ day of _____ 19_____ or on the first available day thereafter. (The words 'or on the first available day thereafter' should be omitted where the application is made in Dublin).

Dated the _____ day of _____ 19_____

SIGNED   _____

Solicitor for the Applicant
(Address)

To: _____

_____

_____

The above named Respondent/Solicitor for Respondent
and
The Secretary, Employment Appeals Tribunal, Department of Enterprise and Employment, 65A Adelaide Road, Dublin 2.

GENERAL NOTE

This Order was added to the Circuit Court Rules by the Circuit Court Rules 1994 (Unfair Dismissals Acts 1977–1993 and Payment of Wages Act 1991) (S.I. No. 279 of 1994) which came into operation on September 30, 1994. These rules, which revoke the Circuit Court Rules (No. 2) 1981 (Unfair Dismissals Act 1977) (S. I. No. 316 of 1981), which in turn revoked the Circuit Court Rules (No. 1) 1979 (Unfair Dismissals Act 1977) (S. I. No. 10 of 1979), prescribe, *inter alia*, Circuit Court procedures in respect of applications brought under section 10 of the 1977 Act and section 11 of the 1993 Amendment Act (*see supra* p.191). Given that section 10 of the 1977 Act was repealed by section 16 of the 1993 Amendment Act the reference in rule 15 to section 10 should be read as a reference to section 11 of the latter Act as regards dismissals occurring after October 1, 1993.

Section 7 of the Courts Act 1964 (as amended by section 22(1) of the Courts Act 1971) provides, in subsection (3), that service of a Circuit Court document (as defined in subsection (1) may be effected by sending a copy of the document by registered personal prepaid post in an envelope addressed to the person to be served at his last known residence or place of business in the State and the document may be posted by the person on whose behalf it purports to be issued or a person authorised by him in that behalf. Subsection (4) provides that service of a Circuit Court document upon a person pursuant to subsection (3) shall, upon proof that the envelope containing a copy of the document was addressed, registered and posted in accordance with the provisions of that subsection, be deemed to be good service upon the person unless it is proved that such copy was not delivered. Subsection (5) provides for substituted service and subsection (6) provides:

> (a) Where service of a document on a person is effected by sending a copy thereof by registered prepaid post in an envelope addressed to the person pursuant to subsection (3) of this section—
> > (i) the document shall be deemed to be served upon the person at the time at which the envelope would be delivered in the ordinary course of post.
> > (ii) the document shall be deemed to be issued at the time at which the envelope is posted.
> > (iii) the addressing, registering and posting, in accordance with the provisions of subsection (3) of this section, of the envelope may be proved by a statutory declaration (which shall be endorsed upon the original document and shall be made, not earlier than ten days after the day on which the envelope is posted, by the person who posted the envelope) exhibiting the certificate of posting of the envelope aforesaid and stating, if it be the case, that the original document was duly stamped at the time of posting and that the envelope has not been returned undelivered to the sender, and
> > (iv) the time, date and place of posting of the envelope shall be endorsed upon the original document.
> (b) Where a document of which service is effected pursuant to subsection (3) of this section falls to be lodged at any court office, the endorsement specified in subparagraphs (iii) and (iv) of paragraph (a) of this subsection shall be effected thereon before lodgement at that office.

210

Order 10 of the Circuit Court Rules 1950 (as amended by S. I. Nos. 202 of 1965 and 155 of 1990), which is headed "Service and Entry", provides in rule 4 that, save where otherwise directed or permitted, service should be effected upon the respondent

> personally wherever he is to be found within the jurisdiction, or at the [respondent's] residence within the jurisdiction personally upon the husband or wife of the [respondent], or upon some relative or employee of the [respondent] over the age of seventeen years and apparently resident there.

It was held by Barron J. in *Morris v. Power Security Ltd* [1990] 1 I.R. 296 that the essence of an appeal under the Unfair Dismissals Act 1977 was not the issue or service of a notice of appeal as such, but the invoking of the Circuit Court's jurisdiction. This was done, he said, by issue of the originating document, in that case a notice of application to the Court in the form prescribed by Order 63 of the Circuit Court Rules. Time ceased to run when the proceedings were issued, not when they were served.

PROTECTION OF EMPLOYEES (EMPLOYERS' INSOLVENCY) ACT 1984

(1984 No. 21)

ARRANGEMENT OF SECTIONS

An Act to confer, on the insolvency of employers, certain rights on employees, to amend certain enactments relating to the rights of employees and to provide for other matters (including offences) connected with the matters aforesaid. [*30th November 1984*]

General Note

This Act implements Council Directive of October 20, 1980 relating to the protection of employees in the event of the insolvency of their employer (80/987/EEC, O.J. 1980 L283/23). The Directive provides that member states should ensure that a fund (referred to as a "guarantee institution") is available from which employees can claim payment of debts, arising from the employment relationship which have not been paid because of the employer's insolvency. It also imposes an obligation on member states to protect the interests of workers in relation to pension schemes. The intent of the Directive is to promote the proper functioning of the

212

Common Market by the harmonisation of the laws of the Member States (Article 100), and to promote co-operation in relation to social policy in matters relating to employment (Article 117). On the Italian and Hellenic Republics' failure to implement Directive 80/987, see the judgments of the Court of Justice of the European Communities in Case 22/87, *Commission v. Italian Republic* [1989] E.C.R. 143 and Case C-53/88, *Commission v. Hellenic Republic* [1990] E.C.R. 1-3931. Furthermore, in Joined Cases C-6/90 and C-9/90, *Francovich and Bonifaci v. Italian Republic*[1991] E.C.R. 1–5357 the Court of Justice ruled that a member state was obliged to make good the damage suffered by individuals as a result of the state's failure to implement Directive 80/987. *See* also Case 334/92, *Wagner Miret v. Fondo de Garantia Salarial* [1993] E.C.R. 1–6911.

In addition, advantage was taken of the Act to standardise the number of normal working hours required by an employee to qualify for rights under worker protection legislation. Employees who work 18 hours a week and who satisfy other requirements are now protected by the Redundancy Payments Acts 1967 to 1984 (previously 20 hours), the Minimum Notice and Terms of Employment Acts 1973 and 1984, and the Unfair Dismissals Act 1977 (previously 21 hours). By virtue of the Worker Protection (Regular Part-Time Employees) Act 1991, the benefits of these Acts have now been extended to regular part-time employees (defined as an employee who has been in the employer's continuous service for at least 13 weeks and who is normally expected to work at least 8 hours a week).

The Scheme of the Act

Eligible employees are entitled to apply to the Minister for Enterprise and Employment for payment of the whole or part of those debts set out in section 6 of the Act, which have remained unpaid because the employer became insolvent on or after October 22, 1983. Article 11 of the Directive put an obligation on Member States to comply with its provisions within 36 months of its notification. Rights under the Act are therefore backdated to cover insolvencies on or after October 22, 1983—the deadline for implementation. The forms which must be used for applications under section 6 are set out in the protection of Employees (Employers' Insolvency) (Forms and Procedure) Regulations 1984 (S.I. No. 356 of 1984) as amended by S.I. No. 349 of 1991. The Minister is authorised by the Act to pay such amount, from the Social Insurance Fund, which, in his opinion, is or was due to the employee.

The debts for which the employee can claim payment under section 6 include up to 8 weeks' arrears of normal pay, sick pay and accrued holiday pay, subject to a weekly maximum (currently £300). A claim can also be made for amounts due to the employee arising from proceedings under worker protection legislation. These include awards in respect of minimum notice, unfair dismissal, areas due under an employment regulation order (failure to pay minimum statutory wages) or entitlements under the Anti-Discrimination (Pay) Act 1974 and the Employment Equality Act 1977. Section 7 of the Act authorises the Minister to use the fund to make payments into the assets of an occupational pension scheme so as to cover contributions not paid on the employer's insolvency. Contributions covered are those

(i) payable by the insolvent employer which he did not pay and
(ii) payable by the employee and for which an equal sum had been deducted from his pay, but had not been paid into the scheme.

The amount paid in respect of the employer's contributions will be the balance unpaid by him on the insolvency date or the certified amount necessary to meet

213

the liabilities of the scheme, whichever is the lesser. The sum payable in respect of deductions from the employees' wages shall not exceed the amount deducted in the 12 months ending on the day preceding the insolvency. An application under section 7 can be made by either an employee or other persons competent to act in respect of the occupational pension scheme. The forms and procedures for an application under section 7 are set out in the Protection of Employees (Employers' Insolvency) (Occupational Pension Scheme) (Forms and Procedure) Regulations 1990 (S.I. No. 121 of 1990).

The rights conferred by sections 6 and 7 depend on the employer's insolvency and on the date of that insolvency. Section 1(3) defines insolvency for the purposes of the Act and allows the Minister to add to the list of insolvency situations by regulation. This is important where business ceases, but no steps are taken to declare the employer insolvent. The date of insolvency is defined in section 4 and it enables the Minister to specify other circumstances in which an employer will be deemed insolvent and the date of its occurrence.

There are other limitations on the claims which can be made under the Act. The categories of employees protected by the legislation are defined in section 3, namely, persons employed in employment which is insurable for all benefits under the Social Welfare (Consolidation) Act 1993, although by virtue of the Protection of Employees (Employer's Insolvency) Act 1984 (Amendment Order) Order 1988 (S.I. No. 48 of 1988), the Act's application is extended to employees who have attained 66 years of age.

Another principal limitation on claiming payment for debts under section 6 is that the employee must have become entitled to arrears of pay during the "relevant period" as defined in section 6(9), or an award, etc. must have been made during or after the "relevant period." The relevant period is defined as 18 months preceding a "relevant date" which varies with the type of debt claimed.

Citation

This Act, section 28 of the Social Welfare Act 1990, and the Worker Protection (Regular Part-Time Employees) Act 1991 may be cited together as the Protection of Employees' (Employers' Insolvency) Acts 1984 to 1991.

Commencement

This Act came into operation on November 30, 1984, having been signed by the President on a date earlier than the fifth day after presentation under Article 25.2.2 of the Constitution.

Statutory Instruments

Protection of Employees (Employers' Insolvency) (Forms and Procedure) Regulations 1984 (S.I. No. 356 of 1984).

Protection of Employees (Employers' Insolvency) (Occupational Pension Scheme) (Forms and Procedure) Regulations 1985 (S.I. No. 123 of 1985).

Protection of Employees (Employers' Insolvency) (Specification of Date) Regulations 1985 (S.I. No. 232 of 1985).

Protection of Employees (Employers' Insolvency) Act 1984 (Amendment Order) Order 1988 (S.I. No. 48 of 1988).

Protection of Employees (Employers' Insolvency) (Variation of Limit) Regulations 1990 (S.I. No. 17 of 1990).

Protection of Employees (Employers' Insolvency) (Occupational Pension Scheme) (Forms and Procedure) Regulations 1990 (S.I. No. 121 of 1990)

Protection of Employees (Employers' Insolvency) (Forms and Procedure) (Amendment) Regulations 1991 (S.I. No. 349 of 1991).

Protection of Employees (Employer's Insolvency) (Variation of Limit) Regulations 1994 (S.I. No. 62 of 1994).

Parliamentary Debates

352 *Dail Debates* Cols. 568–600 (Second Stage)
354 *Dail Debates* Cols. 269–325 (Committee Stage)
354 *Dail Debates* Cols. 387–453 (Committee Stage resumed)
354 *Dail Debates* Cols. 854–887 (Committee Stage resumed)
354 *Dail Debates* Cols. 887–894 (Report and Final Stages)
106 *Seanad Debates* Cols. 378–418 (Second Stage)
106 *Seanad Debates* Cols. 443–471 (Committee and Final Stages)
378 *Dail Debates* Cols. 784–798 (Amendment Order: Motion)
118 *Seanad Debates* Cols. 1558–1573 (Amendment Order: Motion)

Be it enacted by the Oireachtas as follows:

Interpretation

1.—(1) In this Act—

"the Act of 1967" means the Redundancy Payments Act 1967;

"the Act of 1973" means the Minimum Notice and Terms of Employment Act 1973'

"the Act of 1974" means the Anti-Discrimination (Pay) Act, 1974;

"the Act of 1977" means the Unfair Dismissals Act 1977;

"the Act of [1993]" means the Social Welfare (Consolidation) Act [1993]

"company" means, except when the context otherwise require, a company within the meaning of section 2 of the Companies Act 1963, or any other body corporate whether incorporated within or outside the State;

"employee" means a person who has entered into or works under (or, in the case of a contract which has been terminated, worked under) a contract with an employer, whether the contract is for manual labour, clerical work or otherwise, is express or implied, oral or in writing, and whether it is a contract of service or apprenticeship or otherwise and "employer" and any reference to employment shall be construed accordingly;

"holiday pay" means—

(a) pay in respect of a holiday actually taken; or
(b) any holiday pay which had accrued at the date of the termination of the employee's employment and

215

which, had his employment with the employer continued until be became entitled to a holiday, would under the employee's contract of employment in the ordinary course have become payable to him on becoming so entitled;

"the Minister" means the Minister for [Enterprise and Employment];

"occupational pension scheme" means any scheme or arrangement which, forming part of a contract of employment, provides or is capable of providing, in relation to employees in any description of employment, benefits (in the form of pensions or otherwise) payable to or in respect of any such employees on the termination of their employment or on their death or retirement;

"prescribed" means prescribed by regulations under this Act;

"relevant officer" means an executor, an administrator, the official assignee or a trustee in bankruptcy, a liquidator, a receiver or manager, or a trustee under an arrangement between an employer and his creditors or under a trust deed for his creditors executed by an employer;

["the Social Insurance Fund" means the Social Insurance Fund established under section 39 of the Social Welfare Act 1952, and continued in being under section 122 of the Social Welfare (Consolidation) Act 1981 and further continued in being under section 7 of the Social Welfare (Consolidation) Act 1993];

"the Tribunal" means the Employment Appeals Tribunal.

(2) Any reference in this Act to the assets of an occupational pensions scheme is a reference to the funds or other property out of which the benefits provided by the scheme are payable from time to time, including the proceeds of any policy or insurance taken out, or contract entered into, for the purposes of the scheme.

(3) For the purposes of this Act, an employer shall be taken to be or, as may be appropriate, to have become insolvent if, but only if,

(a) he has been adjudicated bankrupt or has filed a petition for or has executed a deed of arrangement (within the meaning of section 4 of the Deeds of Arrangement Act 1887); or

(b) he has died and his estate, being insolvent, is being administered in accordance with the rules set out in Part I of the First Schedule to the Succession Act 1965; or

(c) where the employer is a company, a winding up order is made or a resolution for voluntary winding up is passed with respect to it, or a receiver or manager of its undertaking is duly appointed, or possession is taken, by or on behalf of the holders of any debentures secured by any floating charge, of any property of the company comprised in or subject to the charge, or

(d) he is an employer of a class or description specified in regulations under section 4(2) of this Act which are for the time being in force and the circumstances specified in the regulations as regards employers of such class or description obtain in relation to him.

GENERAL NOTE

"'company'": under the Companies Act 1963 means "a company formed and registered under this Act, or an existing company".

"deed of arrangement": section 4 of the Deeds of Arrangement Act 1887 includes any of the following instruments, whether under seal or not, made by, for, or in respect of the affairs of a debtor, for the benefit of his creditors generally (other than those made under bankruptcy law):

    (a) an assignment of property;

    (b) a deed of agreement for a composition; and in cases where a debtor's creditors obtain control over his property or business—

    (c) a deed of inspectorship entered into for the purpose of carrying on or winding up a business;

    (d) a letter of licence authorising the debtor or any other person to manage, carry on, realise, or dispose of a business, with a view to the payment of debts; and

    (e) any agreement or instrument entered into for the purpose of carrying on or winding up the debtor's business, or authorising the debtor or any other person to manage, carry on, realise, or dispose of the debtor's business, with a view to the payment of his debts.

"his estate, being insolvent": Where the estate of a deceased person is insolvent, section 46(1) of the Succession Act 1965 states that it shall be administered in accordance with rules set out in Part 1 of the First Schedule to that Act. Under these rules, funeral, testamentary and administration expenses have priority. Otherwise bankruptcy rules apply with the date of death being substituted for the date of adjudication in bankruptcy.

"the Minister": this definition was amended by virtue of the Labour (Transfer of Departmental Administration and Ministerial Functions) Order 1993 (S.I. No. 18 of 1993) and the Industry and Commerce (Alteration of Name of Department and Title of Minister) Order 1993 (S.I. No. 19 of 1993).

"occupational pension scheme": the definition is very wide and the Employment Appeals Tribunal has held that it does not demand Revenue approval or a signed deed of trust: see *In re Cavan Rubber Ltd* [1992] E.L.R. 79, 81.

"where a winding up order is made or a resolution for voluntary winding up is passed": a company may be wound up by the court under the Companies Act 1963 following an application by petition (section 215), on a number of grounds (section 213 as amended), by making a winding-up order (section 216). A company can be wound up voluntarily where the company passes a resolution for voluntary winding up under section 251 of the Companies Act 1963. A receiver or manager of the company's undertaking is usually appointed under the terms of a debenture.

Section 1(3) defines the circumstances in which an employer is deemed to be insolvent for the purposes of the Act. It is an important subsection because the rights conferred by sections 6 and 7 are only available to employees employed by employers who become insolvent on or after October 22, 1983 (see sections 6(1) and 7(1)). For the date on which the insolvency is deemed to have occurred, see section 4. For information on bankruptcy law see the Report of the Bankruptcy Law Committee (1972, prl. 2714). A modernisation and consolidation of bankruptcy law was undertaken in the Bankruptcy Act 1988.

The Act deems the employer to be insolvent, for the purposes of the rights conferred on employees, in some situations in which the employer would not be deemed insolvent commercially or for the purposes of other legal rules. Section 1(3) also allows the Minister for Enterprise and Employment to specify by regulations other circumstances in which the employer may be deemed to be insolvent. This can be important to the employee where no steps have been taken to declare the employer insolvent. At Committee Stage, the Minister stated in regard to the definition of insolvency that he was "trying to use the broadest possible definition to ensure that no company, and consequently, no worker, will be able to escape from the consequences of this legislation... Basically we are taking the broadest possible definition of insolvency we know of, such as liquidation or receivership and others where the bank move in." (354 *Dail Debates* Cols. 270–271.) See also General Note to section 4.

Redundancy and Employers' Insolvency Fund

2. [*Repealed by section 39(2) of the Social Welfare Act 1991*]

GENERAL NOTE

The E.C. Directive (80/987/EEC), which this Act implements, requires a fund to be set up which will guarantee payment of certain outstanding claims of employees in the event of the insolvency of their employer. Section 2 met this requirement by extending the Redundancy Fund established by section 26 of the Redundancy Payments Act 1967 and renaming it the Redundancy and Employers' Insolvency Fund. Section 26 of the 1967 Act, however, was repealed by section 29 of the Social Welfare Act 1990, and by virtue of section 28 of that Act the Social Insurance Fund was substituted for the Redundancy and Employers' Insolvency Fund. The amalgamation of the Redundancy and Employers' Insolvency Fund, together with the Occupational Injuries Fund, with the Social Insurance Fund was heavily criticised by the Federation of Irish Employers (see *Industrial Relations News* 44, November 23, 1989). The Fund was financed by a separate employer's redundancy contribution but Part VI of the Social Welfare Act 1991 amalgamated the separate occupational injuries and redundancy contributions with the employer's social insurance contribution. The current rate of employer PRSI contribution is nine per cent of the reckonable earnings of each worker if less than £231 per week and 12.2 per cent up to a ceiling of £21,500 (see section 7 of the Social Welfare Act 1994 and section 6 of the Social Welfare Act 1995). Before their amalgamation the rate of employers' redundancy contribution was 0.4 per cent: see Redundancy Payments (Variation of Employers' Redundancy Contribution) Regulations 1989 (S.I. No. 68 of 1989).

The following table sets out the payments made from the Fund for the years 1986–1991.

Entitlement	1986	1987	1988	1989	1990	1991
Arrears of wages	676,842	643,099	428,491	333,200	414,590	38,012
Holiday pay	1,160,231	1,146,772	652,014	500,349	32,111	590,344
Sick pay	1,127	-	103	638	-	-
Minimum Notice awards	2,949,676	2,229,665	1,834,573	1,105,789	,827283	886,398
Unfair Dismissal awards	48,363	14,860	52,955	62,660	5,611	80,095
Unpaid pension contributions	169,890	-	279,496	87,523	34,703	88,404
TOTAL	£5,006,229	£4,034,396	£3,247,432	£2,390,159	£2,914,298	£1,983,253

In 1993, payments totalled over £3,189,000. The principal components of these payments were minimum notice (£1.5 million), arrears of wages (£0.6 million) and arrears of holiday pay (£0.8 million).

Rebates paid from the Fund under the Redundancy Payments Acts to employers (who get 60 per cent of the redundancy payments legally due and paid to their workers) during 1993 totalled £17,340,000 compared with £13,880,000 in 1992 and 1991, £10,451,622 in 1990, £16,681,065 in 1989, £20,727,849 during 1988, £16,550,452 during 1987 and £16,037,733 during 1986. Where the employer fails to pay, the Fund pays the statutory lump sum direct to the redundant worker and claims the appropriate amount from the employer. In 1993, £2,770,000 was paid to workers in this way, compared with £3,470,000 in 1992, £1,960,000 in 1991, £3,315,647 in 1990, £1,668,131 in 1989, £3,042,432 in 1988, £5,209,225 in 1987 and £5,999,234 in 1986. The closing balance in the Fund on December 31, 1989 was £31,026,820. The balance on the same date in 1988, 1987 and 1986 was £22,183,302, £14,434,801 and £7,721,766 respectively (*Source*: Department of Labour Annual Reports 1986–1991, Department of Enterprise and Employment Annual Report 1993).

Application of Act

3.—Subject to section 11 of this Act, this Act applies to employees employed in employment which is insurable for all benefits under the Social Welfare (Consolidation) Act [1993].

GENERAL NOTE

This section defines the categories of employees protected by the Act–namely, those in employment which is insurable for all benefits under the Social Welfare Acts. This group consists of PRSI Class A Contributors. The Minister explained that the effect of the section would be that the benefits provided by the Act will be available to persons covered by the Redundancy Payments Acts. Both schemes of legislation only apply to persons who are normally expected to work 18 hours a week or more. Considerable dissatisfaction was expressed at Committee Stage at the fact that part–time workers would be excluded from the benefits of the Act. The Minister pointed out that section 3 was linked with what is now section 11, and that the latter section empowers the Minister to include other categories of workers within the ambit of the Act. He also pointed out that a part-time worker with no other source of income could get benefits by establishing his case with the Department of Social Welfare (354 *Dail Debates* Cols. 293–299). By virtue of the Protection of Employees (Employers' Insolvency) Act 1984 (Amendment Order) Order 1988 (S.I. No. 48 of 1988), the application of the Act is extended to employees who have attained the age of 66 years and who are in employment which, but for the age of the employees, would be insurable for all benefits under the Social Welfare Acts. By virtue of the Worker Protection (Regular Part-Time Employees) Act 1991, the benefits of the 1984 Act are extended from June 17, 1991 to employees who have been in the employer's continuous service for at least 13 weeks and who are normally expected to work at least 8 hours a week: Worker Protection (Regular Part-Employees) Act 1991 (Commencement) (No. 2) Order 1991 (S.I. No. 144 of 1991).

Insolvency for the purposes of Act

4.—(1) An employer who is for the purposes of this Act insolvent shall for such purposes be regarded as having become insolvent on—

    (a) where the employer has been adjudicated bankrupt, the date of such adjudication,

    (b) where the employer petitioned for arrangement, the date on which the petition is filed,

    (c) where the employer executed a deed referred to in section 1(3)(a) of this Act, the date of such execution,

    (d) where the employer has died, the date of his death,

    (e) where the employer is a company within the meaning of section 2 of the Companies Act 1963—

        (i) in case either a receiver is appointed on behalf of the holder of any debenture secured by a floating charge, or possession is taken by or on behalf of such a debenture holder of any property of the company comprised in or subject to the charge, the date of the appointment of the receiver or possession being taken as aforesaid, as may be appropriate, or

        (ii) in any other case the date which, in relation to the company, is the relevant date within the meaning of section 285 of the Companies Act 1963, and

    (f) where the employer is an employer of a class or description specified in regulations under subsection (3) of this section which are for the time being in force, the day on which under the regulations such an employer is for such purposes to be regarded as having become insolvent.

(2) The Minister may by regulations specify the circumstances in which employers who are of a class or description specified in the regulations are, for the purposes of this Act, to be taken to be, or to have become, insolvent.

(3) The Minister may by regulations specify the day on which any employer who is of a class or description specified in the regulations and who is also an employer who for the purposes of this Act is insolvent, is to be regarded as having become so insolvent.

GENERAL NOTE

The "relevant date" (section 4(1)(e)(ii) above), in the case of a compulsory winding-up, is defined in section 285 of the Companies Act 1963 as the date of appointment of a provisional liquidator, or, if none was appointed, the date of the winding-up order, unless in either case the company had commenced to be wound up voluntarily before that date. In other cases, the "relevant date" is the date of the passing of the resolution for the winding-up of the company.

The date on which an employer is deemed to have become insolvent is specified in this section. This date is important in two respects. It determines whether an insolvency took place before or after October 22, 1983— the date from which the rights under the Act take effect; and it is a means by which some of the employees' claims are limited in that they may have to relate to the eighteen month period prior to the date of the employer's insolvency.

Section 4(2) and (3) allow the Minister by regulations to specify other circumstances in which an employer is deemed to be insolvent, and the day on which an insolvency is deemed to arise. The Minister said at Committee Stage that an employee who discovered that his employer had simply disappeared could have the situation assessed, preferably by his trade union representative, and make a claim to the Department which would make an investigation through its inspectorate, which would in turn make a recommendation to the Minister. If the Minister was convinced by the evidence that it was a case of insolvency he would pay the employee his entitlements (354 *Dail Debates* Col. 392). Of course, the Minister would only be entitled to do this if there was a case of insolvency within the meaning of section 4 and this section does not cover the case of a company which merely ceases trading and closes down. In theory, any employee owed money by the company would be entitled to put the company into liquidation but, as Mervyn Taylor T.D. commented during the Motion to approve the draft of the 1988 Amendment Order (378 *Dail Debates* Col. 794), "[t]o expect an employee who has lost his job since the company closed down, and who has been deprived of his rights and benefits under the legislation, to be able to undertake the expense to put that company into liquidation is expecting far too much." He, therefore, suggested that if there were an unsatisfied judgment against a company for a month then the company should be deemed to be insolvent even though it had not formally been put into liquidation (*ibid.*). The Minister's response, however, to the problem of what he described as "informal insolvency" was that any extension of the Act along the lines suggested would give rise to "a range of problems both legal and administrative." Despite extensive consideration of the matter, "a solution has not been found to the difficulties involved" (*ibid.* Cols. 796–797).

Subsequently the Minister has admitted that, after consultation with the Attorney-General's Office, he had come to the conclusion that "the problem could not be satisfactorily dealt with, legally or administratively, by Regulations under the 1984 Act and that new or amending legislation would be necessary to deal with the matter." This legislation would have to be based on an entirely different approach from that inherent in the 1984 Act and would give rise to complex issues. Nevertheless he was considering the feasibility of introducing such legislation but was unable to say whether it would be practicable to do this (*Industrial Relations News* 21, June 2, 1988, p.14). Responding to a question in the Dail as to whether he had any plans to introduce regulations relating to "informal insolvency," the Minister reiterated that, "following detailed and prolonged examination," he had concluded that it would not be feasible to make regulations extending the scope of the Act to so-called informal insolvencies. He stated that any extension of the definition of an employer's insolvency could not be implemented solely for the purpose of payments due to employees under the 1984 Act. An employer could not be deemed to be insolvent for one limited purpose only without reference to wider implications: 399 *Dail Debates* Cols. 106–107 (23 May 1990).

The Minister has twice exercised his power under section 4(3). The Protection of Employees (Employers' Insolvency) (Specification of Date) Regulations 1985 (S.I. No. 232 of 1985) specify the date on which an insolvency is deemed to arise in the case of bodies corporate under the Industrial and Provident Societies Act 1893, such as co-operatives, for example. Such organisations are deemed to have become insolvent for the purposes of the Act on the day on which a receiver or manager is appointed by or on behalf of the holders of debentures secured by a floating charge. These regulations are designed to plug the gap that emerged when former employees of Clover Meats Ltd. had their applications rejected because their employer was a co-operative registered under the 1893 Act. In relation to bodies corporate under the Industrial and Provident Societies Acts 1893 to 1978 see the Protection of Employees (Employers' Insolvency) (Specification of Date) Regulations 1986 (S.I. No. 50 of 1986), the purpose of which is to specify the day on which a winding-up order was made or the resolution for voluntary winding-up was passed as being the day on which such bodies are to be regarded as having become insolvent for the purposes of the Act.

Appointment in certain circumstances of persons to perform functions assigned by Act to relevant officers

5.— (1) Where—

(a) by virtue of section 1(3)(d) of this Act, an employer becomes insolvent for the purposes of this Act, or
(b) an employer otherwise becomes insolvent for such purposes and there is not for the time being in relation to the insolvency a relevant officer,

the Minister may appoint as regards such insolvency a person under this subsection.

(2) Where the Minister makes an appointment under this section the following provisions shall apply:

(a) the functions assigned by this Act to a relevant officer shall, as regards the employer concerned, be performed by, and only by, the person to whom the appointment relates, or, if through illness or because his appointment is revoked or for any other reason the person so appointed is unable to perform such functions, another person so appointed, and

(b) for so long as the appointment remains in force, each of the references to a relevant officer in sections 6, 7 and 8 of this Act shall be construed as including a reference to the person to whom the appointment relates.

GENERAL NOTE

The procedure for assessing claims under sections 6 and 7 requires statements in a prescribed form to be sent to the Minister certifying the claims. These statements are to be made by the "relevant officer," who is defined in section 1(1). He may be an executor, administrator, liquidator, receiver, etc., depending on the nature of the insolvency. Section 5 makes provision for the appointment of a "relevant officer" by the Minister where no such person exists in relation to an insolvency.

For the relevant officer's functions, see section 6(5) and (6); section 7(6) and (7); and the decision of O'Hanlon J. in *Minister for Labour v. Grace* [1993] E.L.R. 50.

Employees' rights on insolvency of employer

6.— (1) If, on an application made to him in the prescribed form by or on behalf of an individual, the Minister is satisfied that–

(a) the person by or on whose behalf the application is made (which person is in this section subsequently referred to as "the applicant") is a person to whom this Act applies, and that he was employed by an employer who has become insolvent, and

(b) the date on which the employer becomes insolvent is a day not earlier than the 22nd day of October, 1983, and

(c) on the relevant date the applicant was entitled to be paid the whole or part of any debt to which this section applies,

the Minister shall, subject to this section, pay to or in respect of the applicant out of the [Social Insurance] Fund the amount which, in the opinion of the Minister, is or was due to the applicant in respect of that debt.

(2)(a) Subject to paragraph (b) of this subsection, the following are debts to which this section applies—

(i) any arrears of normal weekly remuneration in respect of a period, or of periods in the aggregate, not exceeding eight weeks, and to which the applicant became entitled during the relevant period,

(ii) any arrears due, in respect of a period or periods not exceeding eight weeks in all under a scheme or arrangement which, forming part of an employee's contract of employment, provides or is capable of providing in relation to employees in any description of employment, payments payable to any such employees in respect of periods during which they are unable to fulfil their contract of employment due to ill health and to which the applicant became entitled during the relevant period,

(iii) any amount which an employer is required to pay, by virtue of an award under section 12 of the Act of 1973 made not earlier than the commencement of the relevant period, either for the period of notice required by section 4 of the Act of 1973 or by reason of a failure by him to give the period of notice required by the said section 4,

(iv) any holiday pay in respect of a period or periods of holiday not exceeding eight weeks in all, and to which the applicant became entitled during the relevant period,

[(v) any amount which an employer is required to pay by virtue of—

(I) a determination under section 8(1) or 9(1) or an order under section 10(2) of the 1977 Act, or

(II) a decision, determination or order under Part V of the Maternity Protection Act 1994,

and made, in any case, not earlier than the commencement of the relevant period,]

(vi) any amount to which a recommendation under section 8(1) of the Act of 1977 relates, being a recommendation which was made not earlier than the commencement of the relevant period,

(vii) any amount which an employer is required to pay by virtue of an employment regulation order within the meaning of Part IV of the Industrial Relations Act 1946, being an amount by reference to which proceedings

224

have been instituted against the employer for an offence under section 45(1) of that Act,

(viii) any amount—

 (I) specified in a recommendation issued under section 7(3) of the Act of 1974, or section 19(3) of the Employment Equality Act 1977,

 (II) which an employer is required to pay by virtue of a decision or determination of an appeal by the Labour Court under subsection (1) of section 8 of the Act of 1974 or subsection (2) of section 21 of the Employment Equality Act 1977 or, where appropriate, a decision of the High Court given by virtue of either subsection (3) of the said section 8 or subsection (4) of the said section 21,

(ix) damages awarded under section 24(3)(a) of the Employment Equality Act 1977,

(x) a fine imposed under section 8(4)(c)(i) or paragraph (a) (inserted by section 30 of the Employment Equality Act 1977) of section 9(3) of the Act of 1974 or under section 25(3)(a)(iii) or 26(3)(a)(iii) of the Employment Equality Act 1977, and

(xi) compensation directed to be paid under section 10(1)(d) (inserted by section 31 of the Employment Equality Act 1977) or section 10(3)(a) (inserted by the said section 31) of the Act of 1974 or under section 26(1)(d)(iii) of the Employment Equality Act 1977.

(b) Any amount, damages, fine or compensation referred to in subparagraphs (viii), (ix), (x) or (xi) or paragraph (a) of this subsection shall be regarded as being a debt to which this section applies if, and only if, the relevant recommendation, decision, determination, award or order was made during, or after the expiration of, the relevant period.

(3) Where—

(a) legal proceedings are instituted by or on behalf of an employee and on foot of all or any of the following—

(i) a claim for arrears described in subparagraph (i) or (ii) of subsection (2) of this section,

(ii) a claim for holiday pay described in subparagraph (iv) of the said subsection (2),

(iii) a claim for damages at common law for wrongful dismissal,

225

an award is made by the court in favour of the employee, and

    (b) had the employee made an application under subsection (1) of this section in respect of any of the matters referred to in subparagraph (i), (ii) or (iii) of paragraph (a) of this subsection he would have satisfied the requirements of paragraphs (a), (b) and (c) of the said subsection (1),

subject to subsection (4)(a) of this section, there shall be paid out of the [Social Insurance] Fund, to or in respect of the employee, an amount equal to—

    (i) the amount of the award, or

    (ii) the maximum which would have been payable out of the said Fund by virtue of this Act had the employee successfully sought redress under section 8(1) or 9(1) of the Act of 1977.

(4)(a) The amount payable to an employee in respect of any debt mentioned in subsection (2) or award mentioned in subsection (3) of this section shall, where the amount of that debt is or may be calculated by reference to the employee's remuneration, not exceed [£300] in respect of any one week or, in respect of any period of less than a week, an amount bearing the same proportion to [£300] as that period bears to the normal weekly working hours of the employee at the relevant date.

    (b) An amount payable under this section in respect of a debt mentioned in subsection (2)(a)(ii) of that section as regards a particular period, shall not exceed the difference between the amount of any disability benefit or injury benefit payable under the Act of [1993] to the employee concerned as regards the period (together with, in either case, the amount of any pay-related benefit payable to such employee under the Act of [1993] as regards the period) and the amount of his normal weekly remuneration as regards the period.

    (c)(i) A payment shall not be made under this section in respect of an amount which an employer is required to pay by virtue of a determination having been made under section 8(1) or 9(1) of the Act of 1977, unless—

        (I) if proceedings are instituted under [section 11(3) of the Unfair Dismissals (Amendment) Act 1993], the proceedings are withdrawn, or

        (II) in case an appeal is brought under [section 11(1) of the Unfair Dismissals (Amendment) Act 1993] from

the determination, the appeal has been either withdrawn or determined, or

(III) in case there is no such appeal, the time for bringing
such an appeal has expired.

(ii) A payment shall not be made under this section in
respect of an amount to which a recommendation
under section 8(1) of the Act of 1977 relates unless—

(I) in case an appeal from the recommendation is
brought under section 9(1) of the Act of 1977, the
appeal is withdrawn, or

(II) in case there is no such appeal, the time for bringing
such an appeal has expired.

(iii) A payment shall not be made under this section as
regards a recommendation referred to in subsection
(2)(a)(viii)(I) of this section unless—

(I) in case an appeal is brought under section 8(1)(a) of
the Anti-Discrimination (Pay) Act 1974, or section
21(1) of the Employment Equality Act 1977, against
the recommendation, the appeal is withdrawn, or

(II) in case there is no such appeal, the time for bringing
such an appeal has expired.

[(iv) A payment shall not be made under this section in
respect of an amount to which a decision under Part V
of the Maternity Protection Act 1994 relates unless—

(I) in case an appeal from the decision to the Tribunal is
brought under the Part in question, the appeal is
withdrawn, or

(II) in case there is no such appeal, the time for bringing
such an appeal has expired.

(v) A payment shall not be made under this section in
respect of an amount to which a determination under
Part V of the Maternity Protection Act 1994, relates
unless—

(I) in case an appeal from the determination is brought
to the High Court under the Part in question, the
appeal is withdrawn, or

(II) in case there is no appeal, the time for bringing such
an appeal has expired.]

(5) The provisions of subsections (6) and (7) of this section shall
apply in a case where a relevant officer is either appointed or
required to be appointed.

(6) Subject to subsection (7) of this section, the Minister shall not
in a case which is a case referred to in subsection (5) of this section

make any payment under this section in respect of any debt until he has received a statement in the prescribed form from the relevant officer of the amount of that debt which appears to have been owed to the employee on the relevant date and to remain unpaid: and the relevant officer shall, on a request being made in that behalf, by the Minister, provide him, as soon as is reasonably practicable, with such a statement.

(7) Where—

(a) a period of six months has elapsed since the application for a payment under this section was received by the Minister, but no such payment has been made,

(b) the Minister is satisfied that a payment under this section should be made, and

(c) it appears to the Minister that there is likely to be further delay before he receives a statement referred to in subsection (6) of this section regarding the debt in question,

then, the Minister may, if the applicant so requests, or if the Minister thinks fit, without such a request make a payment under this section notwithstanding the fact that no such statement has been received.

(8) Where an application is made to the Minister under this section and in relation to any or each of the debts to which the application relates, the Minister is satisfied that—

(a) there was an agreement between the applicant and the employer concerned that the whole or any part of the debt would be the subject of an application under this section, and

(b) when the agreement was made such employer had the means to pay such debt or the part thereof,

the Minister may either refuse the application or disallow it in so far as it relates to such debt or part.

(9) In this section—

'normal weekly remuneration" has the meaning assigned to it by Schedule 3 to the Act of 1967 for the purposes of that Schedule save that any reference in that Schedule to the date on which an employee was declared redundant may, where appropriate, be construed as including a reference to the relevant date;

'the relevant date" means—

(a) in relation to a debt which is an amount, damages, fine or compensation referred to in subparagraph (ii),

> (v), (vi), (viii), (ix), (x) or (xi) or subsection (2)(a) of this section, the date on which the relevant employer became insolvent or the date on which the relevant recommendation, decision, determination, award or order is made, whichever is the later,
> (b) in relation to any other debt to which this section applies—
> (i) in case the relevant applicant's employment is terminated as a result of the relevant employer's insolvency, the date on which such employment became insolvent, or the date of such termination, whichever such applicant shall as regards the debt nominate, or
> (ii) in any other case, the date on which such employer became insolvent;
> 'the relevant period" means in relation to a debt to which this section applies, the period of 18 months immediately preceding the relevant date.
> (10) No reference in subsection (3) of this section to an award shall be construed as including a reference to any amount allowed as regards costs.

GENERAL NOTE

In section 6(2)(a)(i) for "normal weekly remuneration" see note to section 6(9). In *Minister for Labour v. O'Toole* [1990] I.L.R.M. 180 Murphy J. answered in the affirmative the question as to whether sums deducted from the weekly wages of an employee by the employer in respect of the employee's trade union membership, which said sums were not paid over for their designated purpose, was a debt to which section 6(2)(a)(i) applied. The "deduction notice" signed by the employee did not operate as an assignment and Murphy J. held that the employee had not divested herself of the right to recover the money. It was thus part of her normal weekly remuneration and Murphy J. saw no reason why the debt had not been paid out of the Fund.

In section 6(2)(a)(iii) "an award under section 12 of the Act of 1973" refers to an award of compensation made to an employee by the Employment Appeals Tribunal under section 12 of the Minimum Notice and Terms of Employment Act 1973. Such an award may be made against an employer for failing to give the employee the required notice under section 4 of that Act, or for the employer's failure to comply with the provisions of section 5 in relation to the rights of the employee during the period of notice. On the 1973 Act see generally *Bolands Ltd v. Ward* [1988] I.L.R.M. 382.

In section 6(2)(a)(v) "a determination under section 8(1) or 9(1) or an order under section 10(2) of the Act of 1977" refers to a determination made by the Employment Appeals Tribunal on a claim by an employee for redress for unfair dismissal, and to an order by the Circuit Court to an employer to make such redress to an employee. In *Freeney v. Ardiff Securities Ltd.* UD149/1987 the Tribunal held that the claimant had been unfairly dismissed and ordered that he be reinstated. On presenting himself for work he was told that the company was going

229

into liquidation and that everyone was being made redundant. Freeney subsequently claimed that he was entitled to be paid out of the Fund a sum representing accumulated arrears of salary and that such sum fell within the terms of section 6(2)(a)(v). The Tribunal rule, however (I 118/1987), that the payment was subject to the eight-week limit in section 6(2)(a)(i).

In section 6(2)(a)(vi) "a recommendation under section 8(1) of the Act of 1977" refers to a recommendation by a rights commissioner in relation to an employee's claim for redress for unfair dismissal under the Unfair Dismissals Act 1977.

Section 6(2)(a)(vii) refers to a situation where an employment regulation order has been made to fix statutory minimum remuneration under Part IV of the Industrial Relations Act 1946. An employer who pays an employee a sum less than the statutory minimum 1946. An employer who pays an employee a sum less than the statutory minimum remuneration is guilty of an offence under section 45(1) of that Act and can also be ordered remuneration is guilty of an offence under section 45(1) of that Act and can also be ordered by the court to pay the employee a sum representing the difference between the statutory minimum remuneration and the remuneration actually paid. On the interpretation of section 45 see *Minister for Labour v. Costello* [1988] I.R. 135.

Section 6(2)(a)(viii)(I) concerns, first, an amount which was specified to be paid to an employee in a recommendation issued by an equality officer arising out of a dispute over equal pay under section 7(3) of the Anti-Discrimination (Pay) Act 1974; or, secondly, an amount to be paid under a recommendation of an equality officer arising from a dispute amount to be paid under a recommendation of an equality officer arising from a dispute over discrimination under section 19(3) of the Employment Equality Act 1977. On both Acts see Curtin, *Irish Employment Equality Law* (1989).

Section 6(2)(a)(viii)(II) refers to situations in which appeals have been made against recommendations of the equality officer (see above), or where appeals have been made for a determination that the equality officer's recommendations have not been implemented. The employee can claim from the Social Insurance Fund for an amount required to be paid to him by his employer following the decision or determination of the appeal by the Labour Court, or where a further appeal is made, following the decision of the High Court.

Section 6(2)(a)(ix) refers to a claim for damages which arises where a Labour Court determination, following an appeal from the recommendation of an equality officer on alleged discrimination, has not been implemented. In such an event a complaint can be made to the Labour Court which can order implementation to be effected. If implementation is not achieved within two months the person concerned is guilty of an offence and may be fined. The court can award damages to the plaintiff for remuneration lost in connection with the discrimination, but not exceeding 104 weeks' remuneration in total.

Section 6(2)(a)(x) allows claims to be made for fines arising under the Anti-Discrimination (Pay) Act 1974 and the Employment Equality Act 1977 which are payable to the employee. These fines arise:

(1) where an employer has failed to implement a determination of the Labour Court on an equal-pay dispute and a complaint to that effect has been made to the Labour Court which has ordered implementation. An offence is then committed by failure to carry the order into effect within two months. A fine amounting to arrears of remuneration may be imposed on the employer which is payable to the employee.

230

(2) where an employer is convicted of the offence of the offence of dismissing an employee for bringing an equal-pay claim. This fine, which is in addition to any other fine, amounts to a sum for remuneration which would have been paid had dismissal not occurred, but not exceeding 104 weeks' remuneration. A similar fine is payable to the employee where the employer has been prosecuted for dismissing the employee for pursuing certain matters under the Anti-Discrimination Pay Act 1974 or Employment Equality Act 1977. A similar fine is also payable where the employee complains to the Labour Court that he or she was dismissed due to his or her pursuing these rights and the employer was prosecuted for an offence in not implementing an order of the Labour Court to pay compensation to the dismissed employee within two months.

Section 6(2)(a)(xi) refers

(1) to compensation payable to an employee following a complaint to the Labour Court of having been dismissed for having made an equal-pay claim;

(2) to a fine payable to the employee where the employer was convicted of the offence of not paying within two months the compensation ordered by the Labour Court in (1) above;

(3) to compensation payable to an employee following a complaint to the Labour Court of having been dismissed for having pursued certain matters under the Anti-Discrimination (Pay) Act 1974 or the Employment Equality Act 1977.

Subsection (1)

This subsection sets out the conditions which employees must satisfy to be eligible to receive payment of certain debts due to them because of their employer's insolvency.

The applicant must have been entitled to all or part of the debt claimed on the "relevant date" (see section 6(9)). The relevant date varies, however, with the type of claim made. In the case of claims arising out of legislation governing minimum notice, unfair dismissal, pay discrimination or employment equality, the relevant date is the date on which the employer became insolvent or the date the relevant body granted the claim, whichever is the later. In other cases, such as in claims for arrears of pay, the relevant date depends on whether the applicant's employment was terminated by his employer's insolvency or not. The "relevant period" is defined as the period of 18 months immediately preceding the relevant date (section 6(9)). Claims for arrears of pay are limited in that they must have arisen during the relevant period. In the case of other claims, they must not have arisen earlier than the commencement of the relevant period (see note on subsection (2) below).

Subsection (2)

A claim can only be made in respect of awards arising under the Minimum Notice and Terms of Employment Act 1973, the Unfair Dismissals Act 1977, the Anti-Discrimination (Pay) Act 1974 and the Employment Equality Act 1977, where such awards were made during or after the commencement of the "relevant period". The "relevant period" is the period of 18 months immediately preceding the "relevant date". The "relevant date" in respect of these debts is the date of the employer's insolvency or the date of the award, whichever is the later (see section 6(9)). In other words, no application can be made until the award is made and the employer is insolvent, and the award must not have been made more than 18 months prior to the application. *Quaere* whether awards under the Payment of Wages Act 1991 come within the scope of section 6.

231

A claim in respect of other debts, such as arrears of pay, can only be made where they accrued due during the "relevant period". In this case the "relevant period" is also the 18 months immediately preceding the "relevant date". The "relevant date", however, depends on whether the applicant's employment was terminated by his employer's insolvency. If it was, the applicant can choose the insolvency date or the date of termination of his employment as the "relevant date". If the employee was entitled to the debt on the date chosen, and if it had accrued due in the preceding 18 months, he satisfies the requirements of the Act. Where the applicant's employment was not terminated by the insolvency, the relevant date is the employer's insolvency. In other words, the applicant cannot in this case make a claim until the date of the employer's insolvency and the debt must have accrued due in the preceding 18 months. Paragraph (v) was substituted by virtue of section 41(2) of the Maternity Protection Act 1994. Section 40(a) of the Adoptive Leave Act 1995 provides that the references in subparagraph (v) of paragraph (a) to a "determination or order" should be construed as including references to a decision, determination or order under Part V of that Act.

Subsections (3) and (4)

Under section 6(3) a claim can be made from the Fund in relation to an award by the court arising out of civil proceedings under which an employee claimed arrears of remuneration, sick pay, or holiday pay, or in which he claimed common-law damages for wrongful dismissal. If the employee satisfies the conditions of eligibility for protection under section 6(1) he is entitled to be paid out of the Fund the amount of the court award or the maximum payable had he sought redress under the Unfair Dismissals Act 1977.

Section 6(4), however, limits the amount payable in respect of any debt claimed, which is calculated by reference to the employee's remuneration, to a maximum of £300 in respect of one week or *pro rata* for periods less than a week. In *Cronin v. Red Abbey Garage (PMPA) Ltd.* UD871/1984 the claimant, whose gross weekly wage was £357.64, was awarded compensation of £5,251.40. The company went into liquidation and the claimant sought payment of his award from the Fund under section 6(2)(a)(v). The Minister referred to the Tribunal the question of the amount payable bearing in mind the then limit of £211.54. The Secretary of the Division of the Tribunal which heard the claimant's unfair-dismissal case gave evidence that it was agreed that the claimant's net weekly wage was £207.80 and that the award was based on this figure. Accordingly the Tribunal ruled (I 13/1987) that it was satisfied "that the award was calculated within the parameters of section 6(4)(a)" and it made a declaration that the Minister was liable to make payment to the claimant in the amount of £5,251.40. The amount recoverable in relation to any sick-pay scheme is also limited to the difference between normal weekly remuneration and the sum of any disability or injury benefit and any pay-related benefit payable for the period. The limit on wage-related payments (now £300) is the same as that provided for under the Redundancy Payments Acts. It was increased by order (see General Note to section 11) from £211.54 and then £250 and the increased ceiling will apply to debts arising under the Act where the date of termination of employment or the date of insolvency is on or after May 1, 1994: Protection of Employees (Employers' Insolvency) (Variation of Limit) Regulations 1994 (S.I. No. 62 of 1994). The Tribunal has held (*Minister for Labour v. Monaghan* I 24/1990) that the limit relates to the amount of the debt, not to the amount of weekly pay.

No payments can be made from the Fund in respect of entitlements arising under the Unfair Dismissals, Anti-Discrimination (Pay) and Employment Equality

Acts which are subject to appeal unless any appeal brought has been withdrawn or determined, or the time for lodging appeals has expired (section 6(4)(c)).

The words in square brackets in subsection 3(c)(i) were substituted by virtue of the repeal of section 10 of the Unfair Dismissals Act 1977 by section 16 of the Unfair Dismissals (Amendment) Act 1993 and that section's replacement by section 11 of the 1993 Act. Section 40(b) of the Adoptive Leave Act 1995 provides that the references in subparagraph (1) of subsection (4)(c) to a "determination" should be construed as including references to a decision or determination under Part V of that Act and that the reference in clause (II) of the said subparagraph to what is now section 11(1) of the Unfair Dismissals (Amendment) Act 1993 should be construed as including a reference to section 35 or 36 of the 1995 Act. Subparagraphs (iv) and (v) of subsection (4)(c) were inserted by virtue of section 41(3) of the Maternity Protection Act 1994.

Subsection (9)

Under section 6(2)(a)(i) a claim can be made for up to eight weeks' arrears of "normal weekly remuneration." In *Doorley v. Minister for Labour* I 14/1987 the claimant's employer had gone into liquidation just before Christmas and the claimant consequently did not receive his annual Christmas bonus. He contended that his entitlement to this £100 bonus should be dealt with separately under the Act. The Department contended, however, that under section 6(9) the way to treat the bonus was to regard it as a payment which was not paid in respect of one particular week but which accrued over the 52 weeks of the year. The Department's submission that the correct calculation of the amount due was on the basis of £100 divided by 52 and multiplied by 8 was upheld by the Tribunal. Section 6(9) defines normal weekly remuneration as having the meaning assigned to it by Schedule 3 to the Redundancy Payments Act 1967 save that the "relevant date" replaces the "date on which an employee was declared redundant." Paragraphs 13 and 14 of Schedule 3 provide as follows:

Normal Weekly Remuneration

13. For the purposes of this Schedule, in the case of an employee who is paid wholly by an hourly time rate or by a fixed wage or salary, and in the case of any other employee whose remuneration does not vary in relation to the amount of work done by him, his normal weekly remuneration shall be taken to be his earnings (including any regular bonus or allowance which does not vary in relation to the amount of work done) for his normal weekly working hours as at the date on which he was declared redundant, together with, in the case of an employee who is expected to work overtime regularly, his average weekly overtime earnings as determined in accordance with paragraph 14.

14. For the purpose of paragraph 13 the average weekly overtime earnings shall be determined by ascertaining the total amount of overtime earnings of the employee concerned in the period of 26 weeks which ended 13 weeks before the date on which the employee was declared redundant and dividing that amount by 26.

The schedule also provides rules for the calculation of normal weekly remuneration in the case of an employee who is paid wholly or partly by piece rates, bonuses or commissions; where he receives additional remuneration for working more than a fixed number of hours; where he works on a shift cycle or has no normal working hours.

Statutory Instruments

Protection of Employees (Employers' Insolvency) (Forms and Procedure) Regulations 1984 (S.I. No. 356 of 1984); Protection of Employees (Employers' Insolvency) (Forms and Procedures) (Amendment) Regulations 1991 (S.I. No. 349 of 1991).

Payment of unpaid contributions to occupational pension scheme

7.— (1) If, on an application made to him in the prescribed form by an employee or by the persons competent to act in respect of an occupational pension scheme, the Minister is satisfied that—

(a) an employer (being in case the application is made by a person otherwise than in his capacity as the person competent so to act the employer of the applicant) has become insolvent,

(b) the date on which for the purposes of this Act the employer became insolvent is a day not earlier than the 22nd day of October, 1983, and

(c) on that day there remained unpaid relevant contributions remaining to be paid by the employer to the scheme,

on the date on which the employer became insolvent, being a date not earlier than the said 22nd day of October the Minister shall, subject to this section, pay into the assets of the scheme out of the [Social Insurance] Fund the sum which in his opinion is payable in respect of the unpaid relevant contribution.

(2) In this section "relevant contributions" means contributions falling to be paid by an employer in accordance with an occupational pension scheme, either on his own account or on behalf of an employee; provided that for the purposes of this section a contribution of any amount shall not be treated as falling to be paid on behalf of an employee unless a sum equal to that amount has been deducted from the pay of the employee by way of a contribution from him.

(3) The sum payable under this section in respect of unpaid contributions of an employer on his own account to an occupational pension scheme shall be the lesser of the following amounts—

(a) the balance of relevant contributions remaining unpaid on the date on which he became insolvent and payable by the employer on his own account to the scheme in respect

234

of the period of 12 months ending on the day immediately preceding that date,

(b) the amount certified by an actuary to be necessary for the purpose of meeting the liability of the scheme on dissolution to pay the benefits provided by the scheme to or in respect of the employees of the employer.

(4) Any sum payable under this section in respect of unpaid contributions on behalf of an employee shall not exceed the amount deducted from the pay of the employee in respect of the employee's contributions to the occupational pension scheme during the period of 12 months ending on the day immediately preceding the date on which the employer became insolvent.

(5) The provisions of subsections (6), (7) and (8) of this section shall apply in a case where a relevant officer is either appointed or required to be appointed.

(6) Subject to subsection (8) of this section, the Minister shall not in a case which is a case referred to in subsection (5) of this section make any payment under this section in respect of unpaid relevant contributions until he has received a statement in the prescribed form from the relevant officer of the amount of relevant contributions which appear to have been unpaid; and the relevant officer shall, on request made by the Minister provide him, as soon as reasonably practicable, with such a statement.

(7) Subject to subsection (8) of this section, an amount shall be taken to be payable under subsection (3) or to have been deducted in the manner referred to in subsection (3) or to have been deducted in the manner referred to in subsection (4) of this section, only if it is certified by the relevant officer as being so payable, or to have been so deducted.

(8) Where—

(a) a period of six months has elapsed since the application for a payment under this section was received by the Minister, but no such payment has been made,

(b) the Minister is satisfied that a payment under this section should be made, and

(c) it appears to the Minister that there is likely to be further delay before he receives a statement or certificate about the contributions in question,

then, the Minister may, if the applicant so requests or, if the Minister thinks fit, without such a request, make a payment under this section, notwithstanding the fact that no statement or certificate

235

referred to in subsection (6) or (7) of this section has been received.

GENERAL NOTE

This section allows claims to be made from the Social Insurance Fund where an insolvent employer has failed to pay contributions in accordance with an occupational pension scheme: see *In re Cavan Rubber Ltd.* [1992] E.L.R. 79. It covers contributions that should have been paid into the scheme by the employer, and contributions deducted from employees' wages which were not paid into the assets of the scheme by the employer. The maximum sum payable out of the Fund in respect of the employer's unpaid contributions is the lesser of

(a) the balance of unpaid contributions during he 12 months preceding the insolvency date; or

(b) the amount certified by an actuary as being necessary to meet the liability of the scheme to pay the benefits provided by the scheme.

The maximum sum payable in respect of employees' unpaid contributions is the amount deducted and payable in the 12 months immediately preceding the insolvency date. Regulations prescribe forms (known as IP6 and IP7) to be used and procedures to be followed in such applications. The forms require that documentary evidence, details of the subscription rate and a breakdown of the unpaid contributions in the 12 months prior to the date of insolvency should be attached to the application.

Considerable dissatisfaction was expressed in both house of the Oireachtas concerning the limited nature of the protection proposed for employee pension rights in an insolvency situation. An amendment was proposed whereby an employee could claim entitlements arising in the event of losing his ongoing pension payments owing to his employer's insolvency. this was rejected on the grounds that the costs would be substantial and could not be imposed upon employers only. In addition a comprehensive national income-related pension scheme was being considered by the Department of Social Welfare.

The decision of the Tribunal in *O'Sullivan v. Minister for Labour* I 12/1987 revealed an unfortunate lacuna. The claimant and seven other employees were due to be made redundant in May 1986 but the claimant was asked to stay on until the company went into receivership on July 16. On June 10 a cheque for nearly £4,500 was forwarded to the employer from the trustees of the pension fund to cover refunds of the pension contributions of the eight. The claimant never received a refund of her contributions and she sought payment from the Fund under section 6(2)(a)(i). The claimant submitted that, as deductions were made and then refunded to her employer, the net effect to her was that the deductions were not passed to the pension company. The Department argued, however, that the claimant did not come within the scope of sections 6 and 7 because the pension contributions were deducted with the claimant's agreement from her wages and were then passed to the trustees of the pension scheme. The Tribunal agreed with the Department, holding that there was "no provision within the 1984 Act covering the discharge of monies from a pension fund once applied back to the employer/employee."

Statutory Instrument

Protection of Employees (Employers' Insolvency) (Occupational Pension Scheme) (Forms and Procedure) Regulations 1990 (S.I. No. 121 of 1990).

Minister may require certain information and documents

8.— (1) Where an application is made to the Minister under section 6 or 7 of this Act in respect of a debt owed or unpaid contributions to an occupational pensions scheme, the Minister may require—

    (a) the employer concerned, or, in case a relevant officer is or is required to be appointed, that officer, to provide him with such information as the Minister may reasonably require for the purpose of determining whether the application is well-founded, and

    (b) any person having the custody or control of any relevant record kept and retained pursuant to section 10 of the Holidays (Employees) Act 1973, or any register, card, wages sheet, record of wages or other document which an officer of the Minister may reasonably consider to be relevant to the application to produce to such an officer such document for examination by him.

(2) A requirement under this section shall be made by notice in writing given to the person on whom the requirement is imposed and may be varied or revoked by a subsequent notice so given.

Complaints to Tribunal

9.— (1) A person who has applied for payment under section 6 of this Act of a debt described in subparagraph (i), (ii) or (iv) of subsection 2(a) of that section may within the period of six weeks beginning on the day on which the decision of the Minister on the application was communicated to him or, if that is not reasonably practicable, within such further period as the Tribunal considers reasonable, present a complaint to the Tribunal that—

    (a) the Minister has failed to make any such payment; or

    (b) any such payment made by the Minister is less than the amount which should have been paid.

(2) Any person who has applied for a payment to be made under section 7 of this Act into the resources of a pension scheme may, within the period of six weeks beginning on the day on which the decision of the Minister on that application was communicated to him, or, if that is not reasonably practicable, within such further period as the Tribunal considers reasonable, present a complaint to the Tribunal that—

(a) the Minister has failed to make any such payment; or

(b) any such payment made by him is less than the amount which should have been paid.

(3) Where a claim for payment is made under section 6 or 7 of this Act and it appears to the Minister that a doubt exists as to whether or not such a claim is allowable, either in whole or in part, he may refer any matter arising in connection with the claim to the Tribunal for a decision by it as regards the matter.

(4) Where on the hearing of a complaint presented under this section the Tribunal finds that the Minister is liable to make a payment under section 6 or 7 of this act, it shall make a declaration to that effect and shall specify in the declaration the amount of such payment.

(5) Subsection (14) of section 39 of the Act of 1967 shall apply to a decision of the Tribunal on any matter referred to it under this section as it applies to a decision of the Tribunal on a question referred to it under that section.

GENERAL NOTE

This section provides that complaints may be presented to the Employment Appeals Tribunal by employees or persons acting on behalf of a pension scheme where the Minister fails to make a payment or where the payment is considered to be less than the amount which should have been paid. Complaints must normally be presented within six weeks of the communicated decision. In the case of employees, complaints can relate only to claims concerning arrears of remuneration, sick pay and holiday pay. Appeals in relation to entitlements under the Unfair Dismissals Act 1977 and the other worker-protection statutes were not included on the basis that disagreement in relation to the amounts involved would be unlikely to arise. These entitlements would have already been considered by an independent dispute settlement body.

The Minister is also empowered to refer any doubtful claim under sections 6 or 7 to the Tribunal for a decision as to whether it should be allowed. The Tribunal does not have the power to award costs: see *In re Cavan Rubber Ltd.* [1992] E.L.R. 79, 83.

In section 9(5) the reference to "subsection (14) of section 39 of the Act of 1967" refers to the Redundancy Payments Act 1967, where the particular subsection (as amended by section 18 of the Unfair Dismissals Act 1977) states that the decision of the Employment Appeals Tribunal is final and conclusive save that appeals can be made to the High Court on a question of law.

Transfer to Minister of certain rights and remedies

10.— (1) Where, in pursuance of section 6 of this Act, the Minister makes any payment to an employee in respect of any debt to which that section applies, any rights and remedies of the employee in respect of that debt (or, if the Minister has paid only part of it, in respect of that part) shall, on the making of the payment, become rights and remedies of the Minister.

(2) Without prejudice to the generality of subsection (1) of this section, where rights and remedies become, by virtue of subsection (1) of this section, rights and remedies of the Minister, there shall be included amongst them any right to be paid in priority to all other debts under—

(a) [section 81 of the Bankruptcy Act 1988]; or
(b) section 285, as amended by section 10 of the Companies (Amendment) Act 1982 [and section 134 of the Companies Act 1990] of the Companies Act 1963,

and the Minister shall be entitled to be so paid in priority to any other unsatisfied claim of the employee concerned being a claim which, but for this subsection, would be payable to the employee in such priority; and in computing for the purposes of any of the provisions of the said [section 81] or the said section 285, as so amended, any limit on the amount of sums to be paid, any sums paid to the Minister shall be treated as if they had been paid to the employee.

(3) Where in pursuance to section 7 of this Act the Minister makes any payment into the resources of an occupational pension scheme in respect of any contributions to the scheme, any rights and remedies in respect of those contributions belonging to the persons competent to act in respect of the scheme shall, on the making of the payment, become rights and remedies of the Minister.

(4) Any sum recovered by the Minister in exercising any right or pursuing any remedy which is his by virtue of this section shall be paid into the [Social Insurance] Fund.

GENERAL NOTE

This section provides that where payments are made from the Fund to an employee, or into the resources of an occupational pension scheme, any rights or remedies belonging to the employee or to the persons competent to act in respect of the scheme become the rights and remedies of the Minister. The Minister becomes entitled to the same priority as regards such rights and remedies in bankruptcy or liquidation proceedings as the employee had.

Section 81 of the Bankruptcy Act 1988, replacing section 4 of the Preferential Payments in Bankruptcy (Ireland) Act 1889, provides, in relevant part, that, in the distribution of the property of a bankrupt, there shall be paid in priority to all other debts:

(i) all wages or salary, not exceeding £2,500, of any clerk, servant, labourer or workman in respect of services rendered to the bankrupt during the four months before the date of the order of adjudication;

(ii) all accrued holiday remuneration payable;

(iii) all sums due pursuant to any scheme or arrangement for the provision of benefits to employees while absent from employment owing to ill health; and

(iv) all compensation payable under the Minimum Notice and Terms of Employment Act 1973 and the Unfair Dismissals Act 1977.

For preferential payments in the winding-up of limited companies see the similarly worded provisions of section 285 of the Companies Act 1963 as amended by section 13 of the Minimum Notice and Terms of Employment Act 1973, section 12 of the Unfair Dismissals Act 1977, section 10 of the Companies (Amendment) Act 1982 and section 134 of the Companies Act 1990.

Prior to the Bankruptcy Act 1988 the preferential claims of employees in the event of the bankruptcy of their employer were inadequate. Accrued holiday remuneration did no rank as a preferential payment. In respect of wages or salary, "clerks and servants" were limited to £50 and "labourers and workmen" were limited to £25.

Power to amend Act

11.— (1) The Minister may from time to time by order amend section 3 of this Act so as to—

(a) extend the application of this Act to employees who are of a class or description specified in the order,

(b) exclude from such application employees who are of a class or description so specified.

(2) The Minister may from time to time by order amend section 6 of this Act so as to effect either or both of the following—

(a) substitute for the number of weeks specified in all or any of the following subsections, namely subsection (2)(a)(i), (2)(a)(ii) or (2)(a)(iv) a different number of weeks.

(b) substitute for the number of months specified in the definition of "the relevant period" contained in subsection (9) thereof a different number of months.

(3) The Minister may from time to time by order amend section 4(2), as amended by section 17 of the Redundancy Payments Act 1979, and by section 12 of this Act, of the Act of 1967, so as to vary the number of hours specified therein.

(4) The Minister may from time to time by order amend—

(a) paragraph (a) of section 3(1), as amended by section 13 of this Act, of the Act of 1973,

(b) paragraph 8, as amended by the said section 13, of the First Schedule to the Act of 1973,

so as to vary the number of hours specified in that paragraph.

(5) The Minister may by regulation amend section 6 of this Act so as to vary the limit specified in subsection (4)(a).

(6) The reference in section 2(4) of the Act of 1977 to the First Schedule to the Act of 1973 shall be construed as being a reference—

(a) in case an order under this section amending that Schedule is for the time being in force, that Schedule as amended by section 20 of the Act of 1977, by section 13 of this Act and by the order,

(b) in case no such order is so in force, that Schedule as amended both by the said section 20 and the said section 13.

(7) Where an order under this section is proposed to be made, the Minister shall cause a draft of the order to be laid before each House of the Oireachtas and the order shall not be made until a resolution approving of the draft has been passed by each such House.

GENERAL NOTE

This section provides that the Minister may by order amend certain provisions of the Act from time to time. He may alter the classes of employees to whom the Act applies; alter the number of weeks for which normal weekly remuneration, sick pay or holiday pay can be claimed, or the number of months in the "relevant period" within which certain claims must have accrued. The Protection of Employees (Employers' Insolvency) Act 1984 (Amendment Order) Order 1988 (S.I. No. 48 of 1988) extends the protection of the Act to employees over the age of 66 who are in employment which, but for their age, would be insurable for all benefits under the Social Welfare Acts.

It also enables the Minister to alter by order the number of hours an employee must work for the same employer to qualify for eligibility under the Redundancy Payments Act 1967 (section 4(2)), the Minimum Notice and Terms of Employment Act 1973 (section 3(1)(a)), and the Unfair Dismissals Act 1977 (i.e. number of hours to be worked per week for the purpose of computing a period of service and, consequently, eligibility under the Act).

The Minister can change by order the maximum amount payable to an employee (presently £300) in respect of any one week under section 6(4)(a) of this Act, where the amount of the employee's debt is calculated on the basis of his or her remuneration. The original limit of £211.54 was increased to £250 by the Protection of Employees (Employers' Insolvency) (Variation of Limit) Regulations 1990 (S.I. No. 17 of 1990) and to its present level by the Protection of Employees (Employers' Insolvency) (Variation of Limits) Regulations 1994 (S.I. No. 62 of 1994).

241

Writing in (1989) 11 D.U.L.J. (n.s.) 74, Whyte (at page 81) submits that section 11 is contrary to Article 15.2 of the Constitution, "given that it attempts to delegate the power of the Oireachtas to make legislation" and queries the validity of S.I. No. 48 of 1988.

Amendment of section 4 of the Act of 1967

12.— Subsection (2) of section 4, as amended by section 17 of the Redundancy Payments Act 1979, of the Act of 1967 is hereby amended by the substitution of "18 hours" for "20 hours", and the said subsection (2), as so amended, is set out in the Table to this section.

Table

(2) This Act shall not apply to a person who is normally expected to work for the same employer for less than 18 hours in a week.

GENERAL NOTE

This section provides for the reduction of the weekly threshold for eligibility under the Redundancy Payments Acts from 20 hours to 18 hours. See now the Worker Protection (Regular Part-Time Employees) Act 1991 reducing it, in the case of "regular part-time employees", to 8 hours.

Amendment of section 3 of and First Schedule to Act of 1973

13.— The Act of 1973 is hereby amended by—

    (a) the substitution in paragraph (a) of section 3(1) of "18 hours" for "twenty-one hours", and
    (b) the substitution of "18 hours" for "twenty-one hours" in paragraph 8 of the First Schedule;

and the said paragraphs (a) and 8, as so amended, are set out in paragraphs 1 and 2, respectively, of the Table to this section.

Table

1. (a) employment of an employee who is normally expected to work for the same employer for less than 18 hours in a week.
2. 8. Any week in which an employee is not normally expected to work for at least 18 hours or more will not count in computing a period of service.

GENERAL NOTE

This section provides for the reduction of the weekly threshold for eligibility under the Minimum Notice and Terms of Employment Act 1973 and the Unfair Dismissals Act 1977 from 21 to 18 hours. See now the Worker Protection (Regular Part-Time Employees) Act 1991 reducing it, in the case of "regular part-time employees", to 8 hours.

Institution of proceedings for offence

14.— Proceedings for an offence under section 15 of this Act shall not be instituted except by or with the consent of the Minister.

Offences

15.— (1) If any person, in relation to an application under section 6 or 7 of this Act, whether for himself or for some other person,

    (a) knowingly makes any false statement or false representation or knowingly conceals a material fact, or

    (b) produces or furnishes, or causes or knowingly allows to be produced or furnished, any document or information which he knows to be false in a material particular, he shall be guilty of an offence.

(2) If a person refuses or wilfully neglects to provide any information or produce any document which he has been required to provide or produce by a notice under section 8 of this Act he shall be guilty of an offence.

(3) If a person, in purporting to comply with a requirement of a notice under section 8 of this Act, knowingly or recklessly makes any false statement he shall be guilty of an offence.

(4) A person who is guilty of an offence under this section shall be liable on summary conviction to a fine not exceeding £500.

(5) [Subsections (7) and (8) of section 213 of the Act of 1993] shall apply in relation to an offence under this section which is committed by a body corporate as they apply to offences under [the Act of 1993] which are so committed.

(6) [Subsection (9) of section 213 of the Act of 1993] shall be construed and have effect as if the reference therein to proceedings under [the Act of 1993] contained a reference to proceedings under this section.

GENERAL NOTE

Subsections (7), (8) and (9) of section 213 of the Social Welfare (Consolidation) Act 1993 provide as follows:

(7) Where an offence under this Act is committed by a body corporate and, in the case of an offence under subsection (1), where the offence is committed by an employee or officer of the body corporate, and is proved to have been so committed with the consent, connivance or approval of or to have been attributable to any wilful neglect on the part of any person, being a director, manager, secretary or any other officer of the body corporate or a person who was purporting to act in any such capacity, that person, as well as the body corporate, shall be guilty of an offence and shall be liable to be proceeded against and punished as if he were guilty of the first-mentioned offence.

(8) It shall be a defence to a prosecution for an offence under subsection (7) for a person to show that the offence was committed without his knowledge and that he exercised all such diligence to prevent the commission of the offence as he ought to have exercised, having regard to the nature of his position as director, manager, secretary or other officer and to all the circumstances.

(9) Any summons or other document required to be served for the purpose of proceedings under this Act on a body corporate may be served—
   (a) by leaving it at or sending it by post to the registered office of the body corporate,
   (b) by leaving it or sending it by post to any place in the State at which the body corporate conducts business, or
   (c) by sending it by post to any person who is a director, manager, secretary or other officer of the body corporate or is purporting to act in any such capacity at the place where that person resides.

Regulations

16.— (1) The Minister may make regulations for giving effect to this Act.

(2) Without prejudice to the generality of subsection (1) of this section, regulations under this section may make provision requiring an applicant under section 6 or 7 of this Act to make the application within the prescribed time.

(3) The minister may make regulations for prescribing any matter referred to in this Act as prescribed.

(4) Regulations under this section may apply to applications under this Act generally or to such applications which are of a specified class or description.

(5) Every regulation made under this Act by the Minister shall be laid before both House of the Oireachtas as soon as may be after it is made and, if a resolution annulling the regulation is passed by either such House within the next 21 days on which that House has sat after the regulation is laid before it, the regulation shall be

annulled accordingly but without prejudice to the validity of anything previously done thereunder.

Statutory Instruments

Protection of Employees (Employers' Insolvency) (Forms and Procedure) Regulations 198 (S.I. No. 356 of 1984).

Protection of Employees (Employers' Insolvency) Act 1984 (Amendment Order) Order 1988 (S.I. No. 48 of 1988).

Protection of Employees (Employers' Insolvency) (Occupational Pension Scheme) (Forms and Procedure) Regulations 1990 (S.I. No. 121 of 1990).

Protection of Employees (Employers' Insolvency) (Forms and Procedure) (Amendment) Regulations 1991 (S.I. No. 349 of 1991).

Protection of Employees (Employers' Insolvency) (Variation of Limit) Regulations 1994 (S.I. No. 62 of 1994).

Expenses, etc.

17.— (1) The expenses incurred by the Minister in the administration of this Act shall, to such extent as may be sanctioned by the Minister for Finance, be paid out of moneys provided by the Oireachtas.

(2) The Minister may pay out of the [Social Insurance] Fund to a relevant officer or a person to whom an appointment under section 5 of this Act relates, in respect of the functions performed by him under this Act, such fees as the Minister shall, with the concurrence of the Minister for Finance, determine.

Short title and collective citations

18.— (1) This Act may be cited as the Protection of Employees (Employers' Insolvency) Act 1984.

(2) Section 12 of this Act and the Redundancy Payments Acts 1967 to 1979, may be cited together as the Redundancy Payments Acts 1967 to 1984.

(3) Section 13 of this Act and the Act of 1973 may be cited together as the Minimum Notice and Terms of Employment Acts 1973 and 1984.

GENERAL NOTE

Section 1(5) of the Social Welfare Act 1990 provides that section 28 of that Act and this Act may be cited together as the Protection of Employees (Employers' Insolvency) Acts 1984 and 1990. The collective citation— the Protection of Employees (Employers' Insolvency) Acts 1984 to 1991— now includes the Worker Protection (Regular Part-Time Employees) Act 1991 in so far as it relates to those Acts.

PROTECTION OF EMPLOYEES (EMPLOYERS' INSOLVENCY) (FORMS AND PROCEDURE) REGULATIONS 1984

S.I. No. 356 of 1984

1. These Regulations may be cited as the Protection of Employees (Employers' Insolvency) (Forms and Procedure) Regulations 1984.

2. In these Regulations "the Act" means the Protection of Employees (Employers' Insolvency) Act 1984 (No. 21 of 1984).

3. The following forms [or forms to the like effect] shall be used as regards applications under section 6 of the Act.

    (a) in the case of applications for payment in respect of unpaid normal weekly remuneration, entitlements under a sick pay scheme or holiday pay, the form (Form IP1) set out in Part I of the Schedule to these Regulations,

    (b) in the case of applications for payment of unpaid awards made by the Employment Appeals Tribunal as regards entitlements under the Act of 1973, the form (Form IP2) set out in Part II of the said Schedule, and

    (c) in the case of applications for payment of entitlements payable under the Act of 1974, the Act of 1977 or the Employment Equality Act 1977 (No. 16 of 1977), any amount described in subparagraph (vii) of section 6(2)(a) of the Act or applications for payment in respect of a claim described in subparagraph (iii) of section 6(3)(a) of the Act, the form (Form IP4) set out in Part III of the said Schedule.

4. An application under section 6 of the Act shall be made to the Minister—

    (a) in case, in relation to the insolvency of the employer concerned, a person stands for the time being appointed under section 5 of the Act, through that person, and

(b) in any other case—
    (i) where there is for the time being in relation to the employer concerned a relevant officer, through that officer,
    (ii) where there is not for the time being in relation to such employer a relevant officer, by being sent to the Secretary, [Department of [Enterprise and Employment], Davitt House, 65A Adelaide Road, Dublin 2.]

5. (1) Where an application under section 6 of the Act is, pursuant to Regulation 4 of these Regulations, received by a relevant officer or a person appointed under section 5 of the Act, the officer or person, having examined the application, shall, as soon as may be, forward a copy thereof to the Minister accompanied by a statement prepared by such officer or person as regards the application.

(2) The following forms [or forms to the like effect] shall be used as regards statements required by paragraph (1) of this Regulation—

(a) in case the application to which such a statement relates is an application described in paragraph (a) or (b) of Regulation 3 of these Regulations, the form (Form IP3) set out in Part IV of the Schedule to these Regulations,
(b) in case such application is an application described in paragraph (c) of the said Regulation 3, the form (Form IP5) set out in Part V of the said Schedule.

6. (1) Where an application under section 6 of the Act is received by the Minister through a relevant officer or a person appointed under section 5 of the Act, unless the Minister is satisfied that there are particular reasons for making the payment directly to the applicant, any payment falling to be made on foot of the application shall be made to the officer or person through whom it was received.

(2) Where a payment is made by a relevant officer or a person appointed under section 5 of the Act by reason of an application under section 6 of the Act, such relevant officer or person shall, as soon as may be, inform the Minister in writing, of the making of the payment and also whether or not, in relation to the amount payable on foot of the application, any deductions have been made by him as regards income tax, pay related social insurance or pension scheme contributions, and in case any such deductions are made, as regards each such deduction particulars of the amount deducted and the purpose for which the deduction was made.

SCHEDULE
PART I

Form IP1

AN ROINN FIONTAR AGUS FOSTAIOCHTA
DEPARTMENT OF ENTERPRISE AND EMPLOYMENT
EMPLOYEE'S APPLICATION FOR PAYMENT OF ARREARS OF WAGES, SICK PAY AND HOLIDAY PAY OWED BY AN INSOLVENT EMPLOYER
PROTECTION OF EMPLOYEES (EMPLOYERS' INSOLVENCY) ACTS 1984 TO 1991

IMPORTANT: PLEASE READ THESE NOTES BEFORE COMPLETING THIS FORM

1.   After completion, this form should be sent or returned to the insolvent employer's representative.

2.   The insolvent employer's representative is the person appointed in connection with an employer's insolvency (e.g. receiver, liquidator, person appointed by Minister for Enterprise and Employment).

3.   Deductions for income tax, pay-related social insurance and occupational pension scheme contributions, etc., will be made by the employer's representative from payments due to the employees where appropriate.

4.   (A separate) Form IP2 should be completed where payment is being claimed in respect of minimum notice and Form IP4 should be used for claims in respect of arrears of statutory minimum wages or entitlements arising under the Unfair Dismissals Act 1977, the Anti-Discrimination (Pay) Act 1974 or the Employment Equality Act 1977.

5.   The maximum period for which arrears are payable for each individual item is eight weeks. In the case of sick pay, payment will not exceed the difference between any social welfare benefit payable and normal pay.

6.   The amount of the gross weekly wage to be inserted in Part 2(a) should include an average of regular overtime and any other regular commission/bonus, etc. calculated in accordance with the Redundancy Payments Acts. If rates given in Part 2 and Part 4 differ, please explain. Date of commencement of employment, number of hours normally expected to be worked per week, are required to establish entitlement and status of employees under the Worker Protection (Regular Part-Time Employees) Act 1991. For the purposes of calculating arrears a statutory ceiling on gross weekly wages is applied. The current ceiling is £300 per week.

7.   Deductions for union dues, V.H.I. etc. which were made from gross wages and not paid over to the relevant authority should be inserted in Part 2(b).

PART 1   COMPLETE THIS FORM IN BLOCK CAPITALS

EMPLOYEE'S SURNAME   EMPLOYEE'S REVENUE AND SOCIAL
INSURANCE (RSI) NUMBER _____

Class of Insurance: _____

EMPLOYEE'S FIRST NAME   IF OVER 66 YEARS OF AGE OR UNDER 16
_____   YEARS OF AGE, PLEASE GIVE DATE OF

ADDRESS OF EMPLOYEE   BIRTH _____
_____
_____   BUSINESS NAME AND ADDRESS OF
_____   INSOLVENT EMPLOYER

_____
_____
_____

OCCUPATION: (If you are a director or shareholder please indicate)
_____

DATE OF COMMENCEMENT OF EMPLOYMENT   _____

DATE OF TERMINATION OF EMPLOYMENT   _____

PART 2   ARREARS OF WAGES

Number of days normally expected to be worked per week _____

(a)   From _____ To _____

Total Number of
Weeks Due _____

From _____ To _____

Gross Weekly Pay: (See Note 6)   £_____

Number of hours normally expected to be worked per week: _____

Total Arrears of Wages Claimed: £_____ (See Note 5)

(b)   Deductions from Wages: i.e. Union Dues, V.H.I. etc.

Weekly Amount deducted *in each case*	Relevant *Period*	Total No. of weeks due in *each case*	Total amount deducted in *each case*
(i) Union Dues: £	From To		£
(ii) V.H.I.: £	From To		£
(iii) Any other deductions (specify): £	From To		£

Total Arrears of Deductions Due: £

PART 3 **ARREARS DUE UNDER A COMPANY SICK PAY SCHEME**

Total Number of

From _____ To _____   Weeks Due_____

Total Amount of Social Welfare Benefit payable during the period: £_____

Weekly Payment by Employer Under sick Pay Scheme   £_____
(Exclusive of Social Welfare payments)

Gross Weekly Pay *(See Note 6)*   £_____

Total Arrears of Sick Pay claimed *(See Note 5)*   £_____

PART 4 **ARREARS OF HOLIDAY PAY**

Total Number of

(State only your gross basic wage)   Weeks Due _____

From _____ To _____
   (This refers to period in which holiday
   entitlement arose)

Annual Leave Entitlement No. of Days _____

Gross Weekly Pay *(See Note 6)*   £ _____

Total Arrears of Holiday Pay Claimed   £ _____
(See Note 5)

I apply for payment due to me under the Protection of Employees (Employers' Insolvency) Acts 1984 to 1991 and declare that I have made no other applications in respect of the amounts shown above. I am aware that my rights and remedies against my employer in respect of this amount will be transferred to the Minister for Enterprise and Employment when payment has been made.

Signature .... Date.................

WARNING: LEGAL PROCEEDINGS MAY BE TAKEN AGAINST ANYONE MAKING A FALSE STATEMENT ON THIS FORM.

PART II

Form IP2

AN ROINN FIONTAR AGUS FOSTAIOCHTA
DEPARTMENT OF ENTERPRISE AND EMPLOYMENT

EMPLOYEE'S APPLICATION FOR PAYMENT OF AN EMPLOYMENT APPEALS TRIBUNAL AWARD UNDER THE MINIMUM NOTICE AND TERMS OF EMPLOYMENT ACT 1973

PROTECTION OF EMPLOYEES (EMPLOYERS' INSOLVENCY) ACTS 1984 TO 1991

IMPORTANT: PLEASE READ THESE NOTES BEFORE COMPLETING THIS FORM

1. After completion, this form should be sent or returned to the insolvent employer's representative.

2. The insolvent employer's representative is the person appointed in connection with an employer's insolvency (e.g. receiver, liquidator, person appointed by Minister for Enterprise and Employment).

3. This form should be used only for a claim in respect of an unpaid minimum notice award. A separate Form IP1 should be completed where payment is being claimed in respect of unpaid wages, sick pay entitlements or holiday pay and Form IP4 should be used for claims in respect of arrears of statutory minimum wages or entitlements arising under the Unfair Dismissals Act 1977, the Anti-Discrimination (Pay) Act 1974 or the Employment Equality Act 1977.

4. There is a ceiling on gross wages for the purpose of making payment from the Fund. You should refer to the explanatory booklet for the ceiling applicable (presently £300).

PART 1 COMPLETE THIS FORM IN BLOCK CAPITALS

Employee's
Surname: _____

Employee's Revenue and Social Insurance
(R.S.I.) Number: _____

Employee's
First Name: _____

Address of
Employee: _____
_____
_____

Business name and address of insolvent
employer: _____
_____
_____

Occupation: _____

Address of place of
employment: _____

Date of Termination of
Employment: _____

PART 2 AWARD BY THE EMPLOYMENT APPEALS TRIBUNAL UNDER SECTION 12 OF THE MINIMUM NOTICE AND TERMS OF EMPLOYMENT ACT 1973

Date of Employment Appeals Tribunal Award: _____

Reference number of award: _____

Gross Weekly Wage: _____

Total amount claimed/due: _____

PLEASE ATTACH A COPY OF THE TRIBUNAL AWARD

I apply for payment due to me under the Protection of Employees (Employers' Insolvency) Acts 1984 to 1991 and declare that I have made no other applications in respect of the amount shown above. I am aware that my rights and remedies against my employer in respect of this amount will be transferred to the Minister for Enterprise and Employment when payment has been made.

Signature: _____   Date: _____

WARNING: LEGAL PROCEEDINGS MAY BE TAKEN AGAINST ANYONE MAKING A FALSE STATEMENT ON THIS FORM.

PART III

Form IP4

AN ROINN FIONTAR AGUS FOSTAIOCHTA
DEPARTMENT OF ENTERPRISE AND EMPLOYMENT

EMPLOYEE'S APPLICATION FOR PAYMENT OF ARREARS OF STATUTORY MINIMUM WAGES, ENTITLEMENTS UNDER THE ANTI-DISCRIMINATION (PAY) ACT 1974, EMPLOYMENT EQUALITY ACT 1977, UNFAIR DISMISSALS ACT 1977 OR COURT AWARDS IN RESPECT OF UNFAIR DISMISSAL

PROTECTION OF EMPLOYEES (EMPLOYERS' INSOLVENCY) ACTS 1984 TO 1991

IMPORTANT: PLEASE READ THESE NOTES BEFORE COMPLETING THIS FORM

1. After completion, this form should be sent or returned to the insolvent employer's representative.

2. The insolvent employer's representative is the person appointed in connection with an employer's insolvency (e.g. receiver, liquidator, person appointed by Minister for Enterprise and Employment).

3. A separate Form IP1 should be completed where payment is being claimed in respect of arrears of wages, sick pay and holiday pay and Form IP2 should be used for claims in respect of Minimum Notice awards by the Employment Appeals Tribunal.

4. Claims in respect of statutory minimum wages can only be made in respect of employments covered by an Employment Regulation Order. In case of doubt about the application of an Employment Regulation Order, claimants should contact the General Inspectorate Section of this Department.

5. Please attach a copy of Recommendation, determination or order as appropriate, if applicable.

6. Warning: Legal Proceedings may be taken against anyone making a false statement on this form.

PART 1   COMPLETE THIS FORM IN BLOCK CAPITALS

Employee's
Surname: _____

Employee's Revenue and Social Insurance
(R.S.O.) Number: _____

Employee's
First Name: _____

Address of
Employee: _____

_____

_____

Occupation: _____

Date of Termination of
Employment _____

Business name and address of insolvent
employer: _____

_____

_____

Address of place of
employment: _____

_____

Gross Weekly Pay: £_____

PART 2:   ANTI-DISCRIMINATION (PAY) ACT 1974

(1)   Equality Officer Recommendation (note: attach copy of recommendation).

Date of Recommendation: _____   Reference Number: _____

Amount of Recommendation;   £_____

Has an appeal been lodged with the Labour Court? Yes___ No ___ (tick as appropriate)

(Note: If an appeal has been lodged, no payment can be made unless it is withdrawn, or is determined by the Labour Court. If it has been determined by the Labour Court, please complete section 2 following).

(2)   Labour Court Determination (note: attach copy of determination).

Date of Determination: _____   Reference Number: _____

Amount of Award: £_____

Has an appeal been lodged with the High Court? Yes ___ No ___ (tick as appropriate)

(3)   Fine arising out of Civil Court decision (note: attach copy of decision if available).

Date of Decision: _____   Amount of Award £_____

Location of Sitting: _____

(4)   Compensation awarded by Labour Court or Civil Court (note: attach copy of award)

Who awarded the compensation: Labour Court__ Civil Court__ (tick as appropriate)

Date of Decision: _____ Amount of Award: £_____

Reference Number (if any): _____

Location of Sitting (if heard in Civil Court): _____

(5) High Court Judgment (note: attach copy of judgment).

Date of Decision: _____ Amount of Award: £_____

PART 3: EMPLOYMENT EQUALITY ACT 1977

(1) Equality Officer Recommendation (note: attach copy of recommendation).

Date of Recommendation: _____ Reference Number:_____

Amount of Recommendation: £_____

Has an appeal been lodged with the Labour Court? Yes___ No___ (tick as appropriate)

(Note: if an appeal has been lodged, no payment can be made unless it is withdrawn, or is determined by the Labour Court. If it has been determined by the Labour Court, please complete section 2 following).

(2) Labour Court Determination (note: attach copy of determination).

Date of Determination: _____ Reference Number:_____

Amount of Award: £_____

Has an appeal been lodged with the High Court? Yes___ No ___ (tick as appropriate)

(3) Damages/Fine awarded by the Civil Court (note: attach copy of fine/award, if available).

What did the Civil Court award?   Damages__ Fine__ (tick as appropriate)

Date of Award: _____ Amount of Award: £_____

Location of Sitting: _____

(4) Compensation awarded by Labour Court (note: attach copy of award).

Date of Award of Compensation: _____ Reference Number:_____

Amount of Award: £_____

Has an appeal been lodged with the High Court? Yes__ No__ (tick as appropriate)

(5) High Court Judgment (note: attach copy of judgment, if available).

Date of Judgment: _____ Amount of Award: £_____

PART 4: STATUTORY MINIMUM WAGES UNDER AN EMPLOYMENT REGULATION ORDER

Note: A claim under this part is not payable unless proceedings against the employer, under section 45(1) of the Industrial Relations Act 1946, for the amount involved have been instituted.

State title of Employment Regulation Order: _____

Have proceedings been instituted against the employer?   Yes__ No__

(tick as appropriate)

If yes, by whom?: _____

In which court (if applicable): _____

State period in respect of which the claim is being made:

From: _____ To: _____ Total number of weeks: _____

Total Arrears Claimed: £_____

PART 5: UNFAIR DISMISSALS ACT 1977

(1) Rights Commissioner Recommendation (note: attach copy of recommendation).

Date of Recommendation: _____ Amount of Award: £_____

Has an appeal been lodged with the
Employment Appeals Tribunal?   Yes ___ No ___

(tick as appropriate)

(2) Employment Appeals Tribunal Determination (note: attach copy of determination).

Date of Determination: _____ Reference Number:_____

Amount of Award: £_____

Has an appeal been lodged with the Circuit Court?:   Yes__ No__

(tick as appropriate)

(3) Court Order (This part should also be used to claim payment of court awards for damages at common law for wrongful dismissal).

Date of Order: _____ Amount of Award: £_____

I apply for payment due to me under the Protection of Employees (Employers' Insolvency) Acts 1984 to 1991 and declare that I have made no other applications in respect of the amounts shown above. I am aware that my rights and remedies against my employer in respect of this amount will be transferred to the Minister for Enterprise and Employment when payment has been made. I also declare in respect of the amounts claimed above that I have made no appeal in respect of these amounts and I am not aware to the best of my knowledge, that these amounts are the subject of appeal by anybody else.

Signature: _____ Date:_____

PART IV

Form IP3

AN ROINN FIONTAR AGUS FOSTAIOCHTA
DEPARTMENT OF ENTERPRISE AND EMPLOYMENT

APPLICATION BY AN EMPLOYER'S REPRESENTATIVE FOR FUNDS IN RESPECT OF WAGES, SICK PAY, HOLIDAY PAY AND MINIMUM NOTICE AWARDS

PROTECTION OF EMPLOYEES (EMPLOYERS' INSOLVENCY) ACTS 1984 TO 1991

PLEASE COMPLETE THIS FORM IN BLOCK CAPITALS

EMPLOYER'S PAYE REGISTERED NUMBER _____

BUSINESS NAME OF INSOLVENT EMPLOYER _____

BUSINESS ADDRESS _____

_____

_____

NATURE OF BUSINESS _____

Date of Insolvency _____ (e.g. date of appointment of liquid-ator, receiver etc.)

Type of Insolvency _____ (e.g. liquidation, receivership, bank-ruptcy etc.)

257

To: Minister for Enterprise and Employment, Davitt House, 65A Adelaide Road, Dublin 2.

In connection with the provisions of the Protection of Employees (Employers' Insolvency) Acts 1984 to 1991, I have accepted, based on the best information available to me, the entitlement of the employees shown overleaf. No other notification has been made by me in respect of these entitlements. I understand that it may be necessary for you to refer information on the entitlements to the Revenue Commissioners and Government Departments. I hereby give my consent to the disclosure of such information as may be necessary. I also agree to make available to you such records as may be required for examination. I undertake to distribute the appropriate amounts to the employees concerned from the funds received pursuant to this application.

Copies of Forms IP1 and IP2 as appropriate signed by the employees involved are attached.

The Instrument of payment should be drawn in favour of: _____

Address: _____

Signature of Employer's Representative: _____

Date: _____   Telephone: _____

(1) Employee's Name	(2) Revenue & Social Insurance Number	(3) Total Arrears of Wages	(4) Net total arrears of sick pay	(5) Total Arrears of Holiday Pay	(6) Amount of Minimum Notice Award by EAT	(7) Total of Columns (3), (4) (5) & (6)
						GRAND TOTAL

PART V

Form IP5

AN ROINN FIONTAR AGUS FOSTAIOCHTA
DEPARTMENT OF ENTERPRISE AND EMPLOYMENT

APPLICATION BY AN EMPLOYER'S REPRESENTATIVE FOR FUNDS TO PAY ENTITLEMENTS, UNDER AN EMPLOYMENT REGULATION ORDER, UNFAIR DISMISSALS ACT 1977, ANTI-DISCRIMINATION (PAY) ACT 1974 AND EMPLOYMENT EQUALITY ACT 1977

PROTECTION OF EMPLOYEES (EMPLOYERS' INSOLVENCY) ACTS 1984 TO 1991

PLEASE COMPLETE THIS FORM IN BLOCK CAPITALS

EMPLOYER'S PAYE REGISTERED NUMBER _____

BUSINESS NAME OF INSOLVENT EMPLOYER _____

BUSINESS ADDRESS _____

_____

NATURE OF BUSINESS _____

Date of Insolvency _____ (e.g. date of appointment of liquidator, receiver, etc.)

Type of Insolvency _____ (e.g. liquidation, receivership, bankruptcy etc.)

To: Minister for Enterprise and Employment, Davitt House, 65A Adelaide Road, Dublin 2.

In connection with the provisions of the Protection of Employees (Employers' Insolvency) Acts 1984 to 1991, I have accepted, to the best of my knowledge, the entitlement of the employees as shown in this form. No other notification has been made by me in respect of these entitlements. I understand that it may be necessary for you to refer information on the entitlements to the Revenue Commissioners and Government Departments. I hereby give my consent to the disclosure of such information as may be necessary. I also agree to make available to you such records as may be required for examination. I undertake to distribute the appropriate amounts to the employees concerned from the funds received pursuant to this application.

I declare that in respect of the amounts shown on this form for the employees concerned that I have made no appeal in relation to the amounts shown and I am not aware, to the best of my knowledge, that these amounts are the subject of appeal by the employees concerned or anybody else.

The instrument of payment should be drawn in favour of: _____

Address: _____

Signature of Employer's Representative: _____

Date: _____ Telephone: _____

260

FORM IP5

(1) Employer's Name	(2) Revenue & Social Insurance Number	(3) Amount under the Anti Discrimination (Pay) Act 1974	(4) Amount under the Employment Equality Act 1977	(5) Amount under Unfair Dismissals Act 1977 or Court Order for wrongful dismissal	(6) Amount under the Industrial Relations Act 1946 Employment Regulation Order)	(7) Total of Columns (3), (4) (5) & (6)
					GRAND TOTAL	

GENERAL NOTE

The words in square brackets in Regulations 3, 4 and 5 were inserted by virtue of the Protection of Employees (Employers' Insolvency) (Forms and Procedure) (Amendment) Regulations 1991 (S.I. No. 349 of 1991).

These Regulations and the Protection of Employees (Employers' Insolvency) (Occupational Pension Scheme) (Forms and Procedure) Regulations 1990 (S.I. No. 121 of 1990) may be cited together as the Protection of Employees (Employers' Insolvency) (Forms and Procedure) Regulations 1984 and 1990.

The purpose of these Regulations is to prescribe the forms to be used and the procedures to be followed in relation to applications for the payment of certain claims under the act.

PROTECTION OF EMPLOYEES (EMPLOYERS' INSOLVENCY) (SPECIFICATION OF DATE) REGULATIONS 1985

S.I. No. 232 of 1985

1. These Regulations may be cited as the Protection of Employees (Employers' Insolvency) (Specification of Date) Regulations 1985.

2. In the case of an employer who is a company within the meaning of the Protection of Employees (Employers' Insolvency) Act 1984, by virtue of being a body corporate under the Industrial and Provident Societies Act 1893, and which, by virtue of section 1(3)(c) of the said Protection of Employees (Employers' Insolvency) Act 1984, has become insolvent as a result of the appointment of a receiver or manager of its undertaking by or on behalf of the holders of debentures secured by a floating charge, but not being a company within the meaning of section 2 of the Companies Act 1963, the day on which the receiver or manager was appointed is hereby specified as the day on which that employer is to be regarded as having become insolvent for the purposes of the said Protection of Employees (Employers' Insolvency) Act 1984.

GENERAL NOTE

The purpose of these Regulations is to specify the day on which a body corporate under the Industrial and Provident Societies Act 1893 is to be regarded as having been insolvent for the purposes of the Act as being the day on which a receiver or manager was appointed.

PROTECTION OF EMPLOYEES (EMPLOYERS' INSOLVENCY) (SPECIFICATION OF DATE) REGULATIONS 1986

S.I. No. 50 of 1986

1. These Regulations may be cited as the Protection of Employees (Employers' Insolvency) (Specification of Date) Regulations 1985.

2. In the case of an employer who is a company within the meaning of the Protection of Employees (Employers' Insolvency) Act 1984, by virtue of being a body corporate under the Industrial and Provident Societies Act 1893 to 1978, and which, by virtue of section 1(3)(c) of the said Protection of Employees (Employers' Insolvency) Act 1984, has become insolvent as a result of the making of a winding up order or the passing of a resolution for voluntary winding up with respect to the said company, but not being a company within the meaning of section 2 of the Companies Act 1963, the day on which the winding up order was made or the resolution for voluntary winding up was passed is hereby specified as the day on which that employer is to be regarded as having become insolvent for the purposes of the said Protection of Employees (Employers' Insolvency) Act 1984.

GENERAL NOTE

The purpose of these Regulations is to specify the day on which a winding up order was made or the resolution for voluntary winding up was passed as being the day on which a body corporate under the Industrial and Provident Societies Acts 1893 to 1978 is to be regarded as having become insolvent for the purposes of the Act.

PROTECTION OF EMPLOYEES (EMPLOYERS' INSOLVENCY) (OCCUPATIONAL PENSION SCHEME) (FORMS AND PROCEDURE) REGULATIONS 1990

S.I. No. 121 of 1990

1. (1) These Regulations may be cited as the Protection of Employees (Employers' Insolvency) (Occupational Pension Scheme) (Forms and Procedure) Regulations 1990 and shall come into operation on 23rd day of May, 1990.

(2) The Protection of Employees (Employers' Insolvency) (Forms and Procedure) Regulations 1984 (S.I. No. 356 of 1984), and these Regulations may be cited together as the Protection of Employees (Employers' Insolvency) (Forms and Procedure) Regulations 1984 and 1990.

2. In these Regulations—

'the Act" means the Protection of Employees (Employers' Insolvency) Act 1984 (No. 21 of 1984);
'the section" means section 7 of the Act.

3. The following forms shall be used as regards applications under the section:

(a) in the case of applications for payment of—
(i) amounts deducted from the pay of an employee in respect of the employee's contribution to an occupational pension scheme and which were not paid into the occupational pension scheme, and
(ii) the unpaid contributions of an employer on his own account to an occupational pension scheme, the form (Form IP6) set out in Part I of the Schedule to these Regulations, or a form substantially to the like effect, and

(b) in the case of a certificate given by an actuary for the purposes of subsection (3) of the section, the form (Form IP7) set out in Part II of the said Schedule or a form substantially to the like effect.

4. Every application under the section in respect of unpaid contributions of an employer on his own account to an occupational pension scheme shall be accompanied by an actuarial certificate certifying the amount referred to in subsection (3)(b) of the section and such certificate shall be obtained by the relevant officer, or, as may be appropriate, the person appointed under section 5(1) of the Act.

5. Every application under the section in respect of the unpaid contributions of an employer on his own account to an occupational pension scheme shall be accompanied by a certificate given for the purposes of section 7(3) of the Act by an actuary.

6. An application under the section shall be made to the Minister—

(a) in case, in relation to the insolvency of the employer concerned, a person stands for the time being appointed under section 5 of the Act, through that person, and

(b) in any other case—

(i) where there is for the time being in relation to the employer concerned a relevant officer, through that officer,

(ii) where there is not for the time being in relation to such employer a relevant officer, by being sent to the Secretary, Department of [Enterprise and Employment] at his address in Dublin.

7. Where an application under the section is received by a relevant officer or a person appointed under section 5 of the Act, the officer or person, having examined the application, shall, as soon as may be, forward it to the Minister.

8. (1) Where an application under the section is received by the Minister through a relevant office or a person appointed by him under section 5 of the Act, then, unless the Minister is satisfied that there are particular reasons for making the payment directly to the Applicant, any payment falling to be made on foot of the application shall be made to the officer or person through whom the application was received.

(2) Where a payment is made by a relevant officer or a person appointed by the Minister under section 5 of the Act by reason of an application under the section, such relevant officer or person

shall, as soon as may be, inform the Minister in writing of the making of the payment.

9. The Protection of Employees (Employers' Insolvency) (Occupational Pension Scheme) (Forms and Procedure) Regulations 1985 (S.I. No. 123 of 1985), are hereby revoked.

SCHEDULE

PART I

Form IP6

AN ROINN FIONTAR AGUS FOSTAIOCHTA
DEPARTMENT OF ENTERPRISE AND EMPLOYMENT

APPLICATION FOR PAYMENT OF UNPAID
OCCUPATIONAL PENSION SCHEME CONTRIBUTIONS

PROTECTION OF EMPLOYEES (EMPLOYERS'
INSOLVENCY) ACTS 1984 TO 1991

IMPORTANT: PLEASE READ THESE NOTES CAREFULLY BEFORE COMPLETING THIS FORM

1. Part 1 of this form and the schedule should be completed by a trustee, administrator or other person competent to act on behalf of the occupational pension scheme.

2. After completion of Part 1 and the schedule, this form should be sent or returned to the insolvent employer's representative.

3. The insolvent employer's representative is the person appointed in connection with an employer's insolvency (e.g., receiver, liquidator or a person appointed by the Minister for Enterprise and Employment under section 5 of the Protection of Employees (Employers' Insolvency) Act 1984).

4. Part 2 of this form should be completed by the insolvent employer's representative.

5. Where a claim is being made for unpaid contributions payable by an employer on his own account, a completed actuarial certificate, Form IP7, must be obtained by the insolvent employer's representative and attached to the claim.

6. A copy of the terms of occupational pension scheme should be attached to this application, if not already furnished to the Department of Enterprise and Employment.

7. Documentation confirming the existence of the occupational pension scheme should accompany this application, e.g. a Trust Deed and a Deed of Adherence in the case of an industry-wide scheme and a Trust Deed in the case of an individual scheme.

268

8.   The annual subscription rate together with a breakdown of the unpaid contributions in respect of the 12 months prior to the date of insolvency should be attached.

9.   The date of insolvency for the purpose of payments under the above Act is defined in section 4 of the Protection of Employees (Employers' Insolvency) Act 1984.

PART 1   TO BE COMPLETED BY A PERSON COMPETENT TO ACT FOR THE OCCUPATIONAL PENSION SCHEME (See Note 1)

To: _____

NAME OF INSOLVENT EMPLOYER'S REPRESENTATIVE

I am/we are authorised to act on behalf of

_____

NAME OF OCCUPATIONAL PENSION SCHEME

In respect of employee(s) of

_____

NAME OF INSOLVENT EMPLOYER

TYPE OF OCCUPATIONAL PENSION SCHEME
(e.g. Contributory, Non-contributory)

I/We certify that the provisions of the occupational pension scheme, which was in operation for the 12 months prior to the date of the insolvency, provided for contributions as follows:

Total amount of contributions payable on the employer's own account for the 12 months prior to the date of insolvency: £_____

Total amount of contributions payable by the employee(s) for the 12 months prior to the date of insolvency: £_____

I/We apply for payment from the Social Insurance Fund, in accordance with the terms of the Protection of Employees (Employers' Insolvency) Acts 1984 to 1991, of relevant unpaid contributions to the occupational pension scheme.

I/We declare that any money received by me/us as a result of this application will be paid into the resources of the occupational pension scheme.

I/We understand that where payment is made from the Fund in respect of pension contributions, any rights and remedies in respect of those contributions belonging to the persons competent to act in respect of the scheme shall become rights and remedies of the Minister for Enterprise and Employment.

Signature(s):   _____

_____

_____

Date: _____

Designation (Trustee/Administrator, etc.): _____

Name(s): _____

Address: _____

_____

_____

PART 2: TO BE COMPLETED BY THE INSOLVENT EMPLOYER'S REPRESENTATIVE

Employer's PAYE Registered Number _____

Business Name of Employer _____

Business Address _____

_____

_____

Nature of Business _____

DATE OF INSOLVENCY	**TYPE OF INSOLVENCY**
(As defined in section 4 of Employees (Employer's Insolvency) Act 1984)	(e.g. Liquidation,. Receivership, Bankruptcy, etc.)
Day Month Year	

_____   _____

I have examined the claim set out in Part 1 on this form and in the attached schedule. I certify, based on the best information available to me, that the amount of contributions which were not paid into the occupational pension scheme in respect of the 12 months prior to the date of insolvency are:-

Amount unpaid by the insolvent employer on his own account: £_____

Amount deducted from the employees' wages in respect of contributions to the occupational pension scheme but which was not paid into the said scheme: £_____

Did sickness/disability form part of the scheme ☐ Yes ☐ No

If 'yes' state element of contribution: _____

Did Life Assurance form part of the scheme ☐ Yes ☐ No

If 'yes' state element of contribution: _____

An Actuarial Certificate (Form IP7) (See Note 5)   Is attached   Is not attached

☐   ☐

(tick appropriate box)

To: Minister for Enterprise and Employment, Davitt House, 65A Adelaide Road, Dublin 2.

In accordance with the provisions of the Protection of Employees (Employers' Insolvency) Acts 1984 to 1991, I have accepted, based on the best information available to me, the amounts outstanding to the occupational pension scheme as shown in this application. I confirm that all employees in the scheme were insurable at the date of termination of employment for all benefits under the Social Welfare (Consolidation) Act 1993 in accordance with section 3 of the Protection of Employees (Employers' Insolvency) Act 1984. I understand that it may be necessary for you to verify information on the application with other Government Departments. I hereby give my consent to the disclosure of such information as may be necessary. I also agree to make available to you such records as may be required for examination. I undertake to pay to the applicant for payment into the occupational pension scheme concerned any funds received pursuant to this application.

Name of Employer's Representative: _____

Address: _____

_____

_____

Signature of Employer's Representative: _____

Date: _____   Telephone No: _____

WARNING: LEGAL PROCEEDINGS MAY BE TAKEN AGAINST ANY-
ONE MAKING A FALSE STATEMENT ON THIS FORM.

SCHEDULE

Schedule of deductions made from employees' wages (Contributory Pension Scheme) and on behalf of employees (Non-contributory Pension Scheme) in respect of contributions to the Occupational Pension Scheme which were not paid into the Scheme.

NAME OF OCCUPATIONAL PENSION SCHEME _____

(Attach continuation sheets to this schedule if necessary)

NAME OF EMPLOYEE*	RSI NUMBER	PERIOD OF DEBT FROM TO	AMOUNT DEDUCTED BUT NOT PAID INTO SCHEME° £
		GRAND TOTAL	£

*State if any of the employees were directors of the company by placing 'D' after the name above.

°Contributions are payable only in respect of periods of paid employment during the period of debt.

Part II

Actuarial Certificate

Form IP7

AN ROINN FIONTAR AGUS FOSTAIOCHTA
DEPARTMENT OF ENTERPRISE AND EMPLOYMENT

UNPAID OCCUPATIONAL PENSION SCHEME CONTRIBUTIONS

PROTECTION OF EMPLOYEES (EMPLOYERS' INSOLVENCY) ACTS 1984 TO 1991

IMPORTANT: PLEASE READ THESE NOTES BEFORE COMPLETING THIS CERTIFICATE

1. This certificate should be completed by an actuary.

2. This certificate must accompany Form IP6 when a claim in respect of unpaid pension scheme contributions, payable by an Employer on his own account, is being made.

NAME OF OCCUPATIONAL PENSION SCHEME: _____

BUSINESS NAME OF INSOLVENT EMPLOYER: _____

DATE OF INSOLVENCY (as defined in section 4 of the Act): _____

(a) The dissolution provisions of the above occupational pension scheme are as set out in the attached copy of the terms of the occupational pension scheme.

(b) I certify, in accordance with section 7(3)(b) of the Protection of Employees (Employers' Insolvency) Act 1984, that the amount necessary for the purpose of meeting the liability of the scheme on dissolution to pay the benefits provided by the scheme to or in respect of the employees of the employer is: £_____

SIGNATURE OF ACTUARY: _____

DATE: _____

PROFESSIONAL QUALIFICATION:_____

	Last Name	First Name
BUSINESS NAME AND ADDRESS OF ACTUARY:	_____	
	_____	
	_____	
	_____	

273

General Note

The purpose of these Regulations is to revoke the Protection of Employees (Employer's Insolvency) (Occupational Pension Scheme) (Forms and Procedures) Regulations 1985 (S.I. No. 123 of 1985) and to make new Regulations prescribing revised forms IP6 and IP7 to be used and new procedures to be followed in applications made under the Protection of Employees (Employers' Insolvency) Acts 1984 to 1991 following the amalgamation of the Redundancy and Employer's Insolvency Fund with the Social Insurance Fund. The applications concerned refer to:

(a) amounts deducted from the pay of employees in respect of their contributions to an occupational pension scheme but which were not paid into the scheme, and

(b) unpaid contributions by an employer on his own account to an occupational pension scheme.

The prescribed forms were revised to substitute the name of the Social Insurance Fund for the Redundancy and Employers' Insolvency Fund and in accordance with the provisions of the Social Welfare Act 1990.

The revised forms also include some additional requirements to facilitate the processing of applications. These new requirements specify that documentary evidence, e.g. a Trust Deed/Deed of Adherence, details of the subscription rate and breakdown of the unpaid contributions in the 12 months prior to the date of insolvency should be attached to an application. They also require the provision of information about the type of occupational pension scheme, whether any element of contributions cover sickness/disability, the insurability of employees under the Social Welfare Acts and whether any employees were also directors of the company, *etc.*

FORM RP51A
(Part II is overleaf)

FOR OFFICIAL USE		
Case No.		

PART I

NOTICE OF APPEAL TO EMPLOYMENT APPEALS TRIBUNAL UNDER

1. TICK APPROPRIATE BOX OR BOXES

(i) Redundancy Payments Acts 1967 to 1991 ☐

(ii) Minimum Notice and Terms of Employment Acts 1973 to 1991 ☐

(iii) Unfair Dismissals Acts 1977 to 1993 (see Part II) ☐

(iv) Worker Protection (Regular Part-Time Employees) Act 1991 ☐

IMPORTANT: Please read the notes supplied then complete this form in **BLOCK CAPITALS**

2. NAME AND ADDRESS OF PERSON MAKING APPEAL

Phone No:	
Occupation	Sex
RSI No.	

3. EMPLOYER'S FULL LEGAL NAME AND ADDRESS (IF IN DOUBT CONSULT YOUR P60 AND/OR P45.)

Phone No:	
Registered (PAYE) No.	

4. NAME, ADDRESS OR REPRESENTATIVE (UNION OFFICIAL ETC.,) OF PERSON MAKING THIS APPEAL

Phone No:

5. TOWN OR NEAREST TOWN TO PLACE OF EMPLOYMENT

6. GIVE THE FOLLOWING DATES

	Day	Month	Year
Birth			
Employment began			
Dismissal notice received			
Employment ended			

7. NORMAL WEEKLY PAY

	£	p
Basic Weekly Pay		
Regular bonus or allowances		
Average Weekly Overtime		
Any other payments including payments in kind – specify		
Weekly Total Gross		
Net		
Number of hours normally expected to work per week	Number	

8. BASIS OF EMPLOYMENT (PERMANENT, PART-TIME, TEMPORARY, ETC.) AND TYPE OF BUSINESS

9. THE GROUNDS OF MY APPLICATION ARE AS FOLLOWS:

10. APPEALS UNDER REDUNDANCY PAYMENTS ACTS

Has your employer issued you with a Redundancy Certificate   Yes/No
Have you applied to your employer or to the Department of Enterprise and Employment for your redundancy payment   Yes/No

11. REDRESS SOUGHT

12.

Signed:
Date:

275

PART II

IF YOU WISH A CLAIM UNDER THE UNFAIR DISMISSALS ACTS TO BE HEARD BY THE EMPLOYMENT APPEALS TRIBUNAL ANSWER ANY OF THE FOLLOWING QUESTIONS WHICH ARE RELEVANT TO YOU

CLAIM UNDER UNFAIR DISMISSALS ACTS   Insert "Yes" or "No" in each box

Have you sued your employer under Common Law procedures in the matter of your claim in unfair dismissal?

Have you a claim currently with a Rights Commissioner on unfair dismissal?

Do you object to a claim on unfair dismissal being heard by a Rights Commissioner?

(THE TRIBUNAL CANNOT HEAR YOUR CLAIM UNLESS THERE IS AN OBJECTION TO A RIGHTS COMMISSIONER HEARING YOUR CLAIM)

Has your employer objected to a claim on unfair dismissal being heard by a Rights Commissioner?

Are you appealing a recommendation of a Rights Commissioner in regard to your claim on unfair dismissal? If so, state:—

Name of Rights Commissioner _____

Date of the Recommendation _____

Are you referring your claim to the Tribunal following the failure of your employer to implement (within six weeks) a recommendation of Rights Commissioner on unfair dismissal? If so, state:—

Name of Rights Commissioner _____

Date of the Recommendation _____

Return this form to: Secretary
Employment Appeals Tribunal,
Davitt House,
65A Aedlaide Road,
Dublin 2.

INDEX